D0968337

# Holman *QuickSource*™

## GUIDE TO

# UNDERSTANDING CREATION

# Holman *QuickSource™*

## GUIDE TO

# UNDERSTANDING CREATION

## Mark Whorton & Hill Roberts

HOLMAN
REFERENCE

NASHVILLE, TENNESSEE

Holman QuickSource Guide to Understanding Creation
© 2008 by Mark Whorton and Hill Roberts
All rights reserved

ISBN: 978-0-8054-9486-0

A Holman Reference Book
published by
B&H Publishing Group
127 Ninth Avenue, North
Nashville, Tennessee 37234
http://www.broadmanholman.com

Dewey Decimal Classification: 231.765
Subject Heading: BIBLE/CREATIONISM/BIBLE AND SCIENCE/EVOLUTION

Cover Design by Greg Pope
Interior Design by Doug Powell
Acquisitions Editor: Steve Bond, Ph.D.
Editor: Jeremy R. Howard, Ph.D.

Printed in China

1 2 3 4 5 6 • 12 11 10 09 08
D

# Dedicated to

. . .

Our wives and daughters for their love, patience, and support.


**Mrs. Lee Whorton**

**Daughters Rachel, Anna, and Katelyn**


**Mrs. Carol Roberts**

**Daughters Melissa, Brooke, and Rachel**

# Table of Contents

## Part I:
## Ancient Stories about Creation and the Creator

# Part II:
# Revelation in Scripture and Creation

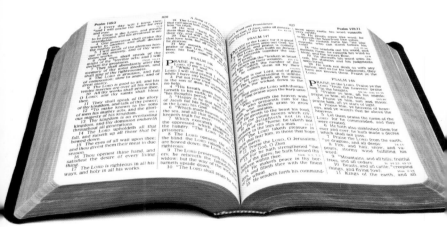

# Part III:
# The Creator's Week of Creation

# Part IV:
# Eden, Fall, and Flood

# Part V:
# Genesis and the Age of Earth

# Part VI:
# Science and the Age of Earth

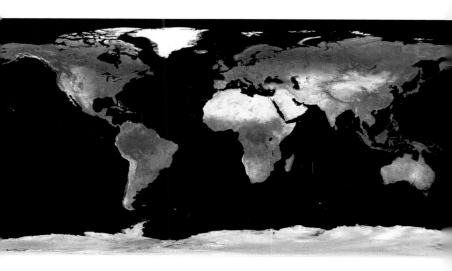

# Part VII:
# Six Impossible Things:
# Nature's Story of Creation

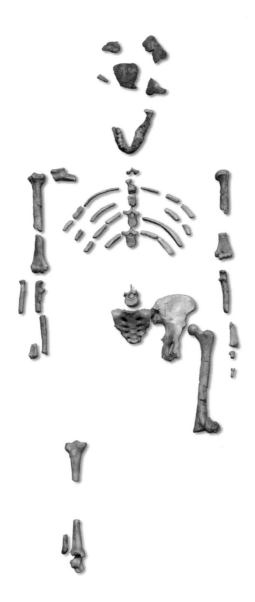

# Part VIII:
# Apes, Bones, and Human Ancestry

# Part IX:
# Concluding Thoughts

# Introduction

A clear and moonless sky filled with brilliant, twinkling stars. Laws of nature tuned with clockwork precision. Living cells packed with enough information to fill a vast library. Complex biochemical machinery engineered into the simplest forms of life. Abstract reasoning, language, and the arts. What do these have in common? Each is a testimony to the majesty of the Maker and an onerous burden to those who say, "There is no God!"

Never before have humans achieved such heights of knowledge about the world around us. As science peels back each layer of ignorance like the skin of an onion, we should gain a more profound sense of awe at the Creator's handiwork. Yet now more than ever Christians are faced with an apparent dilemma: is science the friend or foe of faith?

On one hand the Bible teaches that the heavens declare the glory of God. From the very beginning God

"The heavens declare the glory of God, and the sky proclaims the work of His hands" (Ps. 19:1). Photo: NASA.

has revealed His invisible attributes through what He made. On the other hand critics insist that science proves there is no god. Consequently Christians are tempted to throw up their hands in despair, looking to the preacher for eternal life on Sunday and to the scientist for modern life on Monday. Is this really the way we must live?

## *Back to the Beginning*

Far from a compartmentalized life where faith and reason do not interact, God intends for us to love Him with fully engaged minds (Matt. 22:37). Rather than leaping blindly after an irrational faith, we must base our faith on a reasonable, substantive foundation so we can give a solid defense for our faith. This foundation starts by understanding how everything began. After all, many of the toughest questions faced by believers and seekers today directly relate to the topic of creation:

**"** *Where* did we come from and how did we get here?*

*How do I know that God exists?*

*Can we trust Genesis?*

*Can we reconcile science with the Bible?* **"**

As we face these tough questions, we can strengthen the foundation for our faith and develop a greater sense of wonder for our glorious Creator.

*The Holman QuickSource Guide to Understanding Creation* is designed for seekers who are looking for answers as well as Christians who want to understand more about creation. We believe that studying creation from the biblical and scientific perspectives helps establish a positive basis for the Christian faith while also highlighting significant weaknesses and errors in competing worldviews. But it's no easy task to study creation, for one must span a broad spectrum of disciplines including theology, ancient languages, and scientific disciplines ranging from astrophysics to zoology. Countless books have been written about the minutest aspects of creation. Such breadth and depth presents an imposing challenge to Bible students. Even scientists move quickly out of their specialty when studying the multifaceted subject of creation.

This *QuickSource Guide* simplifies the quest to understand creation by walking you through the scientific and theological issues while providing a thorough overview of each pertinent topic. This single resource provides a comprehensive overview of the theology and science of creation. It's your one-stop source for getting a good grasp on the issues and understanding the perspectives different Christians take as they try to arrive at a solid understanding of the biblical and scientific testimonies about creation.

## *The Importance of the Big Questions*

Some Christians may think that faith means living with unanswered questions, and to some extent it does. Yet while biblical faith is an assurance of things not yet seen, it is never to be a blind or irrational faith. Christianity finds its uniqueness in its objective truth, not merely subjective sentimentality. The biblical message is set forth into the public marketplace of ideas and invites critical investigation. This openness to examination is important, for the heart cannot embrace beliefs or claims that the mind justifiably rejects.

It is by God's design that we think this way. He wants us to use the mental faculties He gave us. Indeed, we are instructed to test everything and hold on to the good (1 Thess. 5:21). In this book we take the approach that the inerrant biblical message about creation is foundational to our faith and that scientific truths about creation will not contradict the Bible. We also believe that understanding creation helps us answer the Big Questions that challenge our faith. Questions such as:

*In this book we take the approach that the inerrant biblical message about creation is foundational to our faith and that scientific truths about creation will not contradict the Bible.*

## Who?

To separate truth and myth about the Creator, we will sift through ancient stories and modern discoveries about the beginning and the Beginner.

## What?

To delve deeper into the Bible's story of what the Creator has done, we will survey the first three chapters of Genesis and other biblical creation accounts.

## Why?

A study of the biblical doctrines linked to creation and the role of creation in God's eternal plan will help us gain an understanding of God's big plan for creation.

## When?

When was Earth created? An overview of the primary evangelical views on the creation time frame aims to help get you started toward a satisfactory answer. Restricting our study to those views that hold to biblical inerrancy and the historicity of the creation account, we summarize and present the strengths and weaknesses of the Recent Creation (Calendar Day) view, the Ancient Creation (Day-Age) view, the Fiat Days view, the Analogical Days view and the Framework Hypothesis.

## How?

God has revealed Himself not only through His written

Word but also through His created world. Nature bears witness to the invisible attributes of God (Rom. 1:20) and provides compelling reasons to believe the biblical account of creation. The biblical testimony provides the same confidence for belief in God and His role as Creator. For this reason our book will examine the science and theology of creation with a view to exploring how God created the universe.

All of the topics covered in this book are important, fascinating and exhilarating. Some of them are also very controversial. For instance, the age of Earth is often a divisive topic even among Christians who agree on all the vital doctrines of the faith. Our hope is that we can

> *Our hope is that we can demonstrate respect and charity as we survey each viewpoint, and we hope you will read with a discerning mind.*

demonstrate respect and charity as we survey each viewpoint, and we hope you will read with a discerning mind. With that said, we invite you to join us in unpacking this fascinating thing we call creation.

## A Note on the Use of "Earth" and "earth"

There is no universally accepted convention for capitalization of *earth*. In this book we capitalize *Earth* anytime we have our home planet as a planet in view. So, for instance, we speak of the age of Earth, not the age of earth (land). Conversely, when we are speaking of the land, surface of the planet, or geological elements, we will use lowercase earth or the earth. An exception to this rule will be the familiar biblical refrain, heavens and earth, which has our planet and all the starry hosts in view.

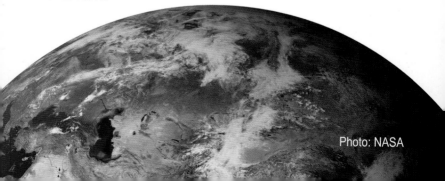

Photo: NASA

# Part I

# Ancient Stories about Creation and the Creator

# Chapter 1
# Creation Myths of Ancient Cultures

Since the beginning of time, people from every culture have asked:

> **"Why** *are we here?*
> **How** *did we get here?*
> **Is** *there a purpose to this life?* **"**

These questions have given rise to a broad array of fantasies, folklore, and myths about creation. Cultures develop these in an attempt to establish their identity in the world. Once these beliefs are disseminated throughout the populace, all of life's vital questions are addressed in the context of this foundation. This chapter examines several of the most important ancient creation stories and compares them to the biblical account.

## Ancient Creation Myths

All nations and cultures share a common quest to understand where they came from. For this reason each culture has forged its own creation myth (cosmogony) to explain the origin of the universe, Earth, and the human race. Records preserved from ancient times testify to the central role questions of origins play in establishing the identity and religious heritage of every nation. Many opponents of the Christian faith assume that the biblical creation account is nothing more than yet another in a long line of such documents, in this case a Hebrew creation myth that sought to establish a preeminent place for Abraham's descendants.

Yet in comparison to all other ancient cosmogonies, the historical accuracy and scientific plausibility of Genesis are striking. The radical thinking of its inspired author, Moses, is clear when compared to the far-fetched myths of the Mesopotamian cultures that surrounded the Israelites. It especially stands in stark contrast to the science and philosophy Moses learned in Egypt's world-class educational institutions.

> *In comparison to all other ancient cosmogonies, the historical accuracy and scientific plausibility of Genesis are striking.*

## Egyptian Cosmogonies

Four different creation mythologies evolved in ancient Egypt, but several common themes run through each of them. It was said that in the beginning the only thing that existed was a primordial ocean called Nu. Out of these waters rose a hill on which a temple stood. In each version of the Egyptian cosmogony, the creator of the world emanated (sprang forth) from this primeval, living temple. For instance the Heliopolitan cosmogony begins with Atum's creating himself on the hill that rose from the waters. He then brought into being all the various lesser gods of the atmosphere, earth, and sky through bodily emanations. It

Atum, the Egyptian god whose myth originated in Heliopolis.

is as if he were budding off new divinities.

A new creation myth developed in the fourth millennium BC when Memphis became the capital of Egypt. Not willing to accept the former account which glorified another city, the Memphian cosmogony trumped the Heliopolitan myth by deeming Ptah, the high god of Memphis, as the creator of Nu (the primeval waters from which Atum was self-realized). This is paramount to saying, "Our god created yours." Yet another creation myth arose in Thebes. The Theban cosmogony said that Thebes was the original city and all other Egyptian gods were in fact derived from their god, Amon. Thus we see that each of the Egyptian cosmogonies was an attempt to bolster the self-image of various cities. Politics, greed, and competitive spirit drove the foundation of these creation accounts.

> *Each of the Egyptian cosmogonies was an attempt to bolster the self-image of various cities. Politics, greed, and competitive spirit drove the foundation of these creation accounts.*

## Babylonian Cosmogonies

Perhaps the most well-known of the Near Eastern creation myths is the Babylonian tale called Enuma Elish. Written in cuneiform (wedge-shaped letters) on seven clay tablets, it tells the story of the god Marduk's rise to power and the establishment of Babylon as the region's preeminent city. Fragments of the seven clay tablets were discovered in the middle nineteenth century by British archaeologist Sir Austen Henry Layard when he unearthed the ruins of King Ashurbanipal's library in Nineveh. Although the version discovered by Layard was likely written as early as the twelfth century BC, older versions

Clay tablet of the Enuma Elish, discovered at the ruins of Nineveh. Photo: British Museum.

date as far back as the time of Hammurabi in the eighteenth century BC. Most scholars believe that its ultimate origin traces even farther back to Sumerian creation myths.

The Babylonian creation myth is an example of polytheism. Polytheism is the belief in many gods who coexist, each having distinct areas of responsibility and various measures

of goodness or evil as well as power. Originally there were two primeval gods according to the Enuma Elish: Apsu, the ocean, and Tiamat, the fresh waters. They mingled and produced numerous other gods. As children often do, the offspring rebelled against parental authority. In time Apsu and Tiamat grew tired of the rebellion and decided to kill the huffy young gods they had begotten. But motherly love got the best of Tiamat, and so she backed out of the plan, leaving the dark task to Apsu alone. But before Apsu could strike, he was killed by one of the offspring, a god named Ea. Realizing her mistake, Tiamat then used her powers to produce a hoard of monsters for the purpose of avenging the death of her husband and taking back control from the younger gods.

Marduk with his pet dragon, from a Babylonian cylinder seal.

Terrified by Tiamat's threats, the gods selected Ea's son Marduk to challenge her. Marduk agreed to the gods' request on the condition that they grant him supremacy over them. After the gods anointed him king, Marduk quickly slew Tiamat. Here is where the story converts to a creation myth: Marduk took an arrow and split Tiamat's corpse into two halves, making the arc of the sky with one portion and dry land with the other. Next he called forth the Tigris and Euphrates Rivers from her sightless eyes. Marduk then went on to slay Tiamat's demon-commander, Kingu, and from his blood he formed the race of humans. The remaining older gods were honored and placed in the sky as the stars that formed the constellations. As we will see more clearly later, the far-fetched Babylonian account, much like the Egyptian account, differs remarkably from Genesis.

## Various Modern Creation Worldviews

*Christian Theism* — Says a personal God exists who created and rules the universe. He created the universe from nothing rather than using some preexisting material or producing an emanation from Himself, and thus He is distinct from and transcends the entire material realm.

*Atheism* — Says God does not exist. The universe was not created by a higher power.

*Pantheism* — Says God and the universe are one all-inclusive unity.

*Naturalism* — Says the universe is the product of strictly natural laws and chance processes with no supernatural involvement.

*Polytheism* — Says many gods coexist, each with distinct areas of responsibility and various measures of goodness, evil, and power.

## Common Features of Ancient Creation Accounts

Many ancient traditions about the creation and early history of Earth share the same general framework found in Genesis 1–11, which includes an account of the world's creation, the subsequent formation of human civilization, and an eventual deluge that wiped out humanity. The closest parallel to Genesis in ancient literature is the Babylonian Epic of Atrakhasis, which was written in the sixteenth century BC and thus predates Moses' fifteenth-century BC authorship of Genesis. This epic is especially significant because, like Genesis, it recounts the beginning of civilization and a flood that destroys all of humanity except for one family. Another significant Babylonian flood story, known as the Gilgamesh Epic, was also found in Ashurbanipal's library.

The Gilgamesh Epic, written in Akkadian on a baked clay tablet.

## *Opening Verses of Genesis and Enuma Elish*

The Enuma Elish:
When the heavens above had not been named,
Firm ground below had not been called by name,
Naught but primordial Apsu (ocean), their begetter,
(And) Mammu-Tiamat (rivers), she who bore them all,
 Their waters commingling as a single body;
No reed hut had been made, no marsh land had appeared,
When no gods whatever had been brought into being,
Uncalled by name, their destinies undetermined—
Then it was that the gods were formed within them.


Genesis 1:1–2:
In the beginning, God created the heavens and the earth.
Now the earth was formless and empty, darkness covered
the surface of the watery depths, and the Spirit of God was
hovering over the surface of the water.


Clearly there are similarities between Genesis and the
various Mesopotamian cosmogonies. In a particularly
striking parallel to Genesis and its six days of creation, the
Enuma Elish includes six tablets detailing the creation of the
gods followed by a seventh tablet describing a restful period
of praise for the preeminent god. Both Genesis and Enuma
Elish begin with a dark and chaotic world covered with water. Then there is a separation of waters, sky, and land, which is a part of the general progression from chaos to order. Stars are appointed to fixed positions to form the constellations from which the seasons of the year are measured; sun and moon are established in the sky; even the Tigris and Euphrates are called out for a place of significance in both Genesis and Enuma Elish. It is hard not to be impressed by the commonalities between all of these accounts. But what does it mean?

*There are many similarities between Genesis and the various Mesopotamian cosmogonies. But what does it mean?*

## *Distinctiveness of the Biblical Creation Account*

Despite the similarity of general themes in these various creation accounts, no ancient creation myth is truly comparable to the biblical creation story. Birthed by the Holy Spirit in a context of polytheistic fantasy, Genesis tells the unique story of the one true God who brought all things into existence by His innate power. Whereas the Enuma Elish tells of a succession of gods who, after being created by the original two gods, slay one another as they vie for power, Genesis presents a self-existent God who by definition cannot war with other gods. After all, no other gods exist! God stands alone as Divine Sovereign of the universe. Whereas the nonbiblical creation stories tell of mythical gods who strive to bring order to the chaotic natural realm, Genesis tells the story of the one true God whose spoken commands are always obeyed. Whereas the Enuma Elish teaches that humans were created to be slaves to the gods and labor in their place, Genesis teaches that humans are created with dignity and freedom.

> *Birthed by the Holy Spirit in a context of polytheistic fantasy, Genesis tells the unique story of the one true God who brought all things into existence by His innate power.*

Warring, vainglorious gods and demigods striving for supremacy; divine and semidivine murderers; female gods who accompany amorous male deities; rowdy pantheons of gods who wrestle with eternal matter to fashion heaven and earth — this is the stuff of the non-biblical creation myths, and it all reads like a dark comic book. Even a cursory reading shows that Genesis does not contain such fanciful elements. Rather, there is an orderly and systematic unfolding of the divine plan of creation. And far from being beasts of burden created to jump at the gods' every beck and call, humans are ultimately created in God's image to fellowship with Him and bring Him glory.

If Genesis were merely authored by humans and inspired by surrounding creation stories, you would expect it to be marked by local prejudices and national character, just as the pagan creation myths were. Such is the case with the Enuma

Elish; the wholly human concern for establishing Babylon as the home of the gods is its theme. Similarly, Egyptian cosmogonies were tailor-made to reflect the aspirations of particular cities. In contrast, there is no mention of Israel or the Jewish temple in the Genesis creation account.

*If Genesis were merely authored by humans and inspired by surrounding creation stories, you would expect it to be marked by local prejudices and national character.*

No jockeying for position or preeminence. All attention is focused on the Creator and His unfolding plan. Local concerns and the ambitions of the Hebrews go unmentioned.

The story of creation in Genesis is a true account. It is credible

*The Creation of Man* by Michelangelo.

and comprehensible to all generations and all cultures. Most importantly, the biblical account presents a worthy conception of the Creator. The one true God acts with righteousness and holiness, independent of all other influences and with no aid outside of Himself. And all these things He does strictly for His own glory.

## Which Came First?

Despite the clear distinctions between Genesis and the Enuma Elish, some historians point to their common features as evidence that Genesis was derived from Enuma Elish and therefore never came from the pen of an inspired writer. One theory holds that Genesis is a compilation of multiple authors (the JEDP theory) and was written much later than the traditional date assigned for Mosaic authorship (around 1440 BC). Since the Hebrews in exile at Babylon in roughly 600 BC would have been exposed to the Enuma Elish, critics claim they adopted and adapted the Babylonian creation myth to create their own cultural identity.

*Moses with the Tablets* by Rembrandt.

However, this theory has been roundly refuted by diligent scholarship. Evidence throughout Genesis demonstrates that it was written from a pre-Israel perspective and thus originated long before the Israelites were exiled in Babylon. Plus, there is a simpler and much more feasible explanation for the relationship between Genesis and other creation accounts such as the Enuma Elish: ancient creation accounts all share similarities because they are all derived from the same true historical events. The original creation story would have passed down through various cultures for centuries, retaining a kernel of truth but also becoming distorted as it was inculcated into each particular culture. But by virtue of divine inspiration, the Genesis account is a uniquely accurate recounting of the creation of the world.

Today there is a broad consensus among evangelical Old Testament scholars that Moses was indeed the author of Genesis and that it was most likely written during the fifteenth century BC. It is intriguing to consider the context in which Moses wrote Genesis. Having been raised as the adopted son of Pharaoh's daughter, he presumably would have received the finest education Egypt had to offer. Thus he would have been indoctrinated in Egyptian cosmogony. And yet nothing

> *All ancient creation accounts share similarities because they are derived from the same true historical events.*

in the Mosaic creation account resembles or is erroneously influenced by the Egyptian creation myths he had been taught. Further, as we will see later, Genesis clearly refutes the Egyptian myths. These facts argue for the divine inspiration and inerrancy of the creation account Moses has given us.

Egypt preceded Israel as a kingdom, but there is no good reason to think Genesis is derived from Egyptian cosmogony. In fact, Genesis is a *response* to Egyptian cosmology

## *Worldview Summary*

### *MONOTHEISM VERSUS POLYTHEISM*

A brief survey of the various ancient creation myths of the Egyptians and Babylonians shows the historical context from which the Hebrew creation account emerged. Egyptian and Babylonian (as well as the earlier Sumerian) creation myths were inherently polytheistic, with teeming masses of powerful but flawed gods competing for the spotlight. Only in the Genesis creation account do we find one true God who brought all things into existence in an orderly and virtuous manner and who stands unopposed in power and majesty.

> *Only in the Genesis creation account do we find one true God who brought all things into existence in an orderly and virtuous manner and who stands unopposed in power and majesty.*

### *HEDONISTIC DEITIES VERSUS A HOLY GOD*

The nonbiblical cosmogonies we surveyed painted very unimpressive moral pictures of the gods. Cohabitation, base motives, and warring between the chief gods led to the incidental creation of other gods as well as the earth, sky, sea,

*The striking uniqueness and moral clarity of Genesis argue for its divine inspiration.*

and all living things. Although several broad themes are held in common by the biblical and nonbiblical creation stories, the striking uniqueness and moral clarity of Genesis argue for its divine inspiration. Every ancient culture had its own version of the creation story, but the biblical witness stands in sharp contrast to all competing creation accounts and towers above all others as the one true story of creation.

# Chapter 2
# From Genesis to Exodus

When reading Genesis, it is easy to miss vital context clues. That is because Genesis was written thousands of years ago to inform and enlighten an ancient audience. This means the author, Moses, used language and references that were suited to that long-gone historical setting.

But Genesis is for modern people as well. By studying the languages and history, we can piece together the meaning God intends to convey. And certainly Genesis is as accurate and relevant today as it was when the ink was still wet, yet we fail to understand it fully if we miss the purpose in its original context. In this chapter we will examine the cultural and historical settings of Genesis in order to better understand the meaning of the creation account.

> *Genesis is as accurate and relevant today as it was when the ink was still wet.*

Briefly, Genesis is part of a larger literary work called the Pentateuch or Torah, which includes Genesis through Deuteronomy. The New Testament also refers to this grouping of five books as The Law. In terms of style, Genesis is a historical narrative with a specific focus. Namely, it tells the story of creation and early human history, centering especially on the life of Abraham and his descendents — Isaac, Jacob, and Joseph. Understanding their life situation will help you read Genesis as the ancients did.

## Key Text

"But the LORD selected you and brought you out of Egypt's iron furnace to be a people for His inheritance, as you are today" (Deut. 4:20).

## A New Start

During Joseph's lifetime Abraham's descendents (the Hebrews) occupied lands in Egypt that had been granted to them by the pharaoh as reward for Joseph's noteworthy service to the nation. The book of Exodus picks up the story several hundred years later when the Hebrews are indentured slaves in an Egypt that has come to despise and fear them. Joseph's heroics were long forgotten. Hearing the Hebrews cry for help, God remembered His covenant with Abraham and sent a deliverer named Moses. Moses led the escape from Egypt toward the lands of Canaan, which God had promised to Abraham's descendents four hundred years earlier.

After Moses led them out of Egypt, the road-worn Hebrews came to rest at the foot of a mountain called Sinai, located somewhere between Egypt and their ultimate destination in Canaan. But for them the drama had only just begun, for God showed up in power at Sinai and christened the Hebrew people with a new name: from this point forward they would be called "Israel." As with any name change, this event involved the modern equivalent of paperwork. Just as America was founded on the basis of a written constitution and documents of law, so also the nation of Israel was founded by God with a binding covenant and the giving of the Law of Moses. More than just a new name, the Hebrews were given a new start.

## A New Nation

Exactly who were these Hebrew escapees that congregated at the foot of Mount Sinai? They were about to form a mutual covenant with God to be His people forever (Exod. 19:1–8). Does this mean they were God-fearing, righteous people who had demonstrated long-standing zealotry for the God of their Fathers? Absolutely not! These people were chosen by God strictly because of His covenant promises to their forefather, Abraham. The people themselves were essentially as wicked and pagan as their late neighbors, the Egyptians. They had Hebrew genes, but Egyptian ways. For all intents and purposes they were Egyptians, as were their fathers, their grandfathers, their great-grandfathers, and so on for many generations back. Their roots in Abraham were largely forgotten.

*Moses had taken the people out of Egypt, now the Law of Moses was intended to take Egypt out of the people.*

So when the Israelites arrived at Sinai, they first had to be "reprogrammed." Coming from the Egyptian culture, they had no adequate concept of who Jehovah God was and what He wanted from them. Hence, the Torah should be read as God's response to all of the questions and confusions the Hebrews had. Moses had taken the people out of Egypt, now the Law of Moses was intended to take Egypt out of the people. The struggles recorded throughout the Old Testament show how hard this proved to be.

## A New Law

After reminding the huddled Israelites at Sinai that He, Jehovah, was the God that brought them out of Egypt, God gave

Mount Sinai mountain range

them the Ten Commandments (Exod. 20:1–17). The first law is foundational to all the rest: honor no other gods but Jehovah. First and foremost, God would not share His glory with any

other so-called god. This must have been counterintuitive to the people, for they had long lived in a pluralistic context. They had also hauled an array of Egyptian idols through the sea and across the desert sands. Now God was saying that these were not allowed in the new kingdom He was establishing. Melt

*The Adoration of the Golden Calf by Nicolas Pousin.*

them, crush them to bits, or throw them into the river; in no case shall you keep them and bow before them.

Not only did Jehovah ban other gods; He also disallowed the use of statues to represent Him. Furthermore, He did not permit His people to craft statues of any skyward objects or any animals of the land or sea. This is important, for it was common among ancient cultures to venerate powerful beasts or wondrous objects in the heavens. The Hebrews had to honor their King and Him alone. A chief means of doing this was to remain connected to the creation story. By observing the seventh day of each week as a hallowed day of rest (a Sabbath day), they harkened back to the creation story and God's wondrous works at the headwaters of history. This served as a weekly reset that reminded them of who they were and what their God expected of them.

## *A New Focus of Worship*

After years of immersion in Egyptian culture and religion, the Israelites badly needed a change of focus. The Egyptians worshipped the heavens and earth, but the God of the Hebrews is far greater than these things. After all, He created the very objects the Egyptians took to be gods. The Egyptians worshipped the light and the dark. But God spoke light into being, illuminating the darkness. They worshipped the seas and the land. But God is the Maker of all land and storm-tossed seas. Beginning to see a pattern?

The Egyptians worshipped the sun, the moon, the stars, and even the changing seasons. Again, these are all God's doing. They worshipped fish. They made idols of birds. They carved images of land ani-

Thoth, god of the moon, before Pharoah.
Photo: Guillaume Blanchard.

mals. God made those as well. And last of all, the Egyptians worshipped man in the form of the pharaoh. They built monumental shrines to their glory that still stand to this day. The Mesopotamians did much the same with their suzerain rulers. In fact, it was the universal practice of ancient cultures to worship their human kings. But such things should not be, for Jehovah God created man and woman in His own image. Hence for the Hebrews, looking at a man might recall God's image in humanity and prompt worship of God, but it should never call forth worship of humans.

*It was the universal practice of ancient cultures to worship their human kings.*

## The Thrust of Genesis 1

Genesis 1 is a short account of a big accomplishment. Sometimes people mistakenly think Genesis 1 addresses all that happened during the creation event. Genesis 2 shows us that this is not a correct assumption. For example, chapter 2 indicates that the making of man and woman involved far more than the brief account reveals in chapter 1. Given the scope of God's work in creating the world, we might question why only these very few created items are mentioned in Genesis 1. Certainly those of us who take great interest in science and nature would like a longer, more detailed account. But if Genesis 1 included even a brief mention of all the life forms that God created and how He did it, we would need a forklift to carry our Bibles around! For example, the most plentiful of all earthly life forms, bacteria, are not mentioned in Genesis. Likewise, the "how" for all of these creation events is not exhaustively detailed in Genesis 1. We are simply told that God spoke and things came into existence.

*Genesis 1 is a direct and maximally effective counter to the false gods of Egyptian and Mesopotamian paganism.*

Given this brevity, we may be tempted to think Genesis leaves vital issues unaddressed, but a proper grasp of the historical context dispels this impression. The fact is Genesis 1 is a direct and maximally effective counter to the false gods of Egyptian and Mesopotamian paganism.

A graphic demonstration of how the biblical creation account presents an intentional contrast to pagan beliefs is found in the summation passage near the end of the Torah. Addressing the whole nation, Moses says:

> You came near and stood at the base of the mountain, a mountain blazing with fire into the heavens and enveloped in a dense, black cloud. Then the LORD spoke to you from the fire. You kept hearing the sound of the words, but didn't see a form; there was only a voice. He declared His covenant to you. He

I THOU SHALT HAVE NO OTHER GODS BEFORE ME

II THOU SHALT NOT MAKE UNTO THEE ANY GRAVEN IMAGE

III THOU SHALT NOT TAKE THE NAME OF THE LORD THY GOD IN VAIN

IV REMEMBER THE SABBATH DAY, TO KEEP IT HOLY

V HONOUR THY FATHER AND THY MOTHER

VI THOU SHALT NOT KILL

VII THOU SHALT NOT COMMIT ADULTERY

VIII THOU SHALT NOT STEAL

IX THOU SHALT NOT BEAR FALSE WITNESS AGAINST THY NEIGHBOUR

X THOU SHALT NOT COVET

commanded you to follow the Ten Commandments, which He wrote on two stone tablets. At that time the LORD commanded me to teach you statutes and ordinances for you to follow in the land you are about to cross into and possess. Be extremely careful for your own good—because you did not see any form on the day the LORD spoke to you at Horeb out of the fire—not to act corruptly and make an idol for yourselves in the shape of any figure:

a male or female form, or

the form of any beast on the earth,

any winged creature that flies in the sky,

any creature that crawls on the ground, or

any fish in the waters under the earth.

Egyptian god Horus depicted as a falcon at the temple built for him in Edfu, Egypt.

When you look to the heavens and see the sun, moon, and stars—all the array of heaven—do not be led astray to bow down and worship them. The LORD your God has provided them for all people everywhere under heaven.

But the LORD selected you and brought you out of Egypt's iron furnace to be a people for His inheritance, as you are today (Deut. 4:11–20).

We must not miss the importance of Moses' maneuver here. When summarizing the most important of all the laws God has given, Moses makes reference back to vital elements in the Genesis creation account as supporting evidence. After reminding them (again!) that the invisible God is the one who brought them out of Egypt, Moses recounts in reverse order the elements of the Genesis 1 creation account. He even elaborates on the details of the fourth day just as He did in Genesis 1. It is as if Moses is marching the people back through time, back through the giving of the commandments at Mt. Sinai, back to Egypt for a review of the rampant idolatry practiced there, and back to the creation event itself, where God formed all things. Moses' intention is clear: he wishes to warn his people against worshipping the things Jehovah God has created. Instead, they were to worship only their Creator. That is the fundamental purpose behind Genesis 1.

*We must be very careful not to force-fit natural history into a text that aims to give a theological history.*

Genesis was not intended to be a science text explaining answers to modern science questions which the ancient Israelites certainly never asked. It was intended to be a direct counter to the pagan culture from which God had just extracted the Hebrews. The aim of the book was to educate them on what it meant to be the people of God. To try to make Genesis into a science text today, thirty-five hundred years after its composition, is to miss the purposes God set out for this text. We must be very careful not to force-fit natural history into a text that aims to give a theological history.

Though Genesis does not answer many of the science questions we could ask of it, God did provide a highly detailed account of natural history elsewhere. It's found in nature

Spiral Galxy. Photo: NASA.

itself. As King David said, "The heavens declare the glory of God, and the sky proclaims the work of His hands. Day after day they pour out speech; night after night they communicate knowledge" (Ps. 19:1–2). God provided natural revelation with the explicit intention that the things He made would provide humanity with irrefutable evidence of His existence, His power, and His goodness.

> "What can be known about God is evident among them, because God has shown it to them. From the creation of the world His invisible attributes, that is, His eternal power and divine nature, have been clearly seen, being understood through what He has made. As a result, people are without excuse" (Rom. 1:19–20).

This means no nation or culture in history has been left without a faithful and true witness to God. Hence, there is no excuse for denying God and the truth He has made evident in nature.

From the beginning of time to our own day, God's message to us in Genesis and in nature has remained the same, while pagan beliefs have come and gone. Since God alone created all things by the power of His Word and according to His plan, He alone is worthy of worship. To do otherwise is to oppose God's clear revelation.

*God provided natural revelation with the explicit intention that the things He made would provide humankind with irrefutable evidence of His existence, His power, and His goodness.*

## Worldview Summary
### DIVINE RIGHTS

As Creator of the universe, God has the right to establish rules for living. In giving the Hebrews the Ten Commandments, God provided a witness to His moral character as well as a guideline telling His people how to relate to Him in a healthy way.

## *THEOLOGY AND NATURAL HISTORY*

Genesis was not written for a scientifically advanced audience. We must be careful not to force Scripture into paradigms that have been created by our modern context, and we must be careful to allow natural revelation to inform our reading of Genesis. This can be a difficult balance to pull off, and not every Christian will reach the same conclusions.

## *PLURALISM AND EXCLUSIVISM*

Images and messages of other religions are very common today. For instance, odds are you live close to persons of the Muslim faith.

Today we can identify with the religious pressures the Israelites experienced in Egypt. We are surrounded by images and messages from a thousand different worldviews. Most likely your neighbor's beliefs about God are vastly different from yours. Perhaps even the people living in your own home have views that contradict your own. How can you maintain your faith in such a society? One way is by taking your cue from God's commandment to observe the Sabbath. Built into the day of rest is a call to reflect on God as Creator. Focusing on God as the one and only Creator helps you stand firm in a world of many religious options.

# Chapter 3
# Biblical Creation Stories

When someone mentions *the* biblical story of creation, most of us immediately think of the account found in Genesis 1:1–2:3. The familiar opening line and the poetic pace of this passage lodge themselves into our minds as *the* story of creation. However, careful readers recognize that another creation account follows immediately after this more famous passage. It is not a contradictory account but rather a recapitulation and expansion of the first one. But what often escapes the attention of even the most attentive reader is that there are other biblical creation accounts outside Genesis that offer additional insights on the truths of Genesis. In this chapter of our book, we provide a survey of the major creation stories in the Bible. In later chapters we will investigate the first three chapters of Genesis in much greater detail.

> *Genesis is a divinely inspired and inerrant declaration that the one true God created all things from nothing.*

## Key Text

"In the beginning was the Word, and the Word was with God, and the Word was God. He was with God in the beginning. All things were created through Him, and apart from Him not one thing was created that has been created" (John 1:1–3).

## Genesis 1:1–2:3

As we have already seen, Genesis is a true historical record that stands in sharp contrast to the myth and fable of the creation stories offered by other ancient religions. Genesis is a divinely inspired and inerrant declaration that the one true God created all things from nothing. Creation unfolds strictly according to a divine plan that was fixed before time began. In unrivaled succinctness and clarity, Genesis explains that all things owe their existence to the only true God, sovereign and wise, who acted for His glory alone.

The account in Genesis 1:1–2:3 chronicles the creation of the heavens and the earth followed by nine creation events that occur over six days. The seventh day is appointed as a day of rest. There is a striking systematic regularity to the six days of

the Creator's work. Each begins with God issuing a fiat command followed by an explanation of the fulfillment. For every day except the second, we are told that after the fulfillment of the day's commands God reviewed His work and pronounced it "good." The sixth day stands out because "God saw all that He had made, and it was very good." Each day of work closes with the phrase "Evening came, and then morning: the ____ day" (Gen. 1:31). Interestingly, the seventh day, the day of rest, has no such closure. This leads some observers to believe that this day is ongoing even today.

Far from writing a simple checklist, Moses uses a rich literary framework to describe the six days of creation. The first group of three days thematically corresponds to the second group of three days in a parallel pattern. For instance, the first three

| Occassion | Event |
|---|---|
| Preface | Heavens created<br>Earth created |
| Day 1 | Light separated from dark |
| Day 2 | Waters separated, making<br>clouds and ocean |
| Day 3 | Waters gathered to one place<br>and dry land appears<br>Land produces vegetation |
| Day 4 | Sun, moon, and stars appear in sky |
| Day 5 | Water swarms with sea creatures<br>Birds fly in the sky |
| Day 6 | Earth produces living creatures<br>Man made in the image of God |
| Day 7 | Rest |

days of the creation week focus on location while the next three focus on inhabitants. More specifically, three days are spent shaping the "formless" planet into a fit habitat, and then the next three days are spent filling the new yet "empty" land with inhabitants.

Recognizing that intentional literary patterns are built into the Genesis account, some have suggested the first three days deal with *creation kingdoms* and the next three days deal with *creature kings*. Others associate the triads with *days of separation* (light from darkness, sky from sea, etc.) and *days of occupation*. Whatever Moses' intention may have been as God inspired him, the parallelism and chronology are laden with meaning.

## Parallel Structure of the Days in Genesis 1

| Separation | Occupation |
|---|---|
| Day 1: Light from dark | Day 4: Sun, moon, and stars |
| Day 2: Sky from sea | Day 5: Sea creatuers and birds |
| Day 3: Sea from land | Day 6: Land creatures and man |
| Day 7: Rest | |

## Genesis 2:4–23

This passage marks the second of the two creation accounts found in the opening chapters of Genesis. But just how distinct are they? Are they contradictory or complementary? One key to answering this question is to determine the meaning of the Hebrew word *toledot*, which first appears in 2:4. *Toledot* is translated "these are the records of." It is used ten other times in the book of Genesis to mark the heading of a new section. It is derived from the word meaning to give birth or generate and also has the meaning of "generations" or "histories." When Moses uses this word throughout the rest of the book of Genesis, he does so in order to begin a historical thread which recounts the life of one of the ancestors.

*Moses* by Michelangelo.

So why does Moses use *toledot* in 2:4? Rather than marking an alternate or competing recollection of the creation event, he uses this word as the heading for Genesis 2:4–4:26, which introduces the opening acts of the human drama. Thus, what begins in Genesis 2:4 is neither the story of a second creation event nor a competing chronological account of creation. Instead, it is the first *toledot* or the "record of the heavens and the earth" as the history of humanity is initiated. The focus has narrowed from the creation of the universe and its creatures to the lives of the first humans.

Another feature that has led some to conclude erroneously that Genesis 2:4–23 is a separate creation account written by a different author is its use of the name Yahweh rather than the more generic name Elohim that is used in the first creation account. Others have noted that the chronology of events in the second account significantly differs from that given in the first account. However, both of these observations point not to different authors but to different themes. The first creation account describes the systematic creation of all things from nothing by a single sovereign Creator. For this

*The two creation accounts of Genesis differ in purpose but not in authorship.*

purpose the use of Elohim (a "generic" name for God) is fitting. On the other hand, the second chapter is more personal and thus calls for the use of Yahweh, the more intimate name for God.

Spring of the Terrestrial Paradise by Nicolas Poussin.

As for variation in chronology between the two accounts, this is driven by the shift of focus from the entire cosmos to a lone garden. The scope of six days is narrowed as the author focuses on the vital sixth day and what follows thereafter. In chapters 2, 3 and 4 we learn things not revealed in Genesis 1, such as God's provision of food for His image bearers, His sole restriction on human freedom (the forbidden fruit), humanity's fall from innocence, a foreshadowing of the provision for man's sin, and the subsequent impact of sin on Adam and Eve, their descendants, and the world around them. In summary, the two creation accounts of Genesis differ in purpose but not in authorship.

## Job 38–42

For millennia the story of Job's suffering and perseverance has gripped us. For a long while he suffers in silence, but then gives vent to the obvious questions. In a scene of incomparable drama, God finally breaks His silence and speaks to Job from the midst of a storm. But rather than answering Job's questions about the problem of pain and suffering, God demonstrates that He is sovereign and worthy of trust even when such questions are not answered.

Beginning in chapter 38 and continuing for four chapters, God turns the tables on Job and asks him a series of questions. God's lecture to Job is His longest speech in the Bible, and it's interrupted only once by Job's brief, humble admission that he should just keep his mouth shut. The Creator peppers Job with a series of more than seventy rapid-fire questions, each

*Job* by William Blake.

of them essentially object lessons aimed at demonstrating the wisdom of God's ways in nature. From weather to mountain goats to the Pleiades and Orion in the night sky, a broad range of examples is included in this comprehensive review of God's power. Huddled there on the ground before his Maker, Job came to understand clearly that nature is full of mysteries. And in seeing that, he understood his own place in the universe.

Interestingly, God's questions to Job begin in a pattern that is reminiscent of the creation account in Genesis. He asks Job where he was when He established the earth on its foundations. The angels watched and sang for joy, but where was Job? And who was it, God asks, that formed the seas and covered the earth with a dark blanket of clouds? Who set a boundary for the seas, commanded the light to separate evening and morning, shook the earth and brought forth dry land and hills like folds in a garment? Where

*God points out to Job that nature itself has revealed Him as the Sovereign over all creation.*

are rain and snow stored? What roads lead to the source of light? The Creator takes it upon Himself to provide prey for the lions. He made the great creatures of the land and sea. In unmatched poetic eloquence, God makes it clear that He has the wisdom and power to providentially care for His creation

Describing the eagle He created, God tells Job, "It lives on a cliff where it spends the night; its stronghold is on a rocky crag. From there it searches for prey" (Job 39:28–29).

and accomplish His purposes. Who shall seek to give such a God advice?

God never answered Job's questions about the problem of suffering. But by pointing to the mysteries of creation, the Lord makes it clear that the robes of cosmic justice are far too weighty for man's narrow frame. God points out to Job that nature itself has revealed Him as the Sovereign over all creation. Better than the answers he had sought from God, Job found that God's questions brought him comfort as he came to see the power and majesty of the Creator through His creation. Even though Job never came to know why God had allowed him to suffer so badly, he did come to understand that God can be trusted and is always worthy of praise.

## Psalm 33:6–15

In this psalm of praise, God's people are told that only He is worthy of praise because He alone is able to provide for them. His power to do this is highlighted by the fact that He created the heavens by His word. Verses 6 and 9 emphasize that regardless of the means and processes involved in creation, it was the power of God's command that brought all things into being. And even though God set out to fashion the most intelligent and capable of all creatures, humans, from a most unlikely source — the lowly dust of the ground — He merely spoke and it was done.

Finally, this creation psalm teaches us that as Creator of humanity, God not only sustains the nations but also actually reigns over the affairs of all peoples. God nullifies the plans and counsel of the nations and ensures that His plans and counsel stand forever. For these reasons the psalmist says God's people rejoice in Him. He is their Creator, their Sustainer, their hope and shield. He sees all things and ordains all things. He alone is worthy of praise and trust.

## A Topical Map of the Biblical Creation Accounts

| Acts of Creation | Gen 1:1–2:3 | Gen 2:4–23 | Job 38–42 | Psalm 33:6–15 | Psalm 104 | Prov 8:22–31 |
|---|---|---|---|---|---|---|
| Heavens created | 1 | 4 | 38:33 | 6 | 2 | 27,28 |
| Earth created | 1 | 4 | 38:4–6 | | 5 | 23 |
| Light separated from dark | 3–4 | | 38:12–13, 19-20 | | 20 | |
| Waters separated, making ocean and clouds | 6–7 | | 38:8–9 | | 6,10, 13 | 24, 27, 28 |
| Waters gathered to one place and dry land appears | 9 | | 38:10–11, 14 | 7 | 7,8,9 | 25, 26, 29 |
| Land produces vegetation | 11-12 | | 38:27 | | 14-17 | |
| Sun, moon, and stars appear in sky | 14–19 | | 38:31–32 | | 19 | |
| Water swarms with sea creatures | 20–21 | | 41:1 | | 25 | |
| Birds fly in the sky | 20–21 | 19 | 39:26 | | 30 | |
| Earth produces living creatures | 24–25 | 19 | 38:39 | | 30 | |
| Man made in the image of God | 26–27 | 7, 22 | 40:15 | 15 | | |

## Psalm 104

Psalm 104 is the most complete biblical allusion to God's creation of the universe outside the book of Genesis. It is not a strict chronology or a literal description of the events described in Genesis, but rather in poetic form Psalm 104 reviews the awesome creative works of God, some of which we are only now beginning to fully appreciate. For instance, the first two verses parallel the creation of light mentioned in Genesis 1:1. The psalmist says of God, "You are clothed with splendor and majesty, covering Yourself with light as with a cloak, stretching out heaven like a tent curtain" (vv. 1–2, NASB). This beautiful image is remarkably similar to the scientific description of the beginning that has emerged from modern astrophysics. Using high-tech instruments such as telescopes and particle colliders, scientists have been able to envision the beginning of the cosmos

Hubble space telescope. Photo: NASA.

as an event when space, matter, and time erupted from nothingness. If we could have been there to record it, scientists say we would have seen something much like what the psalmist describes here. The expanding heavens were completely filled and wrapped in energy and light as newly created matter hurtled off to its appointed destiny.

Verses 3–9 parallel Genesis 1:2–10 and describe a Creator who is Master over the powers of primordial Earth. He rides on the clouds, walks on the winds, and makes messengers of the flaming fire. He tames and transforms Earth, bringing order

God tamed and transformed the early earth, bringing forth order and beauty.

from chaos. God then covered the land with water such that even the mountains were submerged. But this was not to be its final state. As the psalmist says in verses 7 and 8, "At Your rebuke the waters fled; at the sound of Your thunder they hurried away — mountains rose and valleys sank — to the place You established for them." By these commands God called forth the emergence of the continents from the seas, thus establishing a boundary so that the oceans would never return to cover the entire landmass.

The description of early Earth found in these verses closely parallels the modern scientific view. Evidence indicates that, much as the psalmist says, ancient Earth was an infernal world with volcanoes spewing molten lava, lightning arching back and forth across the stormy atmosphere, and flaming debris from space incessantly streaking down through the sky. Over time the bombardment and tumult subsided. As the land cooled, water in the atmosphere condensed and cascaded downward to form an ocean that completely covered the globe. Next, say scientists, dry land emerged from the sea and life appeared.

*Evidence indicates that, much as the psalmist says, ancient Earth was an infernal world with volcanoes spewing molten lava, lightning arching back and forth across the stormy atmosphere, and flaming debris from space incessantly streaking down through the sky.*

In verses 10–18, the psalmist describes how the water cycle that was established on Day Two of creation nourishes the land. For the believer in God, rain is anything but a chance event. Rather, we know that God gives rain to quench the thirst of His creatures and to bring forth food from the land. As verse 13 says, "He waters the mountains from His upper chambers; the earth is satisfied with the fruit of His works" (NASB). Verses 14 and 15 recall Genesis 1:29–30 where God provides grasses, trees, and vegetation to nourish and sustain humans and their animal companions.

Verse 19 points us to Day Four of creation when the moon and sun take their proper places, serving as governors and points of reference for days and seasons. By God's design, earthly life is regulated by rhythms and cycles. For instance, at night the lions seek the prey provided by the Creator; then they return to their dens at morning time (vv. 20–22). For humankind, however, the labor-rest pattern matches that set forth by God in creation week, where day is the time for labor

The moon with a solar carona. Photo: NASA/JPL.

and night is the time of rest.

The psalmist then turns in verses 24–30 to the fifth and sixth days of creation when God animated the sea and land with creatures great and small. And as these verses make clear, God is Ruler of the entire life span. In the first place these creatures exist because God sends forth His Spirit to give the gift of life (v. 30). It is important to note that the psalmist uses the Hebrew word *bara* to indicate that this creation of new life is something that involved God's direct, supernatural action. Life exists because God alone creates it.

Having created life, God now also sustains it. As verse 28 says, "You give to them, they gather it up; You open Your hand, they are satisfied with good" (NASB). Finally, we read that God not only ordains the existence and sustenance of His creatures but also their moment of death. "You hide Your face, they are dismayed; You take away their spirit, they expire and return to their dust" (v. 29, NASB). Far from resembling the finite gods of the pagan cultures, the biblical God is the God of heaven and earth, life and death, beginning and end.

As the psalm draws near a close, verses 31–32 sound a refrain of praise for the power and majesty of this Creator. "Let the glory of the LORD endure forever; let the LORD be glad in His works; He looks at the earth, and it trembles; He touches the mountains, and they smoke" (NASB). All praise and glory to this King of creation!

*Far from resembling the finite gods of the pagan cultures, the biblical God is the God of heaven and earth, life and death, beginning and end.*

## Proverbs 8:22–31

In this passage God's "works of old" (i.e., His work during the creation week) are cited as the author demonstrates wisdom's place of privilege in the universe. God's wisdom is personified as His possession from eternity past and is said to have been with Him before He created the heavens and the earth. Wisdom preceded the first day of creation when "there were no watery depths" and "no springs filled with water" (v. 24). It was with Him before the third day when the "mountains and hills were established" (v. 25). Wisdom was present with Him when He created the heavens and on the second day when He separated the sky from the sea (v. 27). It was also there on the third day when He set a boundary for the sea and established the firm foundation of the continents (v. 29). All of nature testifies to the wisdom of God, proving Him to be a "skilled craftsman" (v. 30). For those who look with the eyes of faith, nature is a cause for delight and rejoicing in the power and goodness of God.

God set the boundary for the sea and established the firm foundation of the continents. Photo: NASA/GSFC/JPL, MISR Team.

## New Testament Passages: Christ's Role in Creation

Each member of the Trinity was involved in the creation of the universe. One passage that teaches this is the first chapter of John's Gospel, which begins with a powerful affirmation of the deity of Jesus. The Son is identified as the Word or Logos. He is portrayed as the breath of God that emanates forth in power. As John says, not only was the Word with God; the Word was (and is) God (v. 1).

The Word was present with God the Father when creation

The Trinity, from van Eyck's *Ghent Altarpiece* (detail).

began, and His role was anything but that of a passive observer. John 1:3 says the Son was the Agent of creation, the One who actually brought all things into being. Nothing has been made apart from Him. The Son was with the Father and Spirit in triune glory at the beginning when "all things were created through Him." This insight is reiterated in Colossians 1:16 (as well as Heb. 1:2), which says, "All things have been created through Him and for Him."

These New Testament passages give fuller meaning to the notion of fiat creation that is introduced in the Old Testament. For instance, when the psalmist says "The heavens were made by the word of the LORD, and all the stars, by the breath of His mouth" (Ps. 33:6), we understand in light of the New Testament that it is Christ who is that "Word" and "Breath." We find this same truth in Hebrews 11:3 (and 2 Pet. 3:5), which reminds us that "the universe was created by the word of God."

*The Word was present with God the Father when creation began, and His role was anything but that of a passive observer.*

## Worldview Summary of the Biblical Creation Accounts

### DIVINE AUTHORITY

As Creator of the entire universe, God naturally holds authority over creation. After all, who could dare oppose God's plans and purposes for the things He has made?

### THE UNIQUENESS OF GOD

There is only one Creator God. All the gods and idols of other religions are mute, lifeless creations formed by the minds and hands of errant humans.

### THE POWER OF GOD

The intricate complexities of the created universe testify to the Creator's unparalleled wisdom, judgment, knowledge, and power (Isa. 40:12–14). Job described God's handiwork in the heavens as "great and unsearchable things" (Job 9:10). In the New Testament we learn of the deity of Christ and His praiseworthiness not just as our Savior but also as the Agent of creation (Col. 1:16; John 1:3; Rev. 4:11). Christ has not only made us but redeemed us.

*The intricate complexities of the created universe testify to the Creator's unparalleled wisdom, judgment, knowledge, and power.*

### THE PROVIDENCE OF GOD

Throughout the Scriptures we are reminded that God is the Creator and Sustainer of all things. We are dependent upon Him for our every breath. The whole universe would cease to exist if God stopped sustaining it by His continual power. Such a God is worthy of praise and trust (Neh. 9:6; Ps. 8:3–4; 19:1–6; 136:6–9; 147:4–5; 148:10; Isa. 45:12,18).

### THE PURPOSES OF GOD

Everyone wants to know what life is all about. It is an unquenchable desire that, for many people, is never fulfilled. The Bible says all meaning and purpose are rooted in one great truth: God's eternal purpose for creation is to bring Himself glory.

# Part II
# Revelation in Scripture and Creation

# Chapter 4
# Revelation in Scripture

No book has impacted the world for good more than the Bible. On the basis of its teachings, people have been moved to push through boundaries and prejudices to take the hope of salvation to remote villages, medicine to the sick, food to the hungry, and education to the uneducated. But what is the Bible? Is it merely a book of religious ideas written by men, or is it actually a revelation of God Himself? The Bible itself answers this question clearly: the Bible is God's Word and is vital for knowing God. In this chapter we examine four key characteristics theologians have used to describe the Bible.

## *Authority*

Throughout the Old Testament we find the familiar refrain, "Thus says the Lord." It is clear that though a human is speaking, it is God's message. These messages often come by way of the prophets, as for instance in 1 Kings 14:18, which says, "According to the word of the LORD He had spoken through His servant Ahijah the prophet." The New Testament is no less explicit in naming God as the true source of Scripture. In 2 Timothy 3:16–17, Paul says, "All Scripture is inspired by God and is profitable for teaching, for rebuking, for correcting, for training in righteousness, so that the man of God may be complete, equipped for every good work." The word translated as "inspired" literally means God breathed. Hence, the Bible is God's spoken word in written form. The apostle Peter affirms Paul's teaching on this matter, for in 2 Peter 1:21 he says, "No prophecy ever came by the will of man; instead, moved by the Holy Spirit, men spoke from God."

> *"All Scripture is inspired by God and is profitable for teaching, for rebuking, for correcting, for training in righteousness, so that the man of God may be complete, equipped for every good work"*
> *(2 Tim. 3:16–17).*

Finally, in an important affirmation of the authority the apostles themselves bore, Peter said of Paul and some of the difficult teachings he includes in his New Testament letters, "He speaks about these things in all his letters, in which there are some matters that are hard to understand. The untaught and unstable twist them to their own destruction, as they also do with the rest of the Scriptures" (2 Pet. 3:16). Having already stated that prophecies (he had the Old Testament in view) come from God, Peter went on to affirm that the apostolic writings also come from God. Hence, the whole Bible comes from God.

An important implication of these teachings is that the Bible is reliable. Drawing from verses such as Numbers 23:19 ("God is not a man who lies, or a son of man who changes His mind") and John 17:17 (where Jesus prays to God the Father, "Sanctify them in truth; Your word is truth" NASB),

theologians have formulated a doctrine known as inerrancy. Evangelical theologian Wayne Grudem says the doctrine of inerrancy means that "Scripture in the original manuscripts does not affirm anything that is contrary to fact."[1]

*Paul* by Rembrandt.

Grudem rightly notes that, taken together, the inspiration and inerrancy of Scripture imply that the Bible is authoritative over our lives. "All the words of Scripture are God's words in such a way that to disbelieve or disobey any word of Scripture is to disbelieve or disobey God."[2] In other words, we are obligated to believe and obey the teachings of the Bible. Clearly it is therefore vital to understand properly what the Bible says, for misreading it leads to mistaken beliefs and practices. One key to avoiding such mistakes is to take note of the fact that inerrancy does not mean the Bible manifests "absolute scientific precision"[3] in all it says. This is especially important where the Bible makes statements that bear on scientific matters. For instance, the Bible speaks of the sun rising (Ps. 50:1) and even of the sun standing still (Josh. 10:12–13). In such instances, the Bible is simply using ordinary language, not scientifically accurate pronouncements, to describe

*Scripture in the original manuscripts does not affirm anything that is contrary to fact.*

*— Wayne Grudem*

events. Grudem sums up the situation nicely when he says, "Biblical statements can be imprecise and still be totally true. Inerrancy has to do with truthfulness, not with the degree of precision with which events are reported."[4]

## Clarity

While the Bible admits that some of its revelations are difficult to understand (recall 2 Pet. 3:15–16), it also says that its vital teachings are understandable to everyone. For instance, Psalm 119:130 says, "The revelation of Your words brings light and gives understanding to the inexperienced." Drawing from such verses, theologians speak of the "clarity" or "perspicuity" of Scripture. According to Grudem, this means "the Bible is written in such a way that its teachings are able to be understood by all who will read it seeking God's help and being willing to follow it."[5] This does not mean believers will be fully unified in what they think the Bible teaches. As history plainly shows, we often disagree. But on the basics (such as God's identity, our fallen nature and need for salvation, the person and work of Jesus Christ) the Bible is clear and can be understood by anyone who wishes to understand it.

> *All the words of Scripture are God's words in such a way that to disbelieve any word of Scripture is to disbelieve or disobey God.*
> — *Wayne Grudem*

## Necessity

While creation itself gives us enough testimony to conclude that God exists and to see something of His divine attributes (Ps. 19; Rom. 1), we rely on the Bible for knowledge of the gospel and greater specifics regarding who God is, who we are, and what God expects of us. General revelation is sufficient for telling us that we are answerable to a holy God, but special revelation is required for clear definition of our sinfulness and for saving knowledge of the Savior, Jesus Christ.

*Peter* by Francesco del Cossa.

## Sufficiency

Theologians also say the Bible is sufficient for conveying to us all we need to know to be saved and obey God.[6] In other words, we do not need a supplement to the Bible to help us learn to live right before God. However, we must not take the sufficiency of Scripture to mean that the Bible is comprehensive. As Grudem says, "There are some subjects about which God has told us little or nothing in the Bible."[7] This means the Bible cannot be our one-stop source

*Special Revelation is required for clear definition of our sinfulness and for saving knowledge of the Savior, Christ Jesus.*

for all knowledge. For some things we must look elsewhere if we wish to gain understanding.

## Summary

The Bible is true in all that it intends to convey. Persons who revere Scripture as God's Word take great care to interpret it correctly. This means we must be careful to understand the original context (the historical setting and the original language) and the author's intent. Carelessness in interpretation can cause us to form wrong beliefs and exercise wrong practices.

## Notes

1. Wayne Grudem, *Systematic Theology: An Introduction to Biblical Doctrine* (Grand Rapids: Zondervan, 1994), 90.

2. Ibid., 73.

3. Ibid., 95.

4. Ibid., 91-92

5. Ibid., 108.

6. Ibid., 127

7. Ibid., 134.

# Chapter 5
# Revelation in Creation

In every age humans have recognized that finite nature is the product of some larger force, something that transcends nature.

Ancient Babylonians heralded Marduk as the conquering divinity who slew Tiamat, forming the land and sky from her corpse and humans from the blood of her chief demonic henchman. Egyptians credited Atum for creating land, sky, and all of nature after emerging from the hilltop temple that rose from the primeval waters called Nu. According to Chinese traditions, Pan Gu awoke from a long slumber to break through the primordial egg and create the heavens and the earth from the shards of the shell. And so goes the story for civilization after civilization.

We may wink at the fantastic nature of many of these creation myths, but the ubiquity of

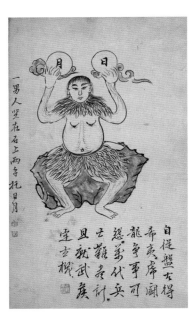

Chinese deity Pan Gu.

such myths is an encouraging sign pointing to the universal recognition that something greater than us exists and is involved in our story. This fits with the Christian expectation, for our Bible says that since the beginning of time it has been evident to all people that the heavens and the earth were created by a deity with power over the natural realm.

## Key Text

"From the creation of the world His invisible attributes, that is, His eternal power and divine nature, have been clearly seen, being understood through what He has made. As a result, people are without excuse" (Rom. 1:20).

## Mistaken Mythologies

Since all peoples have equal access to nature, every civilization in history has shared the foundation of truth revealed by the Creator through His creation. Without any further revelation from God, ancient pagan cultures built upon this foundation with their own imaginations, with the result that they crafted their own creation mythologies. That this sort of procedure would lead to mistaken beliefs about God and the universe is no surprise. Fortunately, we are not stuck with nature as our sole source for information about God. While God has clearly revealed His existence and power through what has been made, He has also told us much more about Himself than is

*As finite creatures, we can only know about the infinite Creator the things He condescends to reveal. We know Him on His terms or we do not know Him at all.*

detailed in nature. Exactly how and where God has revealed Himself and how these revelations relate to one another are topics that lie at the crux of the boundary between science and Christianity.

## *Two Types of Revelation*

It is a remarkable fact that largely goes unrecognized: we would know nothing about God if He chose not to reveal Himself. After all, God is not like the things scientists investigate in their laboratories. We cannot go out and round Him up. He cannot be sliced by cross section and examined under a

*John the Evangelist on Patmos* by Hans Memling.

microscope. His true nature does not come through when put to the fire of the Bunsen burner or loaded into the centrifuge. He will not smile for cameras peering through giant telescopes on remote mountaintops. We cannot bind Him with an oath on a cosmic witness stand and force Him to answer our questions. As finite creatures, we can only know about the infinite Creator the things He condescends to reveal. We know Him on His terms or we do not know Him at all.

Fortunately, as we saw in the previous chapter, God has chosen to reveal Himself through the prophets and apostles of old, through His Son, and through His Word. Theologians call this special revelation because it entails God's direct involvement for the purpose of conveying specific information about Himself and His plan. God has also spoken to us through His natural world. Theologians call this general revelation because the revelation in nature is given to all people at all times. The apostle Paul affirms the significance of general revelation in Romans 1:20 when he writes that God's power and divinity are clearly seen through what He has made. His "invisible attributes" have been evident to all people from the very beginning. Before there was ever a prophet or a preacher, before the first words of Scripture were penned, the heavens told of the glory of God.

*General revelation (nature) conveys inescapable impressions about God's power and divinity while special revelation (the Bible) tells us definitive information about such things as His saving grace in the person of Jesus Christ.*

In summary, general revelation (nature) conveys inescapable impressions about God's power and divinity while special revelation (the Bible) tells us definitive information about such things as His saving grace in the person of Jesus Christ.

## The Reliability of God's Revelation

Our modern world has reaped the fruit of ever-advancing technology and relegated the Bible to the archives of antiquated worldviews. Preachers in turn rail against the godless philosophy of scientific naturalism and its corrupting implications for society. All of this begs a question: If God reveals Himself through both nature and the Bible, why is there so much conflict between science and faith?

To understand the causes of this conflict, we must first understand the nature of God and His revelation. God is holy and righteous. There is no shadow of deception or hint of error in His ways. Because He is the author of all revelation, all revelation must be consistent and true. Thus the perfection

| General Revelation | Special Revelation |
|---|---|
| Communicated in Nature | Communicated in Bible |
| Broader in Scope | Deeper in Depth |
| Given to All People of the World | Given to God's People |
| Reveals the Creator's Power and Divinity | Reveals the Redeemer's Grace |
| Its Message Brings Condemnation | Its Message Brings Salvation |

of His character demands that there can be no contradiction or conflict between the different modes of revelation He has chosen to use. Just as the message of Genesis must be consistent with the book of Revelation, likewise there can be no final conflict between the truths of general revelation in nature and those found in the special revelation of Scripture.

Of course the fact that God's revelations cohere rather than conflict does not mean theologians and scientists will always agree. Just as science is the work of interpreting nature, theology is the work of interpreting Scripture. Both of these are human endeavors, and as such they are subject to error. General revelation provides data for scientists to investigate, and special revelation

**Two Witnesses**

provides data for theologians to investigate. So while the facts from both fields are ultimately consistent with one another, the interpretations may be prone to error. Hence, apparent conflicts between science and faith do not indicate that there are genuine conflicts between God's messages. Rather, the problem lies with our incomplete grasp of the data, our biases, modes of interpretation, and our sinfulness.

It is also important to recognize that science and theology are generally occupied with different types of questions. But in those cases where the domains overlap, there is real potential for conflict between various theories we have formed in science and theology. There is also potential for greater learning as participants in both fields interact and

> *The facts of nature yield positive help in many ways for interpreting Scripture statements correctly, and the discipline of wrestling with the problem of relating the two sets of facts, natural and biblical, leads to a greatly enriched understanding of both. — J. I. Packer[1]*

seek to inform one another, for when the facts of Scripture address a theme that also falls within the scope of natural revelation, we have two witnesses to a common truth. This is significant because our doctrines must be systematically and consistently integrated across all revelation.

## *Science and Scripture: Mutually Helpful*

So while the Bible alone is the inerrant and infallible Word of God, theology does not always take precedence over science when it comes to discerning truths about the natural world. Scientists and theologians have often locked horns, but neither have a perfect track record. Remember, we are capable of misunderstanding God's Word and His world. For this reason, we are instructed to diligently study the revelation God has given and trust His Spirit to guide us in all domains of His revelation.

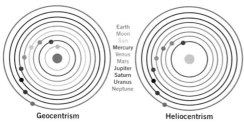

Geocentrism Heliocentrism

The classic example of how science helps shape Bible interpretation is heliocentrism: the fact that Earth and all the planets in our solar system orbit the sun. If you were locked inside a windowless room all your life with only a Bible to occupy your time, you would be of the opinion that the sun moves around the Earth. That's because all biblical references to the Sun are written from the anthropomorphic perspective,

*The classic example of how science helps shape Bible interpretation is heliocentrism: the fact that Earth and all the planets in our solar system orbit the sun.*

which describes the sun as we see it moving across the sky. If you were then granted leave from your room and had the chance to make observations and take note of advances in science, you would discover that it is Earth, not the sun, which moves. In this case science has not overturned the Bible, but rather it has helped you make the correct assessment of the Bible's witness.

The best modern example of how the Bible can correct science is naturalistic evolution (the view that all things naturally evolved without supernatural involvement). The Bible simply does not permit such a theory, and so Christians know that scientists have erred if they accept creation theories that do not involve God.

## Revelation and the Fall

Some people argue that natural revelation is inferior to the Scriptures when it comes to learning truth about the natural world because the entire physical realm was cursed due to the sin of man. This view is primarily based on Romans 8:20–22, which says, "For the creation was subjected to futility—not willingly, but because of Him who subjected it—in the hope that the creation itself will also be set free from the bondage of corruption into the glorious freedom of God's children. For we know that the whole creation has been groaning together with labor pains until now."

Taking their cue from the fact that the natural world has been "subjected to futility" and is in the "bondage of corruption," some commentators conclude that natural revelation became suspect or even misleading after Adam's fall.

Yet to dismiss general revelation as a genuine source of truth seems to unintentionally contradict the doctrine of biblical inerrancy. After all, if Paul really meant to say in Romans 8 that natural revelation is tainted and that its truth content is corrupted, then he would be contradicting the premise he established in Romans 1 about creation supplying irrefutable evidence of God's nature. To state the matter from another angle, if God holds all people accountable to His self-revelation in na-

*If God holds all people accountable to His self-revelation in nature, then by necessity that revelation cannot have been fatally altered or diminished by the fall of humanity.*

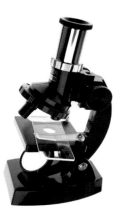

ture, then by necessity that revelation cannot have been fatally altered or diminished by the fall of humanity. Otherwise, rejecting what nature communicates about God's attributes would be excusable. Yet Paul says that all humans are without excuse when they reject God's truth revealed in nature. Therefore, the doctrine of biblical inerrancy demands that we uphold Romans 1 and Romans 8 in such a way that they do not negate one another. This means we must esteem the Creator's Word *and* His world as true revelations.

### A GROANING WORLD

When Paul says the world is "groaning" and is in "bondage," what does he mean? First, let us note that when he speaks of the "creation" in Romans 8:19–22, he uses a word that generally means the created world, but in some cases refers only to humanity or human institutions. So there is a range of possible meanings here. Most likely Paul primarily has the created world in view when he says "creation," but in a sense that is personified as eagerly waiting and groaning. "Futility" generally connotes emptiness, frustration, or transience. It implies that the world is in some sense incomplete and that it is a means to an end rather than an end in itself. Likewise, "corruption" means a state of decay or perishing. The world in its present condition is wasting away.

But just how futile has creation become? There are three general views on this. Young Earth creationists maintain that all physical decay processes (such as the second law of thermodynamics) began at the fall and that wholesale changes to the laws of nature occurred then as well. On their view, environmental conditions and living systems are now fundamentally different than they were before Adam's sin. Support for this view is drawn from the text of

*As part of the curse, we have become neglectful and abusive toward the environment.*

the curse in Genesis 3:14–19. As we will see later, the curse did profoundly affect the physical realm. Young Earth creationists believe that *all* imperfections in the physical realm stem from this.

A second view holds that Paul may have used words like "futility" and "corruption" in a more limited way. Instead

of indicating a direct effect of the curse, these things may be an indirect result of the curse through the effect of man's sin on the physical realm. In that sense, Paul is referring to the degradation of the world due in large part to humanity's failure to faithfully execute our duty as a steward

Some believe God's curse on creation primarily refers to our tendency to abuse and neglect nature.

over the physical world. Whereas Adam was originally faithful to his responsibility to cultivate, keep, and rule over the world, in their fallen state Adam's descendants have dropped this responsibility and become neglectful and abusive toward the creation.

A third possibility that is often overlooked is that the world may not have been subjected to futility and corruption at the time of the fall. Instead, perhaps God subjected the entire creation to futility and decay from the very beginning. Note that Paul does not specify when the subjection to futility occurred. What is clearly stated is that the reason for the subjection was to fulfill the plan and purpose of the Creator. In that case the creation was "very good" because it was well suited to accomplish God's perfect purpose. This world was not intended to be an eternal state of bliss in which Eden was the sum total of God's plan, but rather it was designed with built-in obsolescence and a plan to reach perfect fulfillment in the future through Christ. This creation is the stage on which the drama of creation, fall, redemption, and consummation is unfolding. And recall that the Bible says God planned all this out before He created anything. After all, Ephesians 1:4 says Christians were chosen in Christ before the

> *Some observers believe that God's pronouncement in Genesis that the creation was "very good" refers to its fitness for carrying out His total plan, not to a supposedly perfect beginning that did not include such things as the laws of decay.*

## The Futility of Creation: Three Views

| Pervasive | Indirect | Original |
|---|---|---|
| This view, commonly held by Young Earth advocates, says that all physical decay procsses began at the fall. It also says natural laws were drastically altered at that time. Nature now is much different than it was before Adam sinned. | This view says that it was not so much creation as creation's caretakers (humans) who were cursed at the fall. Nature suffers now because humans are negligent and abusive. Natural laws did not change when humans sinned. | This view suggests that nature was subjected to futility from its inception, and that this reflects God's eternal purpose to create a world in which the drama of redemption plays out, ending in a new creation. |

world was made, and Revelation 13:8 says our names were in the book of the slain Lamb (Jesus) from before the world was created.

The entire creation is passing away as we eagerly anticipate the completion of God's original and only plan, which is to receive glory and bestow benefit on those who call upon His name. To some observers, this suggests that God's pronouncement in Genesis that the creation is "very good" refers to its fitness for carrying out His total plan, not to a supposedly perfect beginning that did not include such things as the laws of physical decay.

## *An Immutable Revelation*

A common theory advanced in support of a recent creation is that when God subjected the world to futility, He substantially altered the laws of nature and living creatures. All scientific evidences for an ancient creation can be called into

The laws of nature are stable and finely balanced, allowing for intricate and orderly phenomena such as our solar system.

question if the properties of nature were fundamentally altered at the fall or subsequent to Noah's flood. Hence, the scientific principle of uniformity (that the past operations of nature are the same as the present operations, which allows us to study nature today and make extrapolations back to the past) is rejected. Thus, when presented with scientific evidence for an old Earth, a Young Earth creationist will simply say the evidence is misleading or misinterpreted.

While this perspective handily deals with evidence that is contrary to its paradigm, many observers believe it also stands contrary to Scripture. After all, God often cites the physical creation as it exists now, *after the fall*, to make analogies about His own nature. For example, He exemplifies His eternality by pointing to the ancient mountains (Ps. 90:2). He bids us to look up and see who created the stars and brings each one out by His power and calls them all by name (Isa. 40:26). The immeasurable height of the heavens above is a measure of the greatness of His thoughts, His ways, and His love for us (Ps. 103:11).

But interestingly, God also demonstrates His faithfulness to His covenants by analogy with the unchanging laws of nature, which of course are His creation. He says that if the laws of nature were to change, then the covenant with Israel and the throne of David would fail (Jer. 31:35–36; 33:19–26). In Psalm 89:30–37, He says His unalterable covenant with David is analogous to the established laws of the heavens. The immutable properties of nature demonstrate that His covenant will not be violated. These facts may indicate that it is mistaken to speculate that the natural laws were altered after the fall.

## *Worldview Summary*

### *THE NECESSITY OF SPECIAL REVELATION*

Starting with a faint corporate memory of the beginning handed down to them through generations and augmented with their own observations of the world, ancient cultures built their creation myths upon a foundation of historical truth and general revelation mixed with self-serving inference. It is *The Bible teaches that natural revelation is truthful and reliable.* not surprising that this inadequate foundation led to a wide variety of pagan cosmogonies. Special revelation, in which God communicates through spoken and written words, is required to correct humanity's error and convey inerrant truth about creation and its Creator.

### *THE RELIABILITY OF GENERAL REVELATION*

Though special revelation is absolutely necessary for us to form sure beliefs about life's big questions, general revelation in the physical world is adequate for communicating the basics of God's existence and His powerful nature. Christians often disagree over how to use physical data for reconstructing Earth's history. As we have seen, the Bible teaches that natural revelation is truthful and reliable.

## *Note*

1. J. I. Packer, *Fundamentalism and the Word of God* (IVF, 1958), 135.

# Chapter 6
# Models for Relating Science and the Bible

## *Concord or Accommodation?*

The most common approach for reconciling science and the Bible is called concordism. Concordism is the view that the Bible and science tell the same story and will agree when interpreted correctly. It is not always easy to see how this can be so, and disagreements arise as scientists and theologians accuse one another of misinterpreting or force-fitting science and Scripture. This is especially common on issues such as the ages of Earth and humanity as well as the extent of Noah's flood.

A popular alternative approach to reconciling Scripture and science is called accommodationism. It emphasizes that God, who is infinitely greater than we can imagine, communicates truth in the Bible in a way that is suitable to finite human understanding. In other words, God accommodates our limitations by communicating in a way that conforms to our

*God acccommodates our limitations by communicating in a way that conforms to our context.* context. Hence, in matters of science, the Bible often speaks in a way that makes concessions to limited human understanding. In such cases the Bible adequately conveys the central truth God is trying to get across, but it often means scientific accuracy is not the Bible's chief aim.

A New Testament example of accommodation is Jesus' parable comparing the kingdom of heaven to a mustard seed. He said it is "the smallest of all the seeds, but when grown, it's taller than the vegetables and becomes a tree" (Matt. 13:32). The fact is that the mustard seed is *not* the smallest of all seeds, and it produces a *shrub*, not a tree. Of course Jesus did not intend this parable to be a scientifically precise lesson in horticulture; rather, He spoke a spiritual truth and used language and concepts that were understood by the listeners. For His audience, the mustard seed was the smallest seed that they would have sown and harvested.

## The Book of Genesis

We suggest that interpreters should draw from both the concordist and accommodationalist approaches when seeking to reconcile science and Genesis. God has truthfully revealed Himself both in His word and in the world He created, so Scripture and science inform one another. A strict concurrence between Genesis 1–2 and the record of nature is difficult and strained at best. On the other hand, a purely accommodationist

*The Genesis creation narrative is on one hand wonderfully simple. . . . On the other hand, its majestic subject is beyond full comprehension for anyone.*

approach errs on the side of discontinuity between God's two forms of revelation. Hence, we should make use of both models while emphasizing the intent and original audience of the Genesis creation account.

As we have shown in previous chapters, God intentionally responded to the Near Eastern pagan cosmogonies with which the Israelites were familiar. He set the record straight and did so in a way that was relevant and understandable to the ancient Hebrews. In that sense we can say that His intent was not to write a modern scientific account of His work. God accommodated the circumstances, context, and concepts of the Near Eastern peoples to teach a timeless truth that is just as relevant today as it was when it was written.

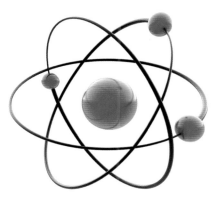

This image readily conveys the idea of "atom" to modern science students, but in reality the atom does not look like this. This model is an accomodation—a simplification of complex reality so that students can understand atoms. God reveals many complex truths about Himself and the world by using a similar accomodationist approach.

God approves of the workman who diligently studies to understand truth (2 Tim. 2:15). The Genesis creation narrative is on one hand wonderfully simple. Its core truths are readily understood by any reader. On the other hand, its majestic subject is beyond full comprehension. Thus, readers should proceed with confidence *and* humility when reading Genesis 1 and 2.

## Some Common Concordist and Accommodationist Readings in Genesis

### THE "WATERS ABOVE THE FIRMAMENT"

*The Concordist View:*

In keeping with the conviction that Genesis and science are saying the same thing when properly understood, Concordist interpreters seek to make one-to-one identifications between features in Genesis and the natural world. Hence, the "firmament" is taken to be the sky, and the "waters above" are said to be a vapor canopy which originally shrouded our planet. Thus, says the concordist, we are given an accurate glimpse at early geological and atmospheric conditions.

### The Accommodationist View:

In keeping with the conviction that Genesis is a direct response to pagan religions, Accommodationist interpreters hold that the terminology in Genesis corresponds to the ancient Near Eastern cosmogonies (especially the Enuma Elish) and is not properly taken to make overt scientific references. Hence, the reference to "waters above the firmament" corresponds not to some precisely described physical feature of Earth but rather to common terminology and concepts of the pagan cosmogonies which taught that  the dome of the sky was a solid firmament. Thus we are given a clear view of the religious context of Genesis and Israel's need to be true to the one true God.

### THE OCEANS

### The Concordist View:

Seeking to align science and Scripture, Concordist interpreters often take Days Two and Three of the creation week to specifically refer to the time when the surface of Earth cooled down enough to sustain an ocean and establish a water cycle, after which the first continental land mass emerged.

### The Accommodationist View:

Accommodationist interpreters note that the terminology Genesis uses here corresponds to the ancient Near Eastern cosmogonies where the primeval deep was split into two parts with the upper half placed above the firmament and the lower half forming the ocean.

### SUN, MOON AND STARS

*The Concordist View:*

Star cluster. Photo: NASA/JPL.

Concordist interpreters who believe Earth is old say that the appearance of the sun, moon, and stars on Day Four (Age Four) corresponds with accepted science models for the formation of the universe and the clearing of space and Earth's atmosphere, such that the sun could be seen from Earth's surface. Concordist interpreters who hold that Earth is young say that a temporary light existed initially and that the sun was not created until Day Four.

*The Accommodationist View:*

Sticking with the intentional parallels to Near Eastern cosmogonies, Genesis notes that God places the luminaries (which pagans mistakenly worship) into the dome framework above Earth. This means the luminaries should never be worshipped.

### THE CREATION OF HUMANS

*The Concordist View:*

Adam was a special and miraculous creation, literally coming from the elements found in the dust of the ground.

*The Accommodationist View:*

A *fully* Accommodationist interpretation says Adam physically descended from other hominid species but was the first true human because God miraculously gave him spirit and mind, which means Adam became the image bearer of God.

A less thoroughgoing Accommodationist view might say Adam was a special creation, not a product of God-guided evolution, but that the "dust of the ground" description should not be taken as a scientifically precise description of Adam's creation.

## *Conclusion*

Neither of these approaches is without difficulties. The Concordist view sometimes leads to forced interpretations which probably do not capture the whole truth of Scripture or science, while Accommodationist interpretations are sometimes too quick to discount true concord between science and the Bible. As always, we must be diligent and humble when seeking to reconcile science and Scripture.

*We must be diligent and humble when seeking to reconcile science and Scripture.*

# Chapter 7
# Three Models of Creationism

All Christians believe that God created the world from nothing, that humans are created in His image, that God is sovereign over the universe, and that the purpose of all created things is to glorify God. The list of creation topics on which we agree is long indeed. However, a basic divide exists over the questions of how and when this happened. Fortunately, these differences do not involve core Christian doctrines such as Christ's deity and resurrection or the sinner's need for spiritual rebirth. Nevertheless, the creation debate is important since it determines what kind of claims we set forth in the modern world. Christians commonly embrace one of two models: Scientific Creationism or Progressive Creationism. Lesser known is the fact that some biblically committed Christians believe God directed macroevolutionary processes. This model is called Evolutionary Creationism. In this chapter we will examine all three models.

> *The creation debate is important since it determines what kind of claims we set forth in the modern world.*

## Scientific Creationism

The view that the days of Genesis 1 are literal 24-hour days and that creation occurred over the span of 144 hours in a 6-day workweek is called Scientific Creationism. On this view, scientific data are properly understood only in the context of a recent creation, the fall of humanity into sin, and a global flood that reshaped geology. Anything that indicates Earth is old is regarded as misleading or misunderstood. Only the Bible gives us trustworthy data about the age of creation.

## Basics of the Scientific Creationism Model

*Scientific Creationism and Special Creation:* God supernaturally created the heavens and earth and all original

"kinds" of plant and animal life. Living things have the capacity to adapt, but this is strictly limited to variations *within* the species. In particular, humans did not evolve from earlier species.

Collage of the solar system. Photo: NASA/JPL.

*Critique:* Progressive Creationism largely agrees on these points. The Evolutionary Creationism model, however, maintains that God created life not by supernatural means but rather by means of the natural laws He designed, upholds, and directs.

*Scientific Creationism and Mature, Recent Creation:* Because the creation events occurred during a 144-hour period, everything was created instantaneously and "full-grown in every respect." The most obvious example is Adam and Eve, who were not created as infants but as mature adults.

*Critique:* Though Genesis implies that Adam and Eve were created as mature adults, it also gives evidence that not everything was created instantaneously and mature. For instance, a straightforward reading of Genesis 2:8-9 indicates that when God created trees He planted them and they grew out of the ground in a normal fashion. No instantaneous creation is implied here. On Day Three, God told the earth to produce vegetation, and "the earth brought forth vegetation" (Gen. 1:11–12). Again, this seems to describe the work of natural

Did God create fully mature trees that had tree rings?

processes which God created. Nothing in Genesis demands that God created everything instantly and in a mature state.

In addition to the fact that Genesis itself does not explicitly state that God created everything instantly and in a mature state, the idea that God created everything with a false appearance of age is troubling to many observers. New trees with age rings testifying to years of drought and plenty that never happened; immense coral reefs and chalk cliffs testifying to ancient marine ecosystems that never existed; starlight created with embedded data (images of past events) that represent fictive history—all of these indicate great age. The example of starlight is especially astounding when one realizes that what we often see in starlight is a record of a star's death. On the Scientific Creationism view, this starlight was created in transit to Earth a few thousand years ago, and so the star never really existed in the first place since the

Nebulae such as these are the remains of stars which have exploded. It takes millions of light-years for these images to reach us, which means the star actually died in the remote past. Photo: NASA, ESA, HEIC, and The Hubble Heritage Team (STScl/AURA).

light show coming to us tells of a death that occurred millions of years ago. So the death of stars that never existed plays out daily on telescopes all over the globe. All of these artifacts would be records of "false history," events that never actually happened. Many Christians doubt that God would create in a way that is so misleading, just as most Christians would not entertain a suggestion that the written history revealed in the Bible is essentially just fiction written to appear as true.

***Scientific Creationism and Catastrophism:*** Earth's geological and fossil records result from catastrophic processes during Noah's flood. Additionally, all of creation is under God's curse. As a consequence, scientific methods that assume the laws of nature have always been constant are mistaken and therefore fail to provide reliable estimates of Earth's age.

***Critique:*** There is no scientific evidence to justify the suggestion that the laws and constants of nature have changed, nor does the Bible say such a thing has happened. In fact, the Bible cites the consistency of nature as a metaphor for God's consistency and His existence (Rom. 1:20; Pss. 19:1–4; 89:37; Jer. 31:36; 33:19–26). Furthermore, a global flood simply does not account for the geological formations, fossil record, and evidences for antiquity as manifested by Earth's natural history. Floods just don't work that way (see chapter 27 of this book).

***Scientific Creationism and Perfect Creation:*** The original creation was a perfect paradise where injury, decay, and death were impossible. Adam and Eve's sin introduced all death and decay into the world. God will restore the universe to Eden-like perfection at the consummation of history.

***Critique:*** Two outstanding concerns must be mentioned in response to the Perfect Creation theory. First, the concept of perfection on which the model relies is questionable. God merely said the world He created was "very good." We read a lot into the text if we take "very good" to mean such things as tigers originally ate grass rather than meat or that monkeys swinging high atop Eden's trees could never fall to their deaths. Second, this model seems to overlook the far-reaching requirements necessary to make it feasible. For instance, it implies continual intervention by God in Eden to preserve His creatures unharmed. It also implies that all current carnivores underwent radical biological redesign after God cursed creation. This means new musculature, new digestive systems, and new instincts arose that switched the animals from grazing herbivores to aggressive predators. Importantly, this would have happened *after* God had already *rested* from His work of creation. Thus, defenders of the Perfect Creation model are left arguing that either there was a second creation which the Bible never mentions (and which interrupts God's Sabbath rest) or else that hyper-evolution kicked in and naturally produced ecologies and ecosystems in the blink of an eye, something which is far more than even the most optimistic evolutionist would suggest.

*Both Scientific Creationists and Progressive Creationists agree that microevolution (variation within species) is part of God's design, but that macroevolution (conversion from one species to another) is impossible.*

The Perfect Creation theory entails that carnivores such as this tiger originally ate grass, not meat.

## *Progressive Creationism*

Christians who believe Earth is old often embrace the Progressive Creationism model, which says that over long periods of time (the "days" of Genesis) new kinds of plant and animal species were created by God through His successive interventions in the normal operations of nature. Progressive creationists accept the timescales and mechanisms of astronomy and geology but reject macro-evolutionary theory.

The fossil record is taken to reflect immense periods of stasis (where there was essentially no biological change) interspersed with occasions where God miraculously introduced new species. The most comprehensive

Progressive Creationists take the fossil record to indicate that God created all things in widely separated eras.

progressive creation model formulated to date is that given by the apologetics ministry, Reasons to Believe (RTB). We outline it below as the best current model for Progressive Creationism. We will refer to this model as TCM for Testable Creation Model.

## *Basics of the Testable Creation Model (Progressive Creationism)*

*Progressive Creationism and Special Creation:* Progressive Creationists agree with Scientific Creationists that the heavens and earth and all of the original "kinds" of plant and animal life were supernaturally created by God. Progressive Creationists typically allow for a broader range of evolutionary development than do Scientific Creationists, but this variation is nonetheless within strict limits when contrasted with a full-blown evolutionary view of species development. Both Scientific Creationists and Progressive Creationists agree that microevolution (variation within species) is part of God's design but that macroevolution (conversion from one kind to another) is impossible. However, Progressive Creationists may accept a substantially broader range of variation for microevolution as compared to the limited range allowed by most Special Creationists.

*Critique:* Scientific Creationists maintain that Progressive Creationists allow science to change the most straightforward reading of Genesis 1 and 2, while Evolutionary Creationists believe they appeal to miracles needlessly.

***Progressive Creationism and Anthropic Development:*** A fundamental principle of Progressive Creationism is the anthropic principle, or the inference that the laws of nature were all finely tuned for the benefit of humans. The TCM asserts that passages such as Job 38–41 and Psalms 104 and 139 indicate that God uses "optimal design" when He creates, which means life is created to match its environment or purpose. This model also posits that as scientists learn more, the number of characteristics that demonstrate fine tuning will increase along with the degree of precision in those instances.

Science has discovered that the natural laws and conditions of the universe are finely tuned for life.

*Critique:* All three models agree that the universe is uniquely designed for life although to different extents and by different means.

***Progressive Creationism and Creation by Intervention:*** The means by which God did the work of creation was divine intervention, either acting outside the laws of nature or by working within them in a special, direct way to produce results that exceed the capacity of the laws themselves. The need for the divine hand is made clearer as scientists continue to discover the fine-tuned characteristics required for life.

*Critique:* A primary distinction between the TCM and Evolutionary Creationism is the TCM's reliance on God's miraculous intervention rather than just His regular, continuous immanence.

***Progressive Creationism and Concordism:*** Because God has truthfully revealed Himself in His word (John 17:17) and in His world (Rom. 1:20; Ps. 19:1), Progressive Creationists believe the truth claims revealed in each must agree. Some Christians fear this approach elevates science to equality with Scripture, but truth is truth no matter how it is revealed, and all truth is God's truth. Thus, studying nature should lead to a better understanding of the truth God has revealed in Scripture when both are carefully studied and properly understood.

Studying nature should lead to a better understanding of the truth God has revealed in Scripture.

Of course, Christians often disagree on who has "properly understood" these issues.

*Critique:* Scientific Creationists share the basic emphasis on concordism between the Bible and science, but they say Progressive Creationists allow science to lead the Bible rather than the Bible to lead science. Evolutionary Creationists favor the Accommodationist approach to reconciling science and Scripture.

## Biblical and Theological Distinctions between the 3 Models

| | Scientific Creationism | Progressive Creationism | Evolutionary Creationism |
|---|---|---|---|
| **When:** | Recent | Ancient | Ancient |
| **How:** | Intervention | Intervention | Concurrence |
| **Interpretive Approach:** | Concordism | Concordism | Accommodationism |

## EVOLUTIONARY CREATIONISM

Dr. Francis Collins, the director of the human genome project, says his scientific studies have strengthened his faith in Jesus Christ. However, that does not mean he is a Scientific Creationist or even a Progressive Creationist. Instead, Collins believes that God providentially guided evolution to create all life.

Renowned conservative theologians such as Benjamin B. Warfield (a staunch advocate of biblical inerrancy in the late 1800s) have shared this belief. We anticipate that many read-

ers will automatically dismiss this model as plainly unbiblical. However, it is important to consider the merits and objections to all the major viewpoints held by thoughtful Christians. Following is a brief description of Evolutionary Creationism.

Many Christians automatically dismiss Evolutionary Creationism as unbiblical, but we must exmine all major views.

## Basics of the Evolutionary Creationism Model

*Evolutionary Creationism and the Works of God:* Everything that exists is contingent on God's continuing activity and sustaining work. "In Him we live and move and exist," and "by Him all things hold together" (Acts 17:28; Col. 1:17). Nature is God's to control, and throughout the Bible we are told that He directs nature. It is clear that God can work naturally or supernaturally. The question for us is, To what extent has God worked concurrently with natural processes or, conversely, *above* natural processes when creating life? Scientific Creationists conclude that all God's creative works were miraculous;

> *Evolutionary Creationists say God achieved creation almost exclusively by working through the natural laws.*

Progressive Creationists hold that all *life* was created miraculously but that other aspects of creation were achieved by God's nonmiraculous guidance of nature; Evolutionary

Creationists say God achieved creation almost exclusively by providentially working through and governing the processes of nature that He created for His purposes.

***Evolutionary Creationism and God's Purposes:*** God formed a plan in eternity past that included Christ's atoning death for the sins of humanity and the consummation of all authority at His throne so that He might be glorified forever. He created this world to accomplish these purposes. Proponents of Evolutionary Creationism say an evolving creation can be thought of as the manifestation of God's plan unfolding in time.

***Evolutionary Creationism and the Process of Creation:*** A strictly Christian view of an evolving creation does not see God as a far-removed deity who sets things in motion and then sits back from a distance to watch things unfold. Nor does He merely intervene on the occasions when nature needs a nudge to stay on course. Rather, God governs creation's development by being continuously and immanently involved in all its affairs. First and foremost then the Evolutionary Creationism view emphasizes the sovereignty of God and the providential outworking of His plan.

Proponents of Evolutionary Creationsism feel that their model is best able to account for the pseudogene evidence that has come to light since the late 1990s. As it now stands, scientists believe pseudogenes may provide the strongest evidence for common descent. Evolutionary Creationists say their model can incorporate the theory of common descent and attribute it to the sovereign hand of God working through history to create all life forms. Of course this is a controversial claim among Christians and non-Christians. In any event, it is vital that all creation models seek to provide an answer to the question of how psuedogenes fit into God's works of creation. An attitude that joins caution to openmindedness is necessary as Christians continue to evaluate incoming data.

***Evolutionary Creationism and Randomness:*** Atheists speak of evolution as a random process, but Christians who embrace Evolutionary Creationism reject naturalism and its dependence on chance. By faith Christians accept that events which appear to be random are in reality guided by God. As Proverbs 16:33 says, "The lot is cast into the lap, but its every decision is from the Lord." God also works in and through human choices to achieve His will, and yet He does so in a way that does not violate our freedom (Acts 4:27–28).

Christians believe there is no such thing as blind chance. God is sovereign even over "incidental" events.

Advocates of Evolutionary Creationism say that in similar ways God achieves His purposes in an evolving creation through His ordinary governance over natural laws.

***Evolutionary Creationism and Causation:*** God is at work even in the mundane realities of existence. He causes springs to flow and grass to grow; He produces crops for man to live on (Ps. 104:10–15). He commands the sun to rise and fastens the belt of Orion (Job 38:12, 31). He even satisfies the appetites

The sun rises at God's command.

of young lions and ravens (Job 38:39–41). Of course to the scientist, these things are purely natural processes. In one sense they are right, but the Bible says God is the ultimate cause. From the biblical standpoint, then, God is the cause even when He employs secondary means (the laws of nature). A sample of passages that teach this include: Psalm 104:11, 14–15, 20, 21, 29–30; Job 38–42; Matthew 5:45; 6:26, 30; Acts 17:24–25; Colossians 1:15–17; Hebrews 1:2–3.

## Objections to the Evolutionary Creationism Model

*Adam and Eve:* Evolutionary Creationists typically say Adam and Eve were hominids who became fully human when God gifted them with soul and mind. Thus, we really did come up from apes, and it took a miraculous act of God to finish creating us and make us uniquely in His image. However, a straightforward reading of the Bible presents Adam and Eve as special creations from the dust of the ground, not some previous hominid species that evolved from apes. To these objections Evolutionary Creationists may reply that Eve was created from a rib, not ex nihilo; that *adam* is a generic word meaning humanity; and that Adam was made from the "dust of the ground," which might seem to indicate that humans were made from the same "earth stuff" as all the other animals. In any view, however, it is vital to retain Adam and Eve as actual historical figures, as Billy Graham does in the following statement on human origins:

> *The Bible presents Adam and Eve as special creations from the dust of the ground, not some previous hominid species that evolved from apes.*

I don't think that there's any conflict at all between science today and the Scriptures. I think that we have misinterpreted the Scriptures many times and we've tried to make the Scriptures say things they weren't meant to say. I think that we have made a mistake by thinking the Bible is a scientific book. The Bible is not a book of science. The Bible is a book of Redemption, and of course I accept the Creation story. I believe that God did create the universe. I believe that God created man, and whether it came by an evolutionary process and at a certain point He took this person or being and made him a living soul or not, does not change the fact that God did create man. . . . Whichever way God did it makes no difference as to what man is and man's relationship to God.[4]

***The Fossil Record:*** Our knowledge of the fossil record will always be incomplete since there will always be fossils that have yet to be unearthed. For this reason we are always one discovery away from new and potentially important knowledge about extinct life forms. As the  record now stands, experts hold different opinions about the range of known transitional fossils and their adequacy for supporting macroevolutionary theory. Some say the evidence is against macroevolution of any variety; others maintain that the fossil record, though incomplete, supports common descent. Also at issue is the relatively rapid introduction of new species witnessed in the fossil record and the ability (or inability) of genetic mutation to drive such rapid change. Certainly this is a stiff challenge to naturalism. For now and always the fossil record bears an important testimony that each creation model must take care to understand.

***No Sabbath Rest:*** The process of creation is seemingly ongoing in the Evolutionary Creationism model. After all, by its own claims the same natural laws that were operative millions of years ago when life arose are still operative today, and so presumably macroevolution itself continues and will hypothetically create new life. So this view implies that God has not rested from His works of creation if "rest" means that all creative processes have come to a halt. Noting that microevolutionary processes are ongoing and in some sense count as creative processes, Evolutionary Creationists elect to say that God's rest from the works of creation does not mean He is not still active in shaping life forms.

***Proof of God's Existence:*** Empirically, this view is indistinguishable from what atheistic evolution would expect to find in nature. Therefore, it is paramount to saying that atheists can appeal to the record of nature just as well as Christians can. But design arguments demonstrate that this is simply untrue. Atheistic views of the universe cannot account for the world as we know it.

## CONCLUSION

From ancient times until today, the Bible has offered a unique, compelling answer to the question of ultimate origins. Modern science has powerfully confirmed the biblical testimony that the universe is both created and designed, not eternal and the result of chance.

## Notes

1. Henry M. Morris, ed., *Scientific Creationism*, 2nd edition (El Cajon, CA: Master Books, 1985), 209.

2. Hugh Ross, *Creation as Science* (Colorado Springs: NavPress, 2006), 80.

3. Ibid., 179.

4. Billy Graham, *Personal Thoughts of a Public Man* (Chariot Victor Publishing, 1999), 72–74.

# Part III

# The Creator's Week of Creation

# Chapter 8
# In the Beginning:
# Genesis 1:1–2

The first two verses of Genesis provide a majestic background for the ensuing six days of creation. They also happen to be among the most striking and oft-quoted verses in the Bible. Here we see God creating the heavens and earth, then shaping them to be an eventual home for humans and the stage for the drama of human history.

## *Key Text*

"In the beginning God created the heavens and the earth. Now the earth was formless and empty, darkness covered the surface of the watery depths, and the Spirit of God was hovering over the surface of the waters" (Gen. 1:1–2).

## *Genesis 1:1—The Biblical Doctrine of Creation*

With its first ten words, Genesis distinguishes itself from all other views on origins. This beautifully succinct sentence lays the foundation for the uniqueness and divine authorship of the biblical story of creation. Three key points are established:

1. *The universe had a beginning.*
2. *The universe was created from nothing.*
3. *The universe was created according to God's will.*

Taken together, these three points comprise the biblical doctrine of creation. Let us examine them more closely.

## *The universe had a beginning.*

The opening phrase of Genesis, "In the beginning," indicates that the universe did not always exist. This would have been an astounding claim in ancient times, for all of the earliest cultures believed that the world had always existed. Recall the ancient Mesopotamian and Egyptian views, which held that such things as primordial waters, hills, and temples had always existed. Genesis 1:1 runs counter to all of this. Only divine authorship could justify such an audacious and counter-intuitive claim in the ancient setting. If the Creator brought the entire universe into existence, then of necessity He must exist outside of the creation. This establishes that God is transcendent, which means He exists independent of, above, and beyond His creation.

*Mesopotamian and Egyptian creation myths held that such things as primordial waters, hills, and temples had always existed.*

## *The universe was created from nothing.*

A second key point in Genesis 1:1 is that the universe was not formed from preexisting matter or energy. Instead, it was created from nothing. Like the first point above, this teaching decisively distinguishes Genesis from all other ancient cosmogonies and points toward its divine inspiration. Creation myths of ancient times told of gods who fashioned

the world from eternal matter. Creation *ex nihilo* (Latin for "out of nothing") was completely foreign to the science and philosophy Moses learned in Egypt.

Creation *ex nihilo* can only be the work of a sovereign God, one who has unlimited power and authority to bring all things into being. The Hebrew verb translated

NASA, ESA, S. Beckwith (STScI) and the HUDF Team.

as "created" in Genesis 1:1 is *bara*, which always describes an unprecedented or exceptional work done only by God. In Genesis it speaks of an act of divine fiat (God's will) rather than the outworking of a natural process.[1] This indicates that

God did not work within the confines of physical laws, nor did He call upon eternal forces of nature to bring about the origin of the material world. God brought all matter, space, energy, and time into being from absolutely nothing and with the aid of nothing.

> *God brought all matter, space, energy, and time into being from absolutely nothing and with the aid of nothing.*

Even time had a beginning. In the New Testament we read that God's grace was given to us "before time began" (2 Tim. 1:9). Many times the Scriptures refer to God acting "before the foundation of the world" (Eph. 1:4; 1 Pet. 1:20; John 17:24). Like the physical universe and the natural laws, time is a creation of God.

## The universe was created according to God's will.

Another implication of creation *ex nihilo* is that God alone determines what kind of world exists. There was no need, lack, or insufficiency in God that drove Him to create. Creation has its origin and purpose in God alone.

*St. John on Patmos* from Very Rich Hours of the duke of Berry.

Proverbs tells us that "the LORD has prepared everything for His purpose" (Prov. 16:4). There is ultimately one purpose for which God created all things. In John's inspired vision of the end times, the twenty-four elders proclaim, "You are worthy to receive glory and honor and power, because You have created all things, and because of Your will they exist and were created" (Rev. 4:11). This world was created for God's glory, not merely our enjoyment.

## Science on Ultimate Origins

The first law of thermodynamics describes how energy is transferred between systems and different forms. This law is also called the "Law of Conservation of Energy" because it indicates that energy cannot be created or destroyed. Einstein's famous equation $E = mc^2$ relates matter (m) to energy (E) through the constant speed of light (c) and hence extends the conservation principle

Albert Einstein (1879–1955). Photo: Oren Jack Turner.

to matter as well as energy. An unavoidable implication is that science cannot say how matter and energy came to exist in the first place because natural law indicates it cannot be created or destroyed. Science can only take matter and energy to be givens. While energy and matter cannot be created or destroyed by natural means, the Bible indicates that God can (and did) supernaturally create all matter, energy, space, and time along with the physical laws that govern them.

### *Genesis 1:2—The Early Earth*

In the second verse the context is drawn down from the entire cosmos to the surface of nascent Earth. We do not know how much time has passed since the events described in verse 1. Moses simply says the earth was "formless and empty" at this time, for God had neither shaped it nor filled it yet. This phrase is a play on words in

> *Science and the Bible bear the same testimony about early Earth conditions.*

Hebrew, using the rhyming words *tohu* (formless) and *bohu* (empty). *Bohu* is a rare word and is more difficult to translate than *tohu*, which in other instances can mean "desert" or "wasteland," places of death for straying travelers. Together

The Hadean Era was marked by harsh, volatile conditions.

these words paint an image of early Earth that is nothing like what we experience today. It was uninhabitable, covered in inky waters and enshrouded in darkness. God had already created light, but it had yet to touch the surface of Earth. These are the conditions of the early Earth as God set out to render the wasteland habitable and fill it with life during the creation week.

Interestingly, this stark image of early Earth matches the predictions that scientists envision. Scientists refer to the early stages of the planet as the Hadean Era (after Hades) since the conditions were so hellish. In this period the solar system was still forming from a cloud of gas, dust, and debris orbiting the sun. (Christians would say, "*God* was still forming the solar system from a cloud of gas, dust, and debris orbiting the sun.") Earth began to coalesce by gravity as lumps of matter collided and aggregated. Heat from these collisions rendered Earth a molten mass. The opaque atmosphere, heavy in water vapor and debris, was impenetrable by light from the young sun. As the collisions subsided, Earth's surface cooled and solidified; water condensed from the vapor layer and fell to the ground, amassing in great pools to form an ocean planet. Like the Bible, science says Earth was "formless and empty," and "darkness covered the surface of the watery depths."

*Scientists estimate that there are roughly one hundred billion galaxies in the observable universe, each having about one hundred billion stars.*

So science and the Bible bear the same testimony about early Earth conditions. Still, many have worried that the time lines for each are very different. In an attempt to solve this, some scholars have sought to reconcile Genesis and the geological record by inserting a gap of unspecified time between the first two verses of Genesis 1. This Gap Theory (or Restitution Theory) renders verse 2 as, "Now the earth became formless and empty" as if some great catastrophe (presumably the fall of Satan and his banishment to Earth) befell Earth after its original perfect and complete creation. On this view the six days of creation actually represent the re-creation of the world after its original demise. This view is not widely supported today

*The Fall of Satan* by Gustave Dore.

because it is neither consistent with the grammar of the text nor supportable from the scientific evidence. Nonetheless, it is impossible to know how much (if any) time elapsed between verses 1 and 2.

Next, we read that "the Spirit of God was hovering over the surface of the waters." The phrase *ruach Elohim* can also be translated as a "mighty wind" or "breath of God," as if a mighty wind were wildly tossing the chaotic abyss. This phrase vividly describes the personal presence of God as He actively watches and nurtures His new creation. He is like an eagle soaring over the surface of the waters, hovering and brooding as He prepares to transform lifeless chaos into order and life (see Deut. 32:11, where "hovering" is used to describe God as an eagle watching over His young). Some speculate that the first life forms were created here while the Spirit of God brooded over the waters, nurturing the new creation as His plan began to unfold on Earth.

The association between life-giving wind and the Spirit of God is carried throughout the Bible. In Genesis 2, this wind is associated with the breath of life which is breathed into Adam by God's Spirit. Breath or wind later becomes the biblical terminology for the Spirit of God (see Job 33:4). Thus, it is perhaps not unreasonable to postulate that when the Spirit of God hovered in waiting, it *Earth is now primed for transformation by the Creator who is intimately involved in its creation.* brought life to the waters. This is not made explicit in Genesis, but the omission of details is not unusual in this sparse, focused creation narrative. In any event, Earth is now primed for transformation by the Creator who is intimately involved in its creation.

When the Hubble Space Telescope was pointed at a dark, empty patch of sky and its cameras recorded the imperceptibly faint light for a million seconds, this image was the result. This Hubble Ultra Deep Field Image shows the oldest, faintest, most distand galaxies ever seen. Photo: NASA/ESA, S. Beckwith (STScI) and the HUDF Team.

## The Beginning as Recorded in the Book of Nature

Ancient civilizations believed the world was fashioned by the gods from eternal matter. Today scientists have conclusive evidence that the physical universe, including time itself, came into being in the not too distant past (in cosmological timescales). Because all matter, space, and time came into being from nothing, whatever brought it into being must exist outside the bounds of our material universe. In a very real sense, science has observed that there must exist a cause that transcends nature, a "super-natural" agent of creation.

Scientists have also learned that our universe is unimaginably immense. Although only a few thousand stars are visible to the naked eye, scientists estimate that there are roughly one hundred billion galaxies in the observable universe, each having about one hundred billion stars. That means there are 10,000,000,000,000,000,000,000 stars in the observable universe, give or take a few. How big is that number? Suppose you were to cover the entire continental United States with decks of playing cards. If the decks were stacked 200,000 deep, then each individual card would represent one star in the observable universe.

Such vast quantities of matter and energy testify to the unfathomable power and wisdom of the Creator. It is no surprise that when God wants to reassure His people that He understands their situation and is able to care for them, He tells them, "Look up and see: who created these? He brings out the starry host by number; He calls all of them by name. Because of His great power and strength, not one of them is missing" (Isa. 40:26). *God calls each star by name!* He then goes on to ask how we could possibly think that He doesn't know, care about, or provide for us. If He knows each star and makes sure that each is fulfilling its destiny, how much more does He watch over us?

Isaiah 40:26 says God calls each star by name. Photo: NASA.

Since the beginning of time, God has revealed His "eternal power and divine nature" through His creation (Rom. 1:20). This testimony of creation, evident to humanity since the beginning, is now even more clearly seen with the advent of modern science.

> ### Modern science affirms two truths established in the first ten words of Genesis:
>
> - *The entire physical universe had a beginning.*
> - *The external cause must transcend creation, meaning it exceeds the universe in power, dimension, wisdom, endurance, etc.*

## Worldview Summary

### GOD IS TRANSCENDENT

From the very first sentence the Bible makes a radical declaration: the universe and all it contains had a beginning.

Only in the Bible do we read of a Creator who exists outside the bounds of matter, space, time, and energy. Only the Bible tells of a Creator who brought all things into being from nothing by His innate power.

## THE IMPORTANCE OF THE DOCTRINE OF CREATION

*The Christian's hope is secured by a sovereign Creator who transcends time and space and holds destiny in His hands.*

All Christian truth is ultimately founded on the biblical doctrine of creation. Because God is not subject to the confines of space and time or limited by anything outside Himself, He is able to fulfill His purposes in the world. The Christian's hope is secured by a sovereign Creator who transcends time and space and holds destiny in His hands.

## *Note*

1. Although *bara* is used with the creation of man, man was not created "out of nothing" since "God formed the man out of dust from the ground" (Gen. 2:7). The physical elements (carbon, iron, oxygen, etc.) of which man is comprised already existed since God had previously created them, but the spiritual being made in the image of God was created ex nihilo.

# Chapter 9
# The First Day:
# Genesis 1:3–5

God's first creation workday begins in the third verse of Genesis with His first spoken words. Beginning with a formless and void water-covered planet, the first command does what only God can do: dispel darkness with light.

## Key Text

"Then God said, 'Let there be light,' and there was light. God saw that the light was good, and God separated the light from the darkness. God called the light 'day,' and He called the darkness 'night.' Evening came, and then morning: the first day" (Gen. 1:3–5).

## Literary Structure of the Days

Readers often overlook it, but the creation account actually follows a well-defined literary pattern. Beginning in verse 3, the creation days follow a structure consisting of commencement, command, commentary, and closure. Slight variances in form appear among some of the days, but on the whole there is a match between each of the six days. For example, on the first day the structure is:

| | |
|---|---|
| **Commencement** | "Then God said" |
| **Command** | "Let there be light" |
| **Commentary** | |
| **Fulfillment** | "and there was light" |
| **Evaluation** | "God saw that the light was good" |
| **Description** | "God separated the light from the darkness. God called the light 'day,' and He called darkness 'night.'" |
| **Closure** | "Evening came, and then morning: the first day." |

Each of the six days is introduced by "Then God said" and closed with "Evening came, and then morning." This structure draws attention to the Creator's words, for His word is the active Agent of creation. It also sets the bounds for defining what works God did on a given day. Importantly, this pattern indicates that Day One begins in verse 3 some unspecified time after God had already created the heavens and earth (v. 1). Go back and read the first three verses of Genesis carefully. It appears that the "first day" of creation may not mark the ultimate beginning of God's work as Creator. Exodus 20:11 supports this possibility, for it says of the creation week, "For the LORD made the heavens and the earth, the sea, and everything in them in six days." The word translated "made" in this verse is the verb *asah*, which emphasizes the process of fashioning material which *already exists*. Since Exodus 20:11 has the six days of creation in view when it uses this verb, it may imply that what God did during the creation week was shape materials He had already created. This may initially sound implausible, but note that in Genesis 1:1 (which precedes the introduction to Day One in Genesis 1:3) the verb *bara* is used to describe God's original, ex nihilo creation of the heavens and earth.

In summary, what shapes up here is the possibility that God

> *It appears that the "first day" of creation may not mark the ultimate beginning of God's work as Creator.*

created the heavens and earth sometime before the "first day" of creation and then shaped them during the creation week. This may indicate that the six days of the creation account are literary vehicles for conveying God's purposes, not precisely chronological accounts of how and when He made the universe. Other commentators disagree with this and hold that the literary structure does not bound the days so precisely and that the heavens and the earth were indeed originally created during what Moses describes as Day One of God's workweek. The Bible seems to allow either view equally.

## Day One: Command

"Let there be light." With these words, God caused light to illuminate the surface of primordial Earth. "Fiat lux" is how the command is translated in the Latin Vulgate; from this we get the term "fiat command." It indicates the power of the Creator's spoken word. The Sovereign speaks and His will is accomplished.

The largest recorded solar flare. Photo: NASA Marshall Space Flight Center (NASA-MSFC).

## Day One: Commentary

On the first day of creation, emphasis is placed on the fiat command rather than the action that brought about the execution of the command. The account is more expansive on the following days, where we are told such things as "the earth brought forth vegetation," which portrays God using secondary means (the land) to create a new thing (vegetation). Grass is His creation, but the land produced it, and it did so by the natural laws and capacities God had designed.

The creation of light brings about the first separation. Light is separated from darkness on the surface of the earth. Throughout Scripture light is used to refer to the presence of

God or the advancement of His kingdom into a world darkened by sin. In John 1:1–5 we learn that Christ is the Word of God through whom all things were created, and in whom is "the light of men" that "shines in the darkness."

The creation verbs used in Genesis indicate that God worked both supernaturally and naturally to create the world. Hence, things like grass are God's creation even though He created it through secondary means (the natural laws and earth He created).

## Creation Verbs in Genesis 1:1–2:3

Seven different verbs are used in Genesis 1:1–2:3 to describe God's creation and fashioning of the world. Together they indicate that God worked independently from the natural realm (supernatural providence) as well as within the natural realm (normal providence) to accomplish His creation purposes.

*bara*—to create, fashion, or form

1 - God "created" the heavens and the earth.

21 - God "created" the large sea creatures.

27 - God "created" humans.

2:3 - His work of "creation."

*hayah*—to exist, be, become, come to pass, happen

3 - "Let there be" light.

6 - "Let there be" an expanse.

14 - "Let there be" light.

*asah*—to do, make, fashion, or accomplish

7 - God "made" the expanse.

11–12 - Trees "bearing" fruit.

16 - God "made" two great lights.

25 - God "made" the wildlife of the earth.

26 - Let us "make" man.

31 - All that he had "made."

2:3 - God created and "made" (NASB).

*raah*—to be seen or to see, appear, be visible

9 – Let the dry land "appear."

(also for God "saw" in v. 4 and others).

*dasha*—bring forth, sprout, shoot, grow green

11 - Earth "bring forth" grass.

*yatsa*—to go or come out, bring forth, lead out

12 - Earth "produce" vegetation.

24 - Earth "produce" living creatures.

*nathan*—give, bestow, permit, put, set, appoint, assign

17 - God "placed" them in the expanse.

29 - I have "given" you plants.

## *Sun and Light: A Closer Look at Days 1–4*

It is striking to note that light appears on Day One, three days before the sun is created on Day Four. Does this mean the light of Day One was not from our sun? Many have thought so, suggesting that a temporary light source was initially created. Others suggest that God's own glory illuminated Earth during those first few days. Regardless of the source of the light, this has long been a point of consternation for interpreters who take a strictly literal approach to the creation account. How can there be a solar day (on Days One, Two, and Three) when the sun does not yet exist? After all, the text says there was "evening and morning" on each of those three days, and evening and morning are periods defined wholly on the basis of solar phenomena. Seemingly, if those first creation days are defined by the ebb and flow of light when there is no sun, the length of those days is undefined. Moreover, this temporary source of light would have to possess many of the properties of the sun to maintain the orbit of Earth and provide the spectrum of electromagnetic radiation needed to sustain the life created on Day Three.

The mystery of the light source for Days One, Two, and Three is one of the primary exegetical reasons many Bible scholars do not regard the first three days to be 24 hours long. Additionally, God's command in Genesis 1:3 for light to appear on the surface of Earth uses the verb *hayah* (let there be), which means "to exist, be, come to pass or happen." Hence, this verb does not have the same connotation as *bara*, which pictures supernatural creation. The heavens (which, of course, have light) and earth had already been created with the *bara* of Genesis 1:1; thus a distinction may be made here between the creation of light in Genesis 1:1 and the first appearance of light on the surface of Earth in Genesis 1:3. In the next section we will explain how this could be.

*Seemingly, if those first creation days are defined by the ebb and flow of light when there is no sun, the length of those days is undefined.*

## Day One: The Record of Nature

The view that the creation days were not necessarily 24 hours long opens the way for matching the Genesis account with discoveries in science. Scientists believe our solar system began from a rotating cloud of gas that aggregated under the forces of gravity and electromagnetism. In this model the early Milky Way was a dusty, rocky disk where sunlight was mostly hidden by debris. What little light that did manage to reach Earth's neighborhood from the veiled sun was further blocked from reaching Earth's surface by the murky atmosphere that was draped over our planet. Thus, Earth's primordial surface was covered in darkness, just as Genesis 1:2 says.

Scientists are not sure exactly what happened to lift the veil from Earth's atmosphere, but the evidence indicates that around four billion years ago the atmosphere changed from opaque to translucent. Further evidence suggests that a collision between Earth and a large body (the size of Mars or larger) about 4.25 billion years ago may have caused this change. This event would have ejected the dense, sun-blocking atmosphere into space, leaving behind a thin atmosphere that would support life and allow sunlight to reach Earth's surface. The sun, moon, and stars could not yet be seen through the translucent atmosphere, but for the first time in Earth's history, daytime could be

Artist's conception of the birth of a planet. Photo: NASA/JPL.

clearly distinguished from night. In space the resulting debris from this impact coalesced to form our moon, providing some light at night. In any case, this scenario from science fits nicely with the interpretation of Genesis mentioned above, namely that the sun was created in Genesis 1:1 but did not illumine the surface of Earth until a later time, as recounted in Genesis 1:3.

## *Worldview Summary*
### *GOD'S PROVIDENCE*

Whether by miracle or by means of His designing and upholding of natural processes, God is the Creator of all things. His work of creating the entire universe from nothing distinguishes Him from all other creation traditions, but His ongoing works in nature are no less magnificent.

# Chapter 10
# The Second Day:
# Genesis 1:6–8

After separating light from darkness, the Creator continues His work of separation by dividing the waters in the sky from the waters on the earth.

## Key Text

"Then God said, 'Let there be an expanse between the waters, separating water from water.' So God made the expanse and separated the water under the expanse from the water above the expanse. And it was so. God called the expanse 'sky.' Evening came, and then morning: the second day" (Gen. 1:6–8).

## Day Two: Command

The Creator's second command fashions an "expanse" to separate "the water under the expanse from the water above the expanse." The Hebrew word for "expanse" occurs 17 times in the Old Testament, nine of which are in the first chapter of Genesis. So what does it mean? Opinions vary.

## *Day Two: Commentary*

Some have suggested the "expanse" (or "firmament") that was created on Day Two was a water vapor canopy that maintained a tropical environment, enabled the longevity of the early patriarchs, and provided water for Noah's flood.

But is this argument persuasive? In verse 8, God names the expanse and calls it "sky," which is the same word used

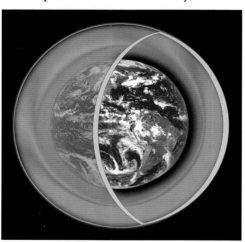

for "heavens" in verse 1. These two Hebrew words (expanse and sky/heavens) appear together again in verses 14, 15, and 17, where the celestial bodies are observed as lights in "the expanse of the sky." In verse 20 "expanse" describes the place where birds fly. David also uses "sky" and "expanse" as synonyms in Psalm 19:1 when he says, "The heavens [sky] declare the glory of God, and the sky [expanse] proclaims the work of His hands."

These broad uses make it especially difficult to define "expanse" specifically as a vapor canopy. David drives the final nail in the vapor canopy theory in Psalm 148. In verse 4 he uses the same Hebrew terminology that is used in Genesis 1:7 when he calls upon the expanse (heavens) and the waters above it to praise the Lord. This means the expanse still existed in David's day. Hence, "expanse" cannot refer to a vapor canopy that collapsed and inundated the earth at the time of Noah's flood.

*Biblical issues plus some outstanding scientific objections have caused most modern commentators to reject the vapor canopy theory.*

These biblical issues plus some outstanding scientific objections have caused most modern commentators to reject the vapor canopy theory.

The best conclusion is that "expanse" is an example of phenomenological language, where things are described not in scientifically verifiable terms but merely as they appear to the casual observer. In the phenomenological sense the atmosphere is accurately depicted as a finite, distinct covering over the surface of the earth through which the birds fly and the sun, moon, and stars run their course.

*The best conclusion is that "expanse" is an example of phenomenological language, where things are described not in scientifically verifiable terms but merely as they appear to the casual observer.*

Two key elements that are necessary for the sustenance of life are now in place after the first two workdays of creation. Light and a stable water cycle provide the conditions needed for the first forms of life to be created. These organisms in turn further prepare Earth for the Creator's special image-bearers, which God will soon create.

### Day Two: The Record of Nature

A stable atmosphere is a vital possession for a planet. Venus and Mars, the second and fourth planets out from our sun, both have atmospheres but remain inhospitable. Venus's carbon-dioxide-rich atmosphere traps heat from the sun, making the planet's surface hot enough to melt lead. Mars

Mars. Photo: NASA, ESA, The Hubble Heritage Team (STScI/AURA), J. Bell (Cornell University) and M. Wolff (Space Science Institute).

also has an atmosphere primarily made of carbon dioxide, but the air is so thin that it barely retains any heat, making the planet too cold for higher life.

Early in Earth history, our atmosphere was transformed

due to several factors. For instance, volcanoes and earthquakes belched gases from deep within the earth, enriching the primordial atmosphere. Continual bombardments from comets (which are made primarily of dirty ice) brought large volumes of water into our atmosphere. All of these factors worked together to shift our atmosphere to the fine-tuned state needed to support complex life.

Venus. Photo: NASA/JPL.

An intriguingly "coincidental" transformation took place simultaneously with our sun and Earth's atmosphere. It is known as the "faint young sun paradox." As the sun's luminosity increased early in the history of the solar system, the carbon dioxide content in Earth's atmosphere changed in sync to maintain a precise range of hospitable temperatures while preventing a runaway greenhouse effect. Scientists theorize that microscopic organisms in the oceans played an important role in clearing carbon dioxide from the atmosphere. These simple organisms absorb carbon dioxide and release oxygen as a byproduct. This continued for billions of years, decreasing the heat retained by the atmosphere as the greenhouse gases diminished in the atmosphere. Eventually the atmosphere became oxygenated enough for more complex forms of life. Whatever the actual mechanisms might have been, the evidence shows that our atmosphere became more hospitable over time. Again, science fits the Genesis account, where Earth transitioned from formless and void to teeming with life.

*Again, science fits the Genesis account, where Earth transitioned from formless and void to teeming with life.*

Today our atmosphere is divided into five distinct layers. The first layer is known as the troposphere, which contains half of Earth's atmospheric gases. Jets fly in the stratosphere, which rides atop the troposphere. Above this is the mesosphere, where meteors typically burn up before they can strike Earth. Next is the sparse thermosphere where low Earth-orbiting satellites, the space station, and the space shuttle orbit. Finally, the atmosphere merges into space in the exosphere. Genesis may appropriately describe these differentiated layers of our atmosphere as "separating water from water," for a key distinction between each layer is their differing amounts of water.

## Worldview Summary

### HUMAN LANGUAGE AND THE WORKS OF GOD

The Bible is the inspired Word of God and accurately conveys all that God intends for it to convey. It is wholly dependable in all of its pronouncements. An important step for any Bible reader is to recognize the use of phenomenological language, where events are described as they appear from the finite human perspective, and reach past this to grasp the objective intention of Scripture. Reverence for God's Word demands that we take this task seriously.

Illustration: NASA.

# Chapter 11
# The Third Day:
# Genesis 1:9–13

It isn't easy to watch new land be born. Standing near the fiery red heat of glowing magma gives you a hint of the energy stored up in Earth's interior. Erupting lava, boiling steam, methane explosions, and pyroclastic flows are just a few of the ways a volcano can ruin your day.

## *Key Text*

"Then God said, 'Let the water under the sky be gathered into one place, and let the dry land appear.' And it was so. God called the dry land 'earth,' and He called the gathering of the water 'seas.' And God saw that it was good. Then God said, 'Let the earth produce vegetation: seed-bearing plants, and fruit trees on the earth bearing fruit with seed in it, according to their kinds.' And it was so. The earth brought forth vegetation: seed-bearing plants according to their kinds and trees bearing fruit with seed in it, according to their kinds. And God saw that it was good. Evening came, and then morning: the third day" (Gen. 1:9–13).

## Day Three: Command

On Day Three, God separates the ocean from dry land. Instead of covering all the land, the ocean is now "gathered into one place." God also begins to fill these newly separated domains. His first step is to command vegetation to spring forth.

> *By naming the key regions of creation, God demonstrates His authority over all things.*

Patagonian Shelf off the coast of Argentina. Photo: The Seawifs Project, NASA/Goddard Space Flight Center, and ORBIMAGE.

## Day Three: Commentary

God's naming of the sky, earth, and seas is a strategy reflecting the antimythological nature of Genesis. To answer pagan cosmogonies that deified creation, Moses demonstrates God's dominion over these by noting that He made them, organized them, and then named them. For ancient societies, the act of bestowing a name demonstrated authority, as when kings renamed those whom they conquered. Moses' point is clear: by naming the key regions of creation, God demonstrates

> *Proponents of a recent creation assert that each act of creation was a miraculous act that occured essentially instantaneously.*

His authority over all things. Importantly, God also delegates authority to His image bearers. This is why Adam was given naming rights and dominion over the animals.

Proponents of a recent creation assert that each act of creation was a miraculous act that occurred essentially instantaneously. In other words all acts of creation were supernatural.

*Advocates of ancient creation believe the verbs used in Genesis indicate that God used both supernatural and natural processes to create the world.*

Those who hold to an ancient creation believe the verbs used in the text indicate that God used both supernatural and natural processes to create the world. Further, proponents of ancient creation point out that God's creative decree on Day Three was indirect. He did not command vegetation to appear; He commanded the *earth* (ground) to "produce vegetation." Ground does not produce vegetation instantly, and there seems to be no indication here that anything out of the ordinary occurred. Hence, Genesis seems to say that in this case God's creative action was accomplished via natural operations. Now, if this is so, does the earth itself get ultimate credit for producing vegetation? Of course not. All it did was act by design – *God's* design!

So Genesis indicates that God demonstrates His power through direct acts of creation as well as indirect acts which follow the natural laws He created. Though science can describe natural causes for events in nature, it is God who causes the earth to produce vegetation, enables creatures to reproduce according to their kinds, and so on. Genesis stresses that all things owe their existence to God alone. God's use of secondary means does not detract from His glory.

Some scientists were talking about how far technology had come. Having split the atom, walked on the moon, and decoded the human genome, they figured humankind no longer needed God. So they let God know that He was free to go now.

God listened and then challenged them to a man-making contest, just like when He made Adam from dust. The scientists agreed and bent over to scoop up some dirt.

God just smiled at the scientists and said, "Wait a minute — get your own dirt!"

Two kinds of vegetation are created on Day Three: seed-bearing plants and fruit trees with seeds in the fruit. Constraints are placed on the vegetation to reproduce "according to their kinds." The word translated "kinds" (*min*) is used as a broad classification for plants, animals, birds, and fish. It is tempting to associate the biblical "kinds" with scientific classifications such as species, but analytical precision is probably not the Bible's intent here. Rather, the kinds point to broad distinctions and procreative bounds between living things.

> *Genesis stresses that all things owe their dependency to God alone. God's use of secondary means does not detract from His glory.*

## Day Three: The Record of Nature

As early as the sixteenth century, observant people recognized that the continents would fit together into one giant landmass if they were brought together like the pieces of a puzzle. Several field discoveries bolstered this conviction. For example, unusual geological structures on the coastlines of South America and Africa match when the continents are hypothetically merged. Furthermore, fossils of dinosaurs and plants found along the coasts of Africa and South America also correspond in placement.

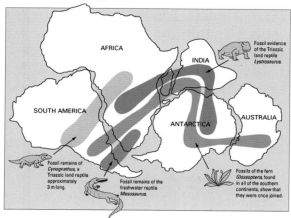

This diagram illustrates how fossils found on different continents correspond to Pangea, when the contents formed one giant landmass. Credit: USGS.

Scientists have since found similar proofs of continental drift. Corresponding coal seams, remnants of semitropical fauna in extreme northern latitudes, and matching glacier scars in Africa and South America all confirm that the continents were originally merged.

Significant advances in the past thirty years have helped scientists understand continent formation. We now know that our planet's surface consists of several plates that "float" atop hotter material beneath the earth's crust. Plate tectonics (the science of plate movement) explains that the shifting of these plates over subterranean magma causes phenomena such as earthquakes and volcanoes. Even mountains are formed as plates rub against one another and push up wrinkles in the land's surface.

| PERMIAN | JURASSIC | PRESENT DAY |
| 225 Million Years Ago | 150 Million Years Ago | |

Credit: USGS.

The seafloor provided the final line of evidence for plate tectonics. Maps of the Atlantic Ocean floor reveal a sharp ridge running down the middle. A deep rift runs through the center of this ridge. Like a scene straight from Genesis, molten magma bubbles up through earth's crust and forms new seafloor as it cools, hardens, and spreads away from the ridge. On one side the new rock moves toward Europe; on the other it creeps toward the Americas. The thickness of the seafloor increases as you move farther out from the ridge because these areas are older and have had more time to collect sediment. Radiometric dating confirms that the age of the seafloor increases linearly with distance away from the ridge. Most telling of all, the seafloor embeds a distinct record of shifting magnetic fields over time. Analysis of this record shows that it agrees with the dates predicted

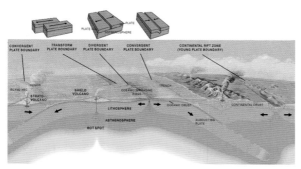

Credit: USGS.

by the plate tectonics model. Finally, the matching fossils on the opposite sides of the ocean date to a time more ancient than the ocean floor itself, which means the continents split apart after these animals went extinct.

What does all of this mean? It means modern science has finally caught up with the inerrant Bible by recognizing that God gathered the oceans together, caused dry land to appear, and then ordained that the dry land be split up into the continents we see today (Gen 1:9–13).

## Does the Bible Teach That Life Began on Land?

Scientific evidence suggests that life began in the seas before vegetation appeared on dry land. Does the Bible teach the reverse? Or did God create the first living organisms while the Spirit of God hovered over the waters? We cannot say for sure. The fact is Scripture does not explicitly say when the first living organisms were created.

Antoni van Leeuwenhoek was the first to observe bacteria.

We should not expect Scripture to emphasize the creation of the first living organism, especially since the simplest life forms were not observed by men until Leeuwenhoek (1632–1723) observed bacteria using his primitive microscope. Before that, humankind would not have comprehended any biblical statements about microscopic life.

*Moses, through God's guidance, chose literary styles and elements that were suited to the purpose at hand: a polemic against pagan creation myths.*

Obviously, Moses could not possibly include every detail in his creation account, so under God's guidance he chose literary styles and elements that were suited to the task. That task included an antimythological polemic, which means the account is written to argue against the pagan creation myths of that day. As we have seen, Genesis is maximally effective in achieving that purpose.

## *Worldview Summary*

### *DIVINE DOMINION*

As Creator of the universe, God has dominion over all things. It is His right to order, direct, and conduct every aspect of creation in order that He may accomplish His purposes. Importantly, one of God's chief purposes is to bestow on humans important freedoms and stewardships. One of the greatest opportunities we have is to be overseers of creation. This world is ours to govern and care for, and we will answer for how well we fulfill our responsibilities.

# Chapter 12
# The Fourth Day:
# Genesis 1:14–19

On Day One God decreed that there should be light, and it was so. Now, on Day Four, God appoints lights in the sky to serve for the regulation of cycles and to guide our journeys.

## *Key Text*

"Then God said, 'Let there be lights in the expanse of the sky to separate the day from the night. They will serve as signs for festivals and for days and years. They will be lights in the expanse of the sky to provide light on the earth.' And it was so. God made the two great lights—the greater light to have dominion over the day and the lesser light to have dominion over the night—as well as the stars. God placed them in the expanse of the sky to provide light on the earth, to dominate the day and the night, and to

"Evening came, and then morning: the fourth day" (Gen. 1:19).

separate light from darkness. And God saw that it was good. Evening came, and then morning: the fourth day" (Gen. 1:14–19).

## Day Four: Command

On Day Four God placed the luminaries in the sky for three purposes:

1. to separate day from night
2. to serve as signs for festivals, days, and years
3. to provide light on the earth

Now that the sun, moon, and stars are present in the night sky, seasons and years can be calculated and precise navigation is also possible.

## Three Views on the Sun, Moon, and Stars of Day 4

| | |
|---|---|
| **Recent Creation** | A temporary light source was created on Day One (a literal day); permanent light sources (sun, moon, and stars) were created on Day Four. |
| **Framework** | The sun, moon, and stars were created on Day One (a nonliteral day); this day coincided with Day Four. |
| **Ancient Creation** | Sun, moon, and stars were created on Day One (a nonliteral day) and were first seen on earth's surface on Day Four. |

## Day Four: Commentary

In keeping with its antimythological theme, Genesis here emphasizes that the heavenly bodies are created servants. Though they are given dominion over day and night, they are not to be worshipped. Recall that in the Babylonian Enuma Elish, the stars are deities which were placed in the sky by Marduk.

An interesting literary parallel exists between Day One and Day Four. Just as *light* was created on Day One to separate light from darkness, on Day Four the *lights* are made to separate day from night. The function is the same both days; the only distinction is that on Day Four the luminaries are emphasized as the objects which carry out this purpose, whereas on Day One we are not told the source for light.

> *The Framework view draws the conclusion that Days One and Four describe events that actually coincided in time and that they are presented as separate days in order to construct a memorable framework which conveys theological truth.*

What is the significance of this parallel? Opinions differ. The Recent Creation view holds that a temporary light source was at work on Day One and was replaced by the sun, moon, and stars when they were created on Day Four. The Framework view draws the conclusion that Days One and Four describe events that actually coincided in time and that they are presented as separate days in order to construct a memorable framework which conveys theological truth. The Ancient Creation view reasons that the actual sun was the source for the small amount of light that reached Earth on Day One but that it was not until Day Four that the sun, moon, and stars themselves were actually discernible from the surface of Earth. (Think of a car sitting in the fog with its headlights on. While the fog is thick, all you see is broadly dispersed light. Then, as the fog dissipates, you can discern that car headlights are the specific source of the light.)

When fog is thick, it is impossible to discern where the sun is located. In a similar manner, when space was occluded with debris, light from the sun was broadly dispersed and dimmed.

The Ancient Creation view enjoys

support from both science and biblical linguistics. Verse 16, which describes God's work on Day Four, says God "made" (*asah*) the lights, and verse 17 says that he "placed" (*nathan*) them in the sky. *Nathan* has a rich variety of uses. It appears over 2,000 times in the Old Testament, and among other things it can mean to "give, put, set, make, set forth, or show." In Psalm 8:1, the psalmist says to God, "[You] have displayed Your splendor above the heavens" (NASB). Genesis 1:17 may use *nathan* in the same way the psalmist does: to say that God displayed the sun, moon, and stars on Day Four. Now that God had finished His work of separation, the atmosphere had been made transparent, and for the first time the sun, moon, and stars could be seen as distinct heavenly bodies from the surface of Earth.

The verb *nathan* is also used in Genesis 9:13 when God says, "I have placed My bow in the clouds." This is especially pertinent since God did not create a rainbow ex nihilo here. After all, a rainbow is a natural result of the optical properties of

water vapor which splits sunlight like a prism. So this phenomenon existed prior to Noah's day, but God ascribed a new meaning to it after the flood. Likewise, one can reasonably suggest that God did not create (*bara*) the sun, moon, and stars on Day Four, but rather that He ascribed a new

Rainbows are natural phenomena that would have occurred long before Noah's flood.

function to them since, given their newly improved visibility from Earth's surface, they could now do more than merely separate day from night.

## Day Four: The Record of Nature

As the solar system continued to mature, the primordial debris orbiting close to the sun dispersed, and the bombardment of our planet abated. Rains began to cleanse the atmosphere of the dusty remnants of celestial collisions. Carbon dioxide levels diminished, and oxygen levels rose as microorganisms and plants absorbed carbon dioxide and released oxygen. Complex life forms demand high levels of oxygen, and so this transformation was a necessary step in the Creator's preparation of Earth for the life He would subsequently create. As the atmosphere cleared, a morning came when the sun could be seen to rise. Although there were no people alive to witness it (Adam was created on Day Six), a night finally came when the stars and

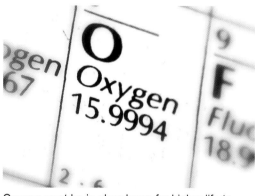

Oxygen must be in abundance for higher life to exist.

the moon first penetrated the cloudy skies. Now the sky was fit to serve the purposes of timekeeping and direction-keeping for Earth's future inhabitants.

## *A Pseudo-Sun?*

Would a temporary light source fit the Genesis account? Not according to Dr. Hugh Ross. In *The Genesis Question*, he says that much more than mere light is required for life. Plants created on Day Three would require a broad range of energy from the electromagnetic spectrum. In fact, plants and animals seem to be optimized for the specific *spectral distribution* of energy that we receive from the sun. Life also strongly depends on the *amount* of energy we receive from the sun. All of these are functions of our sun's highly specific characteristics.

An even bigger problem is that life depends on much more than just light from the sun. Earth's orbit and the orbits of asteroids, comets,

The sun plays a key role in determining Earth's orbital period. NASA Johnson Space Center — Earth Sciences and Image Analysis (NASA-JSC-ES&IA).

and other planets depend on the gravitational attraction of the sun. Additionally, Earth's orbital period, tides, and weather patterns are linked to the mass and gravitational attraction of the sun.

Hence we are left with one of two options for the source of light on Days One, Two and Three:

Illustration: NASA/JPL.

1. Light emanated from a temporary source for the first three days. This implies that either the temporary source had the same mass, chemical composition, and thermonuclear processes as our sun, or that the laws of physics were different on the first three days (which is an argument from silence and so relies on speculation rather than biblical or scientific evidence).

2. Light emanated from the sun for the first three days, but the sun could not be seen from the surface of Earth until Day Four.

Which option seems to fit all the data better? Without question God could have illuminated Earth with a temporary light source, suspended the laws of physics, or even separated light from dark with His own *shekinah* glory. The issue is not what He *could* have done but rather what He actually did do. While the Bible does not aim to answer exhaustive questions about this issue, natural revelation provides a rich text in regard to such questions. This natural text provides a clear testimony to the harmony of God's natural and supernatural revelations, a harmony that Paul cites as the primary apologetic for the existence, power, and divinity of the Creator (Rom. 1:19–20). In this light the second option above seems best.

> *The study of early Earth history calls forth praise of our Creator, not skepticism about His existence.*

## *Worldview Summary*

### *GOD AND THE SCIENCE OF PLANET FORMATION*

Star and planet formation is a complicated field of research. When investigating this field as a nonspecialist, there are two opposite errors you may be tempted to make. First, you may assume scientists are attempting the impossible. The task is just too big, you assume. The opposite error is that you might decide we've pretty much sewn up all the answers by now. The truth lies somewhere in the middle. But one thing is clear: however much we may learn about the physical operations of planet formation, it is overwhelmingly obvious that an Almighty Designer lies behind the whole project. The study of early Earth history, therefore, calls forth praise of our Creator, not skepticism about His existence.

# Chapter 13
# The Fifth Day:
# Genesis 1:20–23

God fashioned the atmosphere and separated the sky from the sea on Day Two. He now moves to fill those domains with creatures.

## *Key Text*

"Then God said, 'Let the water swarm with living creatures, and let birds fly above the earth across the expanse of the sky.' So God created the large sea-creatures and every living creature that moves and swarms in the water, according

"Then God said, 'Let the water swarm with living creatures...'" (Gen. 1:20).

to their kinds. He also created every winged bird according to its kind. And God saw that it was good. So God blessed them, 'Be fruitful, multiply, and fill the waters of the seas, and let the birds multiply on the earth.' Evening came, and then morning: the fifth day" (Gen. 1:20–23).

## Day Five: Command

With a sweeping command, God speaks into existence the creatures that swim in the ocean, crawl on the seafloor, and fly through the sky. He tells the waters to swarm with life.

## Day Five: Commentary

Day Five parallels Day Two insomuch as the realms created on Day Two are now filled with creatures. We also find the first blessing (a gesture of divine favor) in the Bible. In this case the blessing is for creatures to be fruitful, multiply, and fill their domains.

Creatures that are capable of high levels of interaction are originated on Day Five. The Hebrew words *chay nephesh* are translated as "living creatures" here, in 1:24 where the earth produced "living creatures," and in 2:7 where man became a "living being." *Nephesh* is typically understood to be the soul, and some commentators draw a distinction between "soulish" creatures and lesser animals, but here the word is likely used generically to refer to animals.

*God is responsible for all life, whether created by miracle or through the natural processes of reproduction He designed.*

The blessing demonstrates that God alone innately possesses life. More than just granting life to these creatures, God grants them the natural ability to pass life along to successive generations. By granting the ability to self-propagate according to their kinds, God demonstrates that He is responsible for all life—whether created by miracle or through the natural processes of reproduction that He designed.

The phrase "large sea-creatures" stems from the Hebrew word *tanninim*, which means "dragon, sea monster, serpent, or

Baal, the false god of Canaanite mythology.

whale." This word represented the ominous Sea in Canaanite mythology which fought against the Canaanite god, Baal. A similar concept is found in the Enuma Elish, where the Babylonian god Marduk battled Tiamat, the deified primeval waters. In passages such as Isaiah 27:1; 51:9; and Psalm 71:13–14, the word describes dragon-like monsters who symbolize God's enemies.

Here in verse 20 we find the second occurrence of the word *bara*. Recall that this is the Hebrew word that most strongly refers to supernatural acts of creation. *Bara* is only associated with three acts of creation: the heavens and earth (v. 1), the sea creatures and birds (v. 21), and humans (v. 27). It may be that *bara* is reserved for description of the creation of things which the pagans deified. In  this case, *bara* and *tanninim* are used to demonstrate that even the ominous sea monsters are not gods to be feared but merely living creatures formed by the one true God.

## Day Five: The Record of Nature

The events of Day Five would correspond to a very long stretch of the fossil record. For instance, fish are generally associated with the Silurian and Devonian periods of the Paleozoic era, whereas birds do not arrive until the Tertiary period of the Cenizoic era. Marine life in general extends to the earliest geological records of the Cambrian strata.

*The sequence of animal life in Genesis 1 and the sequence of their appearance in the fossil record show an amazing accord.*

Opponents of the biblical creation account attempt to discredit the Bible by asserting inconsistencies in the order of creation between Genesis and the fossil record. In keeping with the purpose of Genesis 1, we must remember that the creation account is intended to be a polemic against pagan mythological deities, not a science treatise. Consequently, while we should expect it to deal with creatures that figured prominently in pagan worship, we should not expect it to be comprehensive of all known animals; neither should we expect it to conform absolutely to the sequences richly detailed in the fossil record. Having noted these limitations, it is nonetheless fascinating to note that the types of creatures that are listed on Days Five and Six do generally conform to the sequence found in the fossil record: various forms of marine life were created, then birds, then various land beasts, and finally humans. At this simplified level of comparison, the sequence of animal life in Genesis 1 and the sequence of their appearance in the fossil record show an amazing accord.

Genesis does not claim to exhaustively record the origination of every species. General classes of creatures are described on specific days, but does that limit God's ability to create other species (left unmentioned) on other days? It seems best not to press the text too narrowly on such points.

Fossil from the Cretaceous Period. Photo: Dave Dyet.

## *The Cambrian Explosion*

Whereas Darwinian evolution presumes a continual development of life through the gradual accumulation of successive mutations and adaptations, the fossil record testifies that life was created in periodic bursts punctuated by vast periods of stasis. For instance, a veritable explosion of life forms is documented in the Cambrian strata. Prior to that the only evidence of life is of algae and other simple life forms. The richness and complexity of the marine life documented in the Cambrian is just as complex as and even more diversified than modern seabeds. These facts present grave problems for naturalism.

*The richness and complexity of the marine life documented in the Cambrian is just as complex as and even more diversified than modern seabeds. These facts present grave problems for naturalism.*

## Worldview Summary

### SOULISH CREATURES AND THE TRIUNE GOD

Being eternally Father, Son, and Holy Spirit, God is a communal Being. Relationship is fundamental to God's nature. As the only species created in God's image, humans are by nature relational creatures. We best reflect God's image when our lives bear out the value of relationship.

# Chapter 14
# The Sixth Day:
# Genesis 1:24–31

Everything that has taken place up until Day Six, whether it took five days or billions of years, was in preparation for the events that now unfold. The fully prepared creation is now ready for the creation of humans, the third and final *bara* creation in Genesis 1. While everything that was done up to now was good, this day's results are deemed very good.

## *Key Text*

"Then God said, 'Let the earth produce living creatures according to their kinds: livestock, creatures that crawl, and the wildlife of the earth according to their kinds.' And it was so. So God made the wildlife of the earth according to their kinds, the livestock according to their kinds, and creatures

God is a God of relationship. He bears this value out in His design for the basic human community: the family.

that crawl on the ground according to their kinds. And God saw that it was good. Then God said, 'Let Us make man in Our image, according to Our likeness. They will rule the fish of the sea, the birds of the sky, the animals, all the earth, and the creatures that crawl on the earth.' So God created man in His own image; He created him in the image of God; He created them male and female. God blessed them, and God said to them, 'Be fruitful, multiply, fill the earth, and subdue it. Rule the fish of the sea, the birds of the sky, and every creature that crawls on the earth.' God also said, 'Look, I have given you every seed-bearing plant on the surface of the entire earth, and

*Surveying the results of His creative decrees on Day Six, God pronounced it to be "very good."*

every tree whose fruit contains seed. This food will be for you, for all the wildlife of the earth, for every bird of the sky, and for every creature that crawls on the earth—everything having the breath of life in it. I have given every green plant for food.' And it was so. God saw all that He had made, and it was very good. Evening came, and then morning: the sixth day" (Gen. 1:24–31).

## Day Six: Commands

*God makes four commands on Day Six:*

Command 1: He tells the earth to produce land beasts.
Command 2: He decrees to create humans in His own image.
Command 3: He tells humankind to be fruitful and multiply.
Command 4: He tells humankind and animals to accept the foods He provides.

The day begins with another indirect command. God instructs the earth to produce living creatures of three general classes: livestock, crawling creatures, and wildlife. We are not to believe that the earth itself wields the power of creation, as if it were divine. Rather, the ground obeys the commands of its Maker.

The Hebrew word translated as "man" in verse 26 is *adam*. It refers not just to the first man but collectively to the entire human race. The word *adam* is also connected to the Hebrew word *adamah*, which is the "red soil" from which Adam was formed in Genesis 2:7.

## *Day Six: Commentary*

In keeping with the parallel triad framework, there are two creation acts on Day Six that correspond to the two creation acts on Day Three, when God formed the dry ground and vegetation. Here the dry ground and vegetation are filled with living, multiplying creatures. As was the case with the animals of Day Five, humankind is told to be fruitful, multiply, fill the land. Adam is also told to subdue the earth and rule over it.

Day Six saw the creation of livestock, creatures that move along the ground, and wild animals. Each of these represents

classes of animals revered and worshipped in the pagan cultures of Egypt and Sumer. Once again God is making a point: I made the things which are falsely worshipped.

God also demonstrates that He is the sole giver of our spiritual life. In verse 26–27 we find the third, fourth and fifth occurrence of the word *bara* (all in reference to humans) after its sparing use in verses 1 and 20. It is no accident that this special word is used multiple times in reference to humankind. After all, we alone bear the image of God.

Much has been made of the first person plural pronouns used by the Creator. He says, "Let *Us* make man in *Our*

*Genesis 1:26 and 3:22 are important precursors to the doctrine of the Trinity, which the New Testament reveals more fully.*

image, according to *Our* likeness" (v. 26). Most likely these plural pronouns indicate plurality within the Godhead. This is an important precursor to the doctrine of the Trinity, which the New Testament reveals more fully. We also know from the Gospel of John (1:1–3, 10) that the Son was present and active in the acts of creation.

> *Our position as stewards over all creation should promote in us an attitude of sober responsibility, not selfish egotism.*

In what way do humans reflect the image of God? God is not flesh and bone but spirit (Matt. 16:17; John 4:1). Therefore, the likeness is not of a physical nature but rather spiritual and personal. As God revealed greater depths of Himself over time, the Bible shows that He is a triune Being: Father, Son, and Holy Spirit. As such, God is inherently relational and personal. He thinks, plans, communicates, and relates. We humans reflect these traits of God. Animals can dimly mimic some of these qualities, but without question humankind is unique. We alone are given dominion over the earth, and we alone are answerable to God for our actions. For this reason our position of privilege should promote in us an attitude of sober responsibility, not selfish egotism.

The nature of the husband-wife relationship, which is God's design, also sets us apart from the rest of creation. Though some few species mate for life, no animal forms anything close to the intimate bond of human marriage.

God closes this final day of creation by pointing out to Adam that He has provided enough vegetation to feed both him and the animals. Some take this as evidence for original animal vegetarianism and animal immortality. The text permits this conclusion, but it is not necessarily the best option. Rather, the Creator's mention of foodstuffs should be seen in contrast to what is coming in chapter two, where Adam is told that he can eat from any tree save one. Therefore, the mention of abundant provision of fruit and vegetation sets the context for the singular prohibition against eating the forbidden fruit.

Now that the work of creation was finished, God surveyed all He had accomplished and said it was "very good." The creation was perfectly suited for His purposes.

*By calling creation "very good," God meant that it was perfectly suited for His purposes.*

## How Long Did the Fulfillment Take?

On the fifth and sixth days of creation, God issued commands that may have taken more than 24 hours to fulfill. After all, creatures cannot multiply instantaneously. To be sure, God can create them instantaneously, but that is not what He commanded here. Thus, it seems that it may have taken a while for God's commands to be fulfilled. The better we understand the natural processes set in place solely by God, the better we might be able to see the timescales involved in the fulfillment of those commands.

This text warns us against using a rigorous literalism in Genesis 1. For example, note that the land is commanded to produce animals. A rigorous literalism would imply that the land literally produced the animals. A more reasonable reading would be that animals are to come forth in the natural order of things, as per God's design.

## Day Six: The Record of Nature

Several aspects of Day Six connect with our understanding of the natural world. In terms of the overall sequence of the appearance of animals and man, the Genesis account fits nicely with the record of nature. Man is widely recognized as the most advanced of the mammals and most recent arrival. This is precisely how the Genesis story places humans in relationship to the rest of the creation. In fact, anthropologists place the age of homo sapiens (humans) in the range of several ten thousands of years, not millions. This is compatible with the popular view among scholars that the Bible constrains the age of humankind to something on the order of a few tens of thousands of years.

*Anthropologists place the age of homo sapiens (humans) in the range of several ten thousands of years, not millions of years.*

Another point of contact between Day Six and the record of nature concerns the statement about multiplying "after their own kind." In past centuries this was taken to mean that all the species of today were created in the beginning with no changes ensuing from then to now. This doctrine was dubbed the "fixity of the species." Now it is known that species adapt to their environment within the genetic limits of their kind. This range of change can be quite broad for some organisms. For example, consider the range of variation exhibited in domesticated dogs. The biblical creation account gives room for this understanding with its use of the broad category, "kinds."

In closing, note that Genesis reflects two key scientific truths that are absent in all other ancient cosmogonies. First, only life gives rise to life. The eternal, inanimate temple of the Egyptian creation myth cannot be the source of temporal, animate life. Second, offspring only come from like-kind parents. Humans do not give birth to salamanders, and so on.

## How Long Was Day Six?

On the sixth day God created livestock, crawling creatures, and wildlife • made Adam • planted a garden in Eden • placed Adam in the garden • instructed Adam to work it and watch over it • commanded Adam to freely eat from any of the trees except for one • told Adam that He would make a helper for him because it is not good for the man to be alone • brought animals and birds to Adam to see what he would call them • put Adam to sleep • formed Eve from one of Adam's ribs • and brought her to Adam.

Clearly, this was a big day, a day like no other. How could all of this happen in 24 hours? Young Earth proponents suggest that this is not a problem because "with God all things are possible" (Matt. 19:26). Certainly God could have instantaneously created the garden, but the problem is with Adam. How could a mere man pack so much into one day? Some suggest that before the fall he had much greater intelligence than men have been given since sin entered the world. Such intelligence, say proponents of this view, would have permitted him to name the animals in a flash.

*Given time, Adam would have witnessed the diversity of creation and understood the wisdom of the Creator as he studiously observed and named the animals.*

Others suggest he only named a few representatives of each "kind." And certainly, they add, the actual work of cultivating the garden could wait until another day.

On the other hand, advocates of an ancient creation point out that the Bible teaches none of these things. Old Earth creationists also fear that compressing all of these events into a portion of a regular day causes the rich meaning of the text to be lost. On their view, if the day were in fact longer than a normal day, Adam would have had plenty of time to obey and serve God as a faithful steward of the creation. He would also have had time to grasp the bounty and beauty of God's provision in contrast with the singular prohibition against the forbidden fruit. Given time, Adam would have witnessed the diversity of creation and understood the wisdom of the Creator as he studiously observed and named the animals.

No matter how far and wide he searched, Adam would not find a companion until God made Eve.

Finally, Adam would also have noted that he was unique and alone in that uniqueness. This is why He exclaimed *"at last!"* when God introduced him to his bride.

## *Worldview Summary*
### *THE TRINITY IN GENESIS*

Some nonbelievers have asserted that the doctrine of the Trinity is entirely absent in the Old Testament. While it is true that the greater emphasis in the Old Testament is on the oneness of God, there are a few significant precursors to Trinity. Two of these are found in Genesis. In Genesis 19:24, which records the destruction of Sodom and Gomorrah, we are

The Triquetra is a traditional symbol of the Trinity.

told that "the LORD rained burning sulfur on Sodom and Gomorrah from the LORD out of the sky." Here the pre-incarnate Son works in communion with the Father in heaven. And in the passage we are presently studying, Genesis 1:26 records an inter-Trinitarian dialogue in which the Godhead decrees to make humankind in "Our image."

# Chapter 15
# The Seventh Day:
# Genesis 2:1–3

After repeating the same literary structure each of the six days of creation, Day Seven breaks from the ranks. There is neither command nor closure on this day. Now that God has breathed life into His image bearer, He ceases creating new life on Earth.

## Key Text

"So the heavens and the earth and everything in them were completed. By the seventh day, God completed His work that He had done, and He rested on the seventh day from all His work that He had done. God blessed the seventh day and declared it holy, for on it He rested from His work of creation" (Gen. 2:1–3).

## Day Seven: A Holy Day

Day Seven (the Sabbath) is distinguished from all others as a day that was blessed and called holy. Kenneth Mathews points out that of the four lines in verses 2–3, the first three are parallel, having seven words each, with "the seventh day" repeated at the midpoint of each. He translates the passage literally as: "So God finished by *the seventh day* his work which he did, and he rested on *the seventh day* from all his work which he did, and God blessed *the seventh day* and sanctified it, because on it he rested from all his work which God created to do."[1] This may seem needlessly repetitious, but the repetition emphasizes the significance and uniqueness of the seventh day.

## Day Seven: A Day of Rest

We are twice told in these verses that God rested on Day Seven. Exodus 31:17 amplifies this and says that "on the seventh day He rested and was refreshed." But can God really need refreshing? Of course not. Talk of God's resting is another instance of anthropomorphism—the use of images and themes familiar to human experience to describe true but essentially ineffable facts about God. When it says God rested and was refreshed, it means He ceased his creative activity and reflected with satisfaction on the results.

*Talk of God's resting is another instance of anthropomorphism—the use of images and themes familiar to human experience to describe true but essentially ineffable facts about God.*

Days, months, and years all have their basis in astronomical events; but the length of the human workweek is defined only

by the pattern of the Creator's workweek. Eventually the pattern was codified in the Mosaic Law (Exod. 20:8–11), which instructs us to remember the Sabbath and keep it holy.

Day Seven has theological and eschatological significance throughout the Scriptures. The idea of "rest" was associated with the holy land when God promised Israel "My presence will go with you, and I will give you rest" (Exod. 33:14). Many commentators have suggested that because there is no closure on the seventh day it has yet to end. Hebrews 4:1–11 may teach that the Creator's Sabbath has not ended. Even though "His works have been finished since the foundation of the world... Sabbath rest remains, therefore, for God's people" (vv. 3, 9). It may well be that the Father's rest will finally end when He creates "a new heaven and a new earth" (Rev. 21:1).

> *Many commentators have suggested that, because there is no closure on the seventh day, it has yet to end.*

## Worldview Summary

### SABBATH REST AND MODERN SCIENCE

Humankind's inclination is to overwork themselves, their animals, and their land. Most likely this is part of our insatiable hunger for *more*. More land, more money, more of every material thing that appeals to our eyes. From the beginning God stressed that this is not in our best interests. By design we need rest. Modern science backs this up. Animals, fields, and humans need rest. The Sabbath, therefore, reflects God's design.

But even more important than meeting physical needs, the Law of the Sabbath meets man's spiritual need for communion with our Creator. Our tendency toward self-absorption and self-serving activity is broken as we step out of the ordinary routine once a week and focus a day on God. From the earliest days of the church, Christians have met weekly to devote themselves to the praise and worship of God, giving special

By design all of God's creatures need rest.

attention to the sacrifice and resurrection of Jesus Christ on their behalf. This should be our practice as well.

## Note:

1. Kenneth Mathews, *Genesis 1–11:26,* New American Commentary, vol. 1A (Nashville: Broadman & Holman, 1996), 177.

# Part IV
# Eden, Fall, and Flood

# Chapter 16
# Genesis 2: Life in Eden

After a systematic account of origins in Genesis 1, the creation week is revisited with a focus on Adam in Genesis 2. Some think the two accounts are contradictory, but it is clear that chapter 2 elaborates on key elements of the same story in a complementary fashion while focusing on how Adam relates to God and His creation.

## *Key Text*

"Then the LORD God formed the man out of the dust from the ground and breathed the breath of life into his nostrils, and the man became a living being" (Gen. 2:7).

God created us male and female in His image.

## *Adam's Creation: Genesis 2:4–7*

A new division of Genesis is introduced in 2:4 with the refrain, "These are the records." This phrase stems from the Hebrew word *toledot*, which typically initiates a section that is thematically connected to the heritage of a significant person.

Its usage in 2:4 is unique because it does not introduce the lineage of a person but rather the original inception of the universe in connection with the history of the first human couple.

This account begins with the primeval Earth covered in a mist (or flood) prior to the creation of plants and animals. The

sky had not yet cleared, clouds had not yet formed, and rain had not yet fallen on the still barren planet. Then the story fast-forwards to Day Six when God creates humans.

Like a potter working with clay, the Creator "formed the man out of the dust from the ground" (Gen. 2:7). Adam's body was formed from existing earthly material by an act of divine craftsmanship. But there was also something distinctly and divinely immaterial about Adam as well. The word for "breath" in 2:7 is only associated

Like a potter working with clay, the Creator "formed the man out of the dust from the ground" (Gen 2:7).

with God and man. Of all creatures only humans possess the breath of the Creator.

## Adam's Home: Genesis 2:8-14

After working as a Potter, now the Creator works as a Planter. He plants "a garden in Eden, in the east," (v. 8) and places Adam in his new home.

In a location now lost to history, God caused trees to grow from the ground. This language implies that God worked through natural processes, not instantaneous

Most of us imagine Eden looked something like this jungle scene. In any case, it had everything Adam and Eve could have reasonably wanted.

miracles, to create Adam's garden home. In other words, God used normal providence rather than supernatural providence. He could have miraculously accelerated its growth, but the text does not imply that conclusion. In fact, the language seems to imply a long period of time was spent preparing the garden for its future inhabitants. In any case, God created it and filled it with beautiful trees, fruit, and precious stones. The garden of Eden had everything that Adam and Eve would ever need or want if only they would avoid taking fruit from the tree of knowledge of good and evil.

## Adam's Tasks: Genesis 2:15–20

Eden was not a magical place of self-perpetuating perfection. Adam was placed in the garden with a job to do: he was to "cultivate it and keep it" (v. 15 NASB). By his daily work, Adam

*Work is not a consequence of the fall. It was part of God's original design.*

served the Creator and expressed gratitude for His goodness. (The word for "cultivate" means "to serve" and is translated as "worship" in Exod. 3:12). An obvious point to be made here

Detail of Adam from Jan van Eyck's Ghent Altarpiece.

is that work is not a consequence of the fall. It was part of God's original design.

At this point Adam is alone, and this displeases God. So God said, "I will make a helper who is like him" (v. 18). But first God parades animals in front of Adam so he can name them, thus initiating his rule over the animal kingdom. The flow of the text gives the impression that God created the animals moments before Adam met them and named them. Critics are quick to argue that this represents a different order of creation from Genesis 1, where animals are created before

Adam. However, the text here in chapter 2 is not necessarily chronological. In verse 19, "formed" can also be translated as "had formed," which would be a reference to the animals God created before Adam. This is most likely the proper reading, though it is possible that God created additional animals here. In any case, "no helper was found who was like him" (v. 20).

## Adam's Bride: Genesis 2:21–25

As Genesis 1:27 tells it, Adam and Eve were created at the same time. However, chapter 2 focuses in more closely on the creation of humans, revealing details previously left unmentioned. Here we learn that God formed the land creatures, created Adam, planted the garden, placed Adam in it, gave him some

*Even though his daily tasks were joyful and worshipful experiences, he had keenly felt that he was alone.*

special instructions, and brought the animals to be named *before* He put Adam to sleep and made Eve from one of his ribs.

When he awoke and met Eve, Adam said, "At last." His wait was over. Even though his daily tasks were joyful and worshipful experiences, he had keenly felt that he was alone. One look at this latest creation and he knew that he and Eve were made for one another. They were joined together in a covenant relationship of perfect unity. Perfect, that is, until the serpent slinked into the garden.

*The Creation of Eve* by Michelangelo.

## Worldview Summary

### MALE AND FEMALE

Genesis emphasizes that sexual union is to be between a husband and a wife in the context of a lifetime covenant. This provides security not only for both partners but for the children born into the marriage as well. The New Testament further reveals that marriage is a picture of the union between Christ and the church.

# Chapter 17
# Genesis 3:
# Serpent, Fall, and Curse

Now the stage is set for the real drama to begin. A new character enters the scene to engage the stars of the show. The fairy tale turns tragic as one of most decisive events in history unfolds.

## *Key Text*

"Now the serpent was the most cunning of all the wild animals that the Lord God had made. He said to the woman, 'Did God really say, "You can't eat from any tree in the garden?"' The woman said to the serpent, 'We may eat the fruit from the trees in the garden. But about the fruit of the tree in the middle of the garden, God said, "You must not eat it or touch it, or you will die."' 'No! You will not die,' the serpent

The serpent (Satan) dropped into the garden paradise and offered a "better" way to Adam and Eve.

said to the woman. 'In fact, God knows that when you eat it your eyes will be opened and you will be like God, knowing good and evil.' Then the woman saw that the tree was good for food and delightful to look at, and that it was desirable for obtaining wisdom. So she took some of its fruit and ate it; she also gave some to her husband, who was with her, and he ate it. Then the eyes of both of them were opened, and they knew they were naked; so they sewed fig leaves together and made loincloths for themselves" (Gen. 3:1–7).

## Temptation and Fall: Genesis 3:1–7

Genesis takes a dark turn as the cunning serpent approaches Eve. While "cunning" is a fitting description of snake behavior, this serpent is actually a manifestation of the supernatural evil one who rebelled against God. None other than Satan (Lucifer) himself had entered the garden to usurp God's plan. His opening words were intended to shock Eve into distrusting God. "What? Surely God didn't really mean you can't eat from any of these trees!" His

*Satan's appeal was tragically effective, and it has continued to be so throughout history.*

tactic is to exaggerate God's prohibition, making the divine will appear too restrictive. As is only proper, Eve initially came to God's defense. But Satan is persistent, and so he immediately brought the full force of his argument against Eve by letting her in on a dirty little secret: God fears you'll become like Him if you eat. Satan's appeal was tragically effective, and it has continued to be so throughout history.

After eating, Eve gave the fruit to Adam as well. She didn't have to beg or even ask. He simply ate, and together their eyes were flung open to a new recognition of evil. Rather than turning to God in repentance, they sought their own means of remediation by covering themselves with fig leaves and hiding. With this act of profound disobedience, sin entered humanity and turned the course of history down a tragic path.

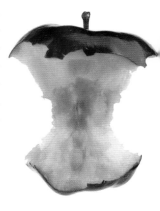

## Did Adam Die the Same Day He Ate the Fruit?

God said Adam would die on the day he ate the fruit. So why did Adam live to be 930 years old? One common explanation

is that Adam did not literally die but instead became mortal at that moment. But God did not say that He would become subject to death or *begin* to die. He said, "On the day you eat from it, you will certainly die" (Gen. 2:17). Moreover, one may argue that the presumption that humans (or animals) were originally immortal is contrary to Scripture. Only God is immortal (1 Tim. 6:16). Adam's life before the

When did Adam die? The day of the curse? 930 years later? Both?

fall was not innately immortal but was indefinitely sustained by the power and provision of God. Recall the purpose of the tree of life. Perhaps if there had been no fall God would have sustained Adam's life forever, but immortality was not part of human nature.

While Adam did not immediately die physically, he did experience spiritual death the day he ate. His unfettered fellowship with God ended, and his spiritual vitality was lost. His sin also eventually led to physical death as he and Eve were banished from the garden and the tree of life.

Some see Adam's longevity as evidence that the days of creation were long periods of time. This echoes the early church fathers Justin Martyr and Irenaeus who argued that since a day with the Lord is like a thousand years, then Adam lived 930 years and still died on the day he sinned. We may not agree with this interpretation, but it does provide precedent for the Ancient Creation position.

## Meeting the Maker: Genesis 3:8–13

Though many of the elements of this passage are not familiar to our experiences, this is no myth or allegory. Instead, it is a real story about a terrible tragedy. The text employs anthropomorphisms, so there are things we can only dimly understand. For instance, we cannot conceive what it was like to walk in the garden with God. God somehow accommodated Himself to the first couple, giving them access to the divine that would astound us. The attempt by Adam and Eve to clothe their nakedness was desperate and irrational, and for the first time their nakedness felt like a vulnerability.

As for God's questions, these do not reflect ignorance on His part. Instead of driving out the answers, He seeks to draw out confessions. Instead of demanding that Adam and Eve present themselves, He gently draws them forth with questions. Eventually the questions become more pointed. God wants to know how they knew they were naked; He also wants to know if they've eaten the forbidden fruit. These questions urge confession, but Adam is in no mood for that. He shifts the blame to the woman God gave him. When God turns the

> *Though many of the elements of the Genesis 3 passage are not familiar to our experiences, this is no myth or allegory.*

*The Garden of Eden* by Lucas Cranach.

questioning to her, she too shifts the blame. It is the serpent's fault, she said. By now God had had enough of their answers. It was time for Him to be heard.

## The Curse: Genesis 3:14–19

God is not fooled by the blame game. He knows the guilt of all three participants, and He announces punishments that match their crimes. First, He tells the serpent that he will forever be subjugated and humiliated. This is a reflection and extension of the banishment Satan already suffered as punishment for his rebellion in heaven. Now his demise is doubly assured. Some have suggested that serpents originally walked on legs which were lost in the curse, but that is not what is intended here. The language about crawling on its belly and eating dust is a symbolic and eloquent description of the fate of the one who possessed the serpent. Having brought man *to* the dust through temptation, Satan now symbolically *eats* dust as an illustration of his doom. This fate is made certain by the future coming of Christ, as foreshadowed in verse 15, the first Messianic prophecy of the Bible.

*Eve's punishment was an intensification of pain, not an* **origination** *of pain. Hence, pain was a real possibility before the fall and curse.*

Next, the curse is directed at Eve. As mother of all the living and the one bearing the seed that will eventually crush the serpent forever, Eve's punishment is an intensification of pain in childbirth. Notice it says *intensification* of pain, not origination. Hence, pain was a real possibility before the fall and curse. Further, Eve's marriage and every subsequent marriage will be characterized by strife as both partners seek their own ambitions and try to usurp rather than lovingly serve each other.

Finally, the attention turns to Adam. All of humanity and the earth itself will suffer because of his sin. Some take Romans 8:20–22 as an explanation of God's curse on the ground and reason that even the physical realm has been corrupted by Adam's fall. Others note that God did not speak directly to the ground and thus suggest that the effect on the ground is indirect. The amoral physical realm did not sin, and God did not pronounce a judgment directly to the ground. On this view, the curse points to the fact that our stewardship of nature is compromised by sin. We promote our own self-interests over the best interests of the environment. The world suffers because of this. In either case, Adam's sin clearly affected the world around him.

Adam's work outside the garden of Eden would be difficult.

Like the serpent's, Adam's curse involves the ground, eating, and dust. Having been cast out of the divinely prepared garden, he must now contend with the thorns and thistles of the unkempt world beyond the garden. The text does not state that God created thorns and thistles as part of the curse; rather, Adam now had to contend with them as part of his labor since he was banished from the idyllic garden. Whereas tending the ground had originally been a pleasing act of worship, now it would be a toilsome and painful burden. Finally, Adam's days as a living, breathing creature are now numbered. He came from the dust, and he will return there in death.

Whatever it looked like, the tree of life was God's provision for Adam and Eve's original immortality.

## *Out of Eden: Genesis 3:20–24*

Following immediately on the heels of judgment is a promise and a provision. Adam gives his wife a name, demonstrating confidence that God's blessings and assignments of responsibility are not entirely withdrawn because of the fall. Life will go on. There is also an implicit prophetic promise as God clothes the couple. This first sacrificial animal provided clothing for them and foreshadowed the Lamb of God who would shed His blood to take away our sins.

Having heard God's pronouncements, Adam and Eve are forced to leave the garden and make it on their own in the untamed world. An angelic guard is placed at the entrance to prevent their return. God's original provision of everlasting life (through the tree of life) would no longer be available, but the time would come when another tree, fashioned into a cross, would be involved in restoring what was lost.

# Chapter 18
# Genesis and the Flood

## *Meaning of the Flood*

The story of Noah's flood is a great way to capture a child's fascination and instill a sense of wonder for God's power and justice, but is it no more than a child's bedtime story? Like most areas where science and faith merge, the nature of Noah's flood is a point of contention. Did it cover the entire planet, reshaping the geology of the earth and forming the entire fossil record in one great cataclysm? Or was it a regional flood that destroyed not all the earth but all of humanity since humans had not yet spread beyond the

Edward Hicks (1780–1849) painted this hypothetical scene of the loading of the ark.

Mesopotamian Plain? What does the Bible say? These are the kinds of questions we will examine in this chapter.

## The Two Major Views

A global flood is an integral part of Scientific Creationism, for in that paradigm the flood was more than an inundation of water; it was a world-making force that altered the continents. Mountains rose up and seafloors sank; countless animals died, were buried, and became fossils. They even say the decay rate of radioactive elements drastically changed. The world Noah saw when he emerged from the ark was drastically different from anything he had seen before.

*In Young Earth creationism the flood was a world-making force that altered the continents.*

On the other hand, advocates of ancient creation do not look to Noah's flood for explanation of geological data. In their view the fossil record did not form in a single global catastrophe but instead reflects millions of years of animal history. Age-old mountains were formed largely through the slow process of continental motion and volcanism, processes that continue today and are well understood by scientists.

*Advocates of ancient creation do not look to Noah's flood for explanation of geological data.*

We will attempt to objectively present both views, emphasizing that proponents of both views aim to uphold the inspiration and authority of the Bible. In chapter 27 we will examine the flood in light of modern scientific discoveries.

*The Deluge by Gustave Dore.*

## Biblical Description of the Flood

Genesis chapters 6–9 tell the story of how God was grieved by the evil of humanity and decided to wipe them from the face of the earth (6:7). In God's words, "I am bringing a deluge—floodwaters on the earth to destroy all flesh under heaven with the breath of life in it" (6:17). But of course He did not destroy all flesh because Noah followed His instructions and built the ark to preserve his family and two of "every living thing of all flesh" (6:19).

*Global Flood View:* A straightforward reading of our English text gives the impression that the flood covered the entire planet. At its peak the floodwaters are said to have covered the highest mountains to a depth of 15 cubits (22.5 feet). After 150 days the waters began to subside. Shortly thereafter the ark came to rest in the mountains of Ararat; and eventually, a year after the flood began, the earth was dry, and the occupants left the ark.

*Local Flood View:* Advocates for local flood cautiously point out that the Hebrew text is not as unequivocal as our English Bible. Because the Hebrew language has relatively few

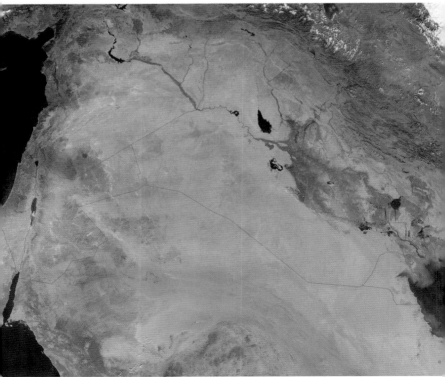

Mesopotamia. Photo: Jeff Schmaltz, MODIS Rapid Response Team, NASA/GSFC.

words, words commonly have multiple meanings. The Hebrew phrase used for "entire earth" is *kol erets*, which is used 205 times in the Old Testament. At least 80 percent of the time, *kol erets* refers merely to a local region, not the whole earth.

*To the Hebrews, the entire world was the region of Mesopotamia. They had no knowledge of the world's remote regions.*

Likewise the phrase *kol shamayim* (translated "entire heavens") can refer to a limited area as well (e.g., Deut. 2:25). This broad usage makes precise interpretation difficult since "entire world" and "entire heavens" can legitimately mean that the flood covered just a local area. Since we moderns think from a global perspective, the "entire world" to us means exactly that. But to the Hebrews, the entire world was the region of Mesopotamia. They had no knowledge of the world's remote regions. From Moses' perspective, therefore, "the entire world" probably

The ancients commonly believed their stretch of the world was in fact the whole world. This world map, a recreation of one composed by Hecataeus in circa 500 BC, is a prime example.

only meant "the world known to him." Of course the Holy Spirit has a global perspective, but the inspired Scriptures often accommodate the limited perspectives of the human author.

## Excursus: Meaning of "the World"

Local areas are commonly described as "the world" in the Bible. Here are a few examples:

***Genesis 41:56–57*** (NASB)—"When the famine was spread over all (*kol*) the face of the earth (*erets*),. . . the people of all the earth (*kol erets*) came to Egypt to buy grain from Joseph."

- Here, "all the earth" merely meant Egypt and the surrounding nations. Joseph clearly did not feed Pacific Islanders or Native Americans from his storehouses in Egypt.

***Genesis 13:9–10***—Abram said to Lot, "Isn't the whole land (*kol erets*) before you? . . . Lot looked out and saw that the entire Jordan Valley . . . was well-watered."

- Again, *kol erets* does not mean the whole earth but "the whole region of the Jordan Valley."

***Leviticus 25:9***—Here God commanded His people to sound a horn "throughout your land (*kol erets*) on the Day of Atonement."

- Naturally, God did not mean for this trumpet blast to be heard around the world.

As you can see, translators often understand "entire earth" to mean a specific region. This must be borne in mind when we study the flood account in Genesis 6–9.

## Causes of the Flood

Where did all the water come from to flood the earth? The Bible names two sources: "the sources of the watery depths" and "the floodgates of the sky" (7:11). The reference to the "watery depths" likely refers to oceans but can also refer to underground stores of water. The floodgates of the sky describe rain poured out by God in an extraordinary fashion. Both causes seem to indicate that the floodwaters came from natural sources being directed by God. But theories on exactly what happened differ.

***Global Flood View:*** Many global flood advocates have sought to precisely identify the water sources. It was once popular to suggest that a vapor canopy hovered over the early earth and held back the water until the flood. As this theory fell out of favor, some global flood

Many Young Earth advocates suggest that the earth was much flatter before Noah's flood.

advocates have speculated that subterranean water rose up through volcanic eruptions, rapid spreading or rising of the seafloor, or other catastrophic motions of the earth's tectonic plates. These suggestions are associated with Young Earth creationists who say the preflood earth was much flatter and thus required less water to flood.

*The Hebrew phrase translated "high mountains" can refer to any elevated landscape, whether high hills or Mount Everest.*

***Local Flood View:*** Even though local flood advocates do not believe the flood covered the entire planet, they still maintain that the flood was directed by God. Subterranean sources coupled with an extraordinary amount of rainfall brought about a providentially directed, once-in-human-history flood event. But how were "all the high mountains under the whole sky" covered by a local flood? The Hebrew phrase translated "high mountains" can refer to *any elevated landscape*, whether high hills or Mount Everest. Furthermore, since the text does not specify exactly what it was that covered the mountains, *The Theological Wordbook of the Old Testament* suggests that it may have been storm clouds rather than water that spread over the highest peaks.[1] And as we saw above, "under the whole sky" often refers merely to a local patch of sky. Hence, from a language standpoint it is possible that Genesis only means to say there was enough water to thoroughly flood the local region.

## Duration and Scope of the Flood

After the rain ceased, the waters continued to cover the earth for 150 days. Then "God caused a wind to pass over the earth, and the water began to subside" (8:1). Exactly five months after the flood began, the ark came to rest on the mountains of Ararat (not necessarily *the* Mount Ararat) and then two and a half months later the tops of the mountains became visible.

Global Flood advocates believe Noah's flood carved out the Grand Canyon.

The water continued to abate and one year and eleven days after it all began, Noah and his family left the ark.

*Global Flood View:* The year of the flood was packed with geological action, say global flood supporters. The high mountains were all formed since earth was previously mostly flat; all the sedimentary layers of the earth were laid; receding floodwaters produced the Grand Canyon, Niagara Falls, Monument Valley, and many other such wonders. A drastic change in climate brought about massive speciation from the "kinds" that survived aboard the ark. Those that could not adapt, such as dinosaurs, rapidly went extinct.

*Local Flood View:* Forty days *after* the mountaintops appeared, Noah released a raven that flew around until it found a place to land. Then he sent a dove out, but it returned to the ark. Why did it return? The Bible says it came back because "water covered the surface of the whole earth" (8:9). So though the mountaintops had been visible for some time and though the raven, apparently more willing to fly to higher elevations, found a place to land, Genesis 8:9 still uses "whole earth" (*kol erets*) to describe the extent of the waters when the dove was released. This is the same phrase used earlier to de-

scribe the extent of the flood before the waters began to recede. Clearly the use of "whole earth" in 8:9 cannot be taken in a strictly literal sense, and it serves as another indicator that the flood even at its height may not have literally covered all the earth.

One week later Noah sent out another dove. This time it returned with an olive leaf in its beak (8:11). Somewhere near the ark an olive tree had survived the flood. Olive trees only grow at low elevations, so most likely the ark did not come to rest near the top of Mount Ararat, and the olive tree would have been down toward the lower regions of the mountain. Would this tree have survived at low elevations if the flood literally covered all the high mountains of the entire earth? Would it even remain rooted? If the flood were global and reached higher than the highest mountains, then somehow the tree survived being covered by thousands of feet of salty, turbulent, debris-filled water for at least half a year as mountains were uplifted and millions of tons of sediment settled into low elevations. Not only did the tree escape intact and avoid being entombed in sludge, it was able to produce fresh leaves a mere week after it emerged from the global devastation.

*The olive tree produced leaves a mere week after it emerged from the global devastation.*

Some suggest that God miraculously protected the tree and allowed it to survive, and indeed it would have taken a miracle, but the Bible does not say the tree had been miraculously preserved. Therefore, the intact olive tree may point to a local flood. For in that case the tree may have been only marginally flooded as it stood somewhere near the flood's perimeter on the mountainside.

The dove Noah released found a healthy olive tree and plucked a sprig from it mere days after the flood.

After the flood God sent a wind to disperse the floodwaters. If the floodwaters covered literally the entire planet, wind would not cause the water to abate. It would only move it around and perhaps saturate the atmosphere, causing torrential rains which would perpetuate the flood. Only some sort of miraculous wind could rid the earth of waters that covered every high mountain. But again the Bible says nothing of miracles here. Thus, a global flood perspective assumes that miracles occurred where the text only names seemingly natural processes. Moreover, as the flood ended the water "was dried up from the earth" (8:7 NASB) and eventually "the earth was completely dry" (8:14 NIV). What does this imply? If the flood had literally covered the entire earth (*erets*), then to be consistent we would have to admit that this present passage says the entire planet was now completely dry. No lakes. No oceans. No water anywhere. To be consistent with a strictly literalistic interpretation of the language, a global flood implies a global desert after the flood. On the other hand, a consistent, biblically justified, local-flood usage of *erets* indicates that the local Mesopotamian area was flooded and afterward became dry again. There are

How much of the land was dry after the flood?

no difficulties in making sense of that conception.

That is not to say there are no difficulties with the local flood interpretation. Despite the indisputable fact that the Bible sometimes uses universal language for merely local references, it is nevertheless difficult for some Bible readers to think that such universal-sounding passages as Genesis 6:7 ("I will wipe off the face of the earth: man, whom I created, together with the animals, creatures that crawl, and birds of the sky") and Genesis 6:13 ("I have decided to put an end to all flesh . . . along with the earth") really have only the Mesopotamian area in view. Further, some scientific aspects of the local flood are hard to work out, such as how the water was able to pool up in this limited area to a depth sufficient enough to drown all inhabitants. These are not insuperable barriers to the local flood view, but they are enough to convince some Bible readers that the global flood view is best.

*It is difficult for some readers to think that such universal-sounding passages as Genesis 6:7 and 6:13 have only the Mesopotamian area in view.*

## The Ark

God told Noah to build a big boat: 450 feet long, 75 feet wide, and 45 feet high. It was three stories tall, filled with rooms, and covered inside and out with pitch. When it was finished, God sent animals and birds of all kinds to the ark to be spared from the coming flood.

***Global Flood View:*** Global flood advocates argue that

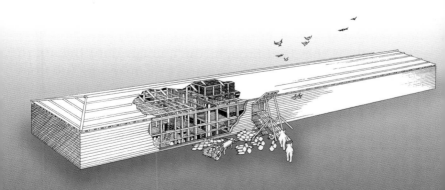

*Noah and the Ark* by Französischer Meister.

if the flood was merely local, Noah had no need to build an ark. He could have just rounded up his family and headed for the distant hills. Similarly, God could have just sent the animals away as well. Why build a big boat and bother with housing smelly animals? Thus, the ark itself demonstrates that the flood would not have been just a local event.

**Local Flood View:** Local flood advocates believe this argument misses a fundamental theological point made by the ark. Jesus used the flood as a vivid picture of God's judgment against sin. But before God sends judgment, He typically preaches repentance. Noah worked for many years building a boat that was a tangible sign of impending judgment. Had he simply packed up and moved on, this poignant message to sinners would have been silenced. The ark is also a beautiful picture of God's provision for deliverance from judgment. Peter draws an analogy where water baptism corresponds to the ark which saved Noah's family (1 Pet. 3:20–21). The ark was a type of Christ, foreshadowing God's provision of salvation.

> *The ark was a type of Christ, foreshadowing God's provision of salvation.*

But what about all the birds and animals? What theological point could their presence on the ark demonstrate? One possibility is that God brought the animals onto the ark to demonstrate the broad consequences of human sin. And from a pragmatic perspective, the global flood argument assumes that all the planet's animals could survive long-distance migrations through foreign ecosystems to reach Noah's ark. The truth is, many species depend on a highly localized territory and could not survive such conditions. It is hard to imagine polar bears, koalas, and kangaroos ranging over thousands of miles of territory not suited to their design, traversing mountains, fording rivers and possibly oceans, all in an attempt to reach Noah's ark so they can immediately embark on a year-long voyage. This is no exaggeration, for the global flood view entails that animals came to the ark from every corner of the globe. The local flood view alleviates this difficulty since it holds that only animals native to the Mesopotamian region boarded Noah's ark.

*The local flood holds that only animals native to the Mesopotamian region boarded Noah's ark.*

Another difficult question for the global flood view is how would all the animals have dispersed to continents widely separated by oceans after the flood? Again, God could have done this miraculously, but this must be read into the Bible in order to defend the global flood view.

## The Promise After the Flood

After the waters subsided and everyone disembarked, Noah made burnt offerings to the Lord. God then made a new covenant with him and promised, "I will never again strike down every living thing as I have done," and "there will never again be a deluge to destroy the earth" (8:21; 9:11). The rainbow is a sign of that covenant between God and man, reminding us of God's promise.

***Global Flood View:*** Global flood advocates claim that if Noah's flood was local, then God has broken His promise since there have been many local floods throughout history.

***Local Flood View:*** Local flood advocates point out that although Noah's flood was local in a geographic sense, it was universal in the sense that it destroyed all humans except

Noah's family. At the time of the flood, humans had not yet spread beyond the region of Mesopotamia (recall that God had to forcibly disperse the population from the Tower of Babel after Noah's flood). Hence, a local flood would have accomplished God's stated purpose to destroy all people. God's promise never to flood the earth again has held true since there has never been another flood that destroyed all of humanity.

## So Which Was It? Global or Local?

### Summary of Objections to a Local Flood

- Read literally, the text says the flood covered the entire earth and all the high mountains.

- Why build an ark when Noah could have just moved away from the localized flood zone?

- Why build an ark when the birds and animals could have just migrated with Noah out of danger?

- God promised there would never again be such a flood, but there have been many local floods.

### Summary of Objections to a Global Flood

- In biblical usage, "entire earth" and "entire heavens" most often refer only to local regions.

- Not enough water to cover all the mountains.

- Nowhere for all that water to go after the flood.

- Since the Bible says that "the earth was completely dry" (Gen. 8:14 NIV) after "the water prevailed upon the earth" (Gen. 7:24 NASB), we have a clue that the flood only covered a local region. After all, the earth was not a waterless desert after the flood.

- There would be no olive leaves to be picked if the flood covered all the high mountains.

- Getting animals to come to the ark and then go back home again to remote, inaccessible locations that were drastically altered by the flood seems to present a strong challenge.

- Animals from diverse ecological niches would not likely survive the trip to the ark, let alone the voyage aboard the ark.

Clearly, there are merits and difficulties for both sides of this debate. All agree that the flood destroyed all of humanity, which is certainly the main point of the flood account. Does it really matter how far the waters extended? Young Earth creationists answer yes because they believe the global flood model allows them to suggest reasons why the scientific consensus about Earth's antiquity is mistaken. Old Earth creationists also believe the debate is important, for they maintain that science and the Bible are compatible regarding the scope of the flood and the age of Earth.

*All agree that the flood destroyed all of humanity, which is certainly the main point of the flood account.*

## Our View

We believe the flood was as big as God wanted it to be. We also believe it was a miraculous, historical event that killed everyone in the world except Noah and his family. While a straightforward reading of the English text supports a global flood, the Hebrew text indisputably allows for a local flood.

Natural processes alone cannot account for the flood, but the flood was not a natural event. The flood was a unique event, brought about by the power of God. Since it was a providentially ordered event, God could have miraculously

*The Deluge* by Michelangelo.

provided the source and removal of enough water for a global flood. It need not be explained through natural processes alone. In summary, we believe what the Bible says: that the flood was a miraculous, historical event that killed everyone in the world except Noah and his family.

## Worldview Summary
### THE JUSTICE OF GOD

Can a just and loving God really wipe out virtually all of humanity with a flood? This perennial question has bothered every generation of believers. The chief difficulty is that we fail to perceive just how serious sin is. God is the essence of holiness, justice, and love. Human

*The truly difficult question is not, How could a Holy God destroy all humans except Noah's family but, Why did He not wipe everyone out?*

rebellion against God merits the strictest punishment. He is not obligated to put up with our sins or forgive us. And by definition His actions are always just. Perhaps the more difficult question is, Why does God not wipe everyone out?

## Note

1. "In Gen. 7:19–20 the hills were 'covered;' the Hebrew does not specify with what. The . . . specification of water goes beyond the Hebrew. The Hebrew may merely mean that the mountains were hidden from view by the storm." From *Theological Wordbook of the Old Testament,* vol. 1., edited by Laird Harris (Chicago: Moody Press, 1980), 449.

# Part V

# Genesis and the Age of Earth

# Chapter 19
# Back to the Beginning

Evangelical Christians face many important issues in the twenty-first century. We are called to take the gospel to a world that is increasingly skeptical. Now more than ever Christians need to stand united in our core beliefs but sadly we spend much of our energy dividing over nonessential differences of opinion. Certainly we should seek truth in all things, but in the process we should live by the maxim, "In essentials, unity; in nonessentials, liberty; and in all things charity."

## Science and Faith Collide

One issue that is heatedly debated in the church today is the length of the creation days. This is not a vital doctrine of our faith, but it is nonetheless important because it affects our understanding of the Bible and how we engage our technological society. Specifically, this debate does much to define the relationship between science and the Christian faith. Scientific advances made in recent decades have caused many to question the relevance of the Bible. Students today are bombarded with a materialistic philosophy that portrays Christian faith as an outmoded worldview. In this context we must follow the lead of the apostle Paul when he wrote: "Set apart the Messiah as Lord in your hearts, and always be ready to give a defense to anyone who asks you for a reason for the hope that is in you" (1 Pet. 3:15).

If we are to take the gospel to the modern world, we must be prepared to demolish the strongholds, arguments, and intellectual impediments that are raised up against the knowledge of God. The modern secular mind is often opposed to the gospel because the Bible is thought to conflict with scientific evidences. This conflict comes to a head on questions such as:

*Students today are bombarded with a materialistic philosophy that portrays Christian faith as an outmoded worldview.*

- Does the Bible teach that everything was created in a 144-hour period around 7,000 years ago?
- What about the scientific evidence for an older Earth?
- Should interpretations of Genesis be influenced by evidence from outside the Bible?

## Early Views on the Days of Genesis

Throughout history there have been two approaches to interpreting the days of Genesis. The common view has been that the days were 24 hours long. However, there have been notable exceptions. The first-century Jewish scholar Philo wrote that the days of creation were figurative because the length of a day had no meaning before the sun was created on Day Four.[1] In the following centuries several significant church fathers also viewed the days figuratively or allegorically. In his *De Principiis* IV.3.1, Origen says, "What person of any intelligence would think that there existed a first, second, and third day, and evening and morning, without sun, moon, and stars?" Basil opposed the allegorical view of Origen and regarded the days as 24-hour days, but he nonetheless acknowledged the problem of the sun's being created on Day Four.[2]

Writing about the creation days, Augustine said in *The City of God* XI.6, "What kind of days these were it is extremely difficult, or perhaps impossible for us to conceive." He further questioned when time itself was created if the sun (by which we measure time) was created on Day Four. This led him to suggest that creation may have been instantaneous and not measurable in time. But like many of the early commentators, it is difficult to ascertain exactly what Augustine fully and finally believed. He also seems to have treated the days of Genesis 1 as being six repetitions of a single day, and elsewhere as being 1,000 years long each (based on

*Historically, the view that the days of Genesis are 24 hours long is most common.*

1 Pet.) since Adam lived to be more than nine hundred years old even though God told him he would die in the "day" he ate of the tree.

*Augustine* by Botticelli.

Centuries later Calvin and other Reformers seem to have held to a 24-hour view, yet esteemed evangelical theologians since the Reformation have commonly held both literal and non-literal views. The history of interpretation alone cannot decide this matter.

## *Modern Science Enters the Picture*

One of the chief questions that early modern scientists faced was how marine fossils came to be on mountaintops. For many the best answer was that Noah's flood had covered the entire earth and deposited them there. But that started to become less attractive in the late 1700s when James Hutton studied the processes of erosion and theorized that slow-acting mechanisms drive the uplift of land masses over vast periods of time, such that seafloors and lake beds can eventually be uplifted to become mountaintops, thus explaining the presence of marine fossils at high elevations. Following Hutton's work, Charles Lyell popularized the theories of gradualism in the 1830s and became known as the father of modern geology. By

now scientists had begun to question Archbishop Ussher's claim that Earth was created on the evening of October 22, 4004 BC. With the advent of plate tectonic theory in the latter half of the twentieth century, Hutton's views were validated.

Largely in response to Lyell, a distinguished Christian marine biologist named Philip Gosse set out to reconcile geology with six 24-hour days of creation. Gosse published his book, *Omphalos* (Greek for "navel"), two years before

Charles Lyell (1797–1875) pioneered modern geology in the 1830s, thirty years before Darwin published his theory of evolution.

Darwin's *Origin of the Species*. His intriguing title hinted at the book's theme: Did God create Adam and the world with artifacts (such as a navel on Adam's abdomen) that implied age and history even though everything was brand-new? Well aware of the scientific evidence against recent creation, Gosse held to his lifelong belief in a recent creation by assuming that

God had indeed created the world with the appearance of age. So even though geologists had found tremendous evidence for an ancient Earth, it only *appeared* to be old. But does this make God a deceiver? Many believed so and heavily criticized Gosse on this count.

Philip Gosse attempted to counter Lyell's geological method.

## The Advent of Flood Geology and Scientific Creationism

Sensing that the tide was turning decisively in favor of ancient creation, Seventh Day Adventist George McCready Price sought scientific support for recent creation in the early twentieth century. A self-taught amateur geologist, Price revived the idea that Noah's flood could account for the earth's geological structure. Price had little following outside his own church until John Whitcomb and Henry Morris resurrected his ideas in their 1961 book, *The Genesis Flood*. Whitcomb, a theologian, was react-ing to the Baptist theo-logian Bernard Ramm's well-received 1954 book, *Christian View of Science and Scripture*, which melded modern science with the biblical record. Seeking to bolster his project with scientific credentials, Whitcomb enlisted the help of Mor-ris, a civil engineer. Their

Recent Creationists believe places like Monument Valley are the result of Noah's flood.

book took the Christian world by storm and laid the founda-tion for the Scientific Creationist movement.

More than science is at stake in the debate over Earth's age. Many participants believe the nature of God and our entire approach to Christian apologetics are on the line. In this light we will investigate the five primary competing interpretations of Genesis 1. Only those views that uphold the inerrancy of Scripture and the special cre-ation of humanity will be con-sidered. Thus the differences are not over inspiration or authority but over correct interpreta-tion of the inspired, inerrant Bible.

> *More than science is at stake in the debate over Earth's age.*

## Five Creation Views

Note that the last four views are not mutually exclusive,

but each of the last four does exclude the first.

| | |
|---|---|
| *Recent Creation* | God created everything that exists over a period of six normal days about six to ten thousand years ago. |
| *Day-Age* | The days of creation literally mean indefinite periods of time much longer than 24 hours. Earth is ancient, but humanity is young. |
| *Analogical Days* | The creation days are God's workdays and are conceptually (not chronologically) analogous to man's workdays. The language of normal days is used to make the analogy and establish the pattern for God's Sabbath law. |
| *Fiat Days* | God spoke the commands to create during six days and the fulfillment of the commands subsequently proceeded over indefinite periods of time. |
| *Framework* | Genesis 1:1–2:3 is a literary framework where the days are arranged in a topical order rather than a chronological order. The "days" are largely irrelevant as time markers of history. |

## Conclusion

Having given a general introduction, let us now turn to an in-depth investigation of each of the viewpoints. It is our prayer that the following chapters will bring light rather than heat to this debate and that you will be better equipped to understand the biblical and scientific aspects of creation.

## Notes

1. Philo Judaeus, *Legum Allegoria*, "Allegorical Interpretations of Genesis 2 and 3," Book 1, Section 2.

2. PCA Report of the Creation Study Committee, Section II, paragraph 7.

# Chapter 20
# The Recent Creation View

The Recent Creation view, also known as the 24-hour day view, Scientific Creationism or Solar Day view, is the view that God created everything in the span of six solar days and then rested on a seventh day. Adam and Eve were created as adults, and the entire physical world was mature and fully functional right out of the gate. These events all occurred several thousand years ago.

*The Young Earth view holds that "very good" in Genesis 1:31 means the early Earth was an utterly perfect paradise.*

This view rests on a straightforward interpretation of the Genesis creation narrative plus a conviction that by calling His creation "very good," God meant to convey that the early Earth was an utterly perfect paradise. All death and suffering, therefore, are strictly a result of the fall of Adam and Eve into sin.

## Arguments for the Recent Creation View

**Simplest Meaning:** The clearest and most straightforward explanation of the Genesis creation text is that the days are normal solar days.

***Critique:*** The simplest and most straightforward literal meaning is not always correct. Hebrew scholars point out that the word translated "day" (*yom*) has various meanings. For example, it has *three different meanings* in the creation narrative itself. Genesis 1:5 has two occurrences of *yom*; it refers to the 12-hour period of daylight in the first usage and then the complete creation day in the second usage. The third different meaning occurs in Genesis 2:4, where *yom* refers back to the entire creation week. This last example illustrates how *yom* can literally mean a long or indefinite period of time. Finally, recall also the biblical use of "the day of the Lord" to refer to the time of God's judgment. With all this in mind, it seems reasonable to suggest that Genesis may use *yom* to mean something besides 24 hours.

**Ordered Sequence:** Each day of the creation week is enumerated in a sequential fashion. When qualified by an ordinal (e.g., "Day One"), *yom* means a 24-hour day.

*Critique:* While *yom* typically means a regular day when used with a number, the ordered sequence of six creation days is unquestionably a unique event in the Bible. Hence, we've really nothing to compare it to. Furthermore, Zechariah 14:7 describes a long period of time as "one day" using the same phrase translated as "the first day" in Genesis 1:5. Hosea 6:2 uses the same phrase as Genesis 1:13 for "third day" when it refers to the coming time of restoration for Israel. Likewise, Deuteronomy 10:10 qualifies *yom* with a number in the expression "first time," but it specifically refers to forty days, not one 24-hour day. These examples suggest that *yom* is not constrained to a 24-hour meaning even when associated with a number.

> *Zechariah 14:7 describes a long period of time as "one day" using the same phrase translated as "the first day" in Genesis 1:5.*

**Evening and Morning:** The use of "evening and morning" for each creation day indicates that these were ordinary, sequential days.

*Critique:* As with the usage of *yom*, this phrase can indicate normal days, or it can metaphorically indicate the beginning and ending of an extended creation period. A metaphorical usage of "day" or "evening and morning" does not deny the historical accuracy of Genesis 1, for it still conveys the same message that God alone commenced and completed creation. Furthermore, some scholars point out that the phrase "evening and morning" does not describe a normal 24-hour day. The Hebrews marked the beginning of a day at sunset. Obviously, only 12 hours pass from sunset to morning. Hence, "evening and morning" refers only to the half-day period from dark to dawn and not the entire creation day. The uniqueness of this phrase in the Old Testament may alert the reader that something other than normal days are in view.

> *A metaphorical usage of "day" or "evening and morning" does not deny the historical accuracy of Genesis 1, for it still conveys the same message that God alone commenced and completed creation.*

**Historical consensus:** The 24-hour interpretation has been the consensus throughout church history.

*Critique:* While it is certainly true that this is the majority view historically, it is also true that from ancient times significant interpreters have held that the days of Genesis could have been something other than 24 hours. Before the time of Christ, Jewish writers recognized that if a day with the Lord is like a thousand years (Ps. 90:4) then Adam died in the "day" he sinned. Similarly, virtually all of the church fathers from the first centuries after Christ allowed latitude on the length of the  days, and those that held stringently to a short creation period often did so for reasons we do not find compelling today, such as the idea that God had to create instantaneously since He is omnipotent.[1] Finally, conservative theologians since the nineteenth century have commonly supported alternative views on the creation days as scientific evidences stacked up, helping inform our interpretation of the Bible. One well-known example is C. I. Scofield, who advocated the Old Earth view known as "gap theory" in his widely acclaimed study Bible.

*Conservative theologians since the nineteenth century have commonly supported alternative views on the creation days as scientific evidences stacked up, helping inform our interpretation of the Bible.*

**Sabbath Rest:** The Solar-Day view provides the theological foundation for the day of "Sabbath rest." Exodus 20:11 confirms that a normal seven-day week was described by the Genesis creation account.

Photo: NASA/JPL.

*Critique:* This is one of the stronger arguments in support of the Solar Day view. God commanded His people to work six days and rest the seventh, "For the LORD made the heavens and the earth ... in six days; then He rested on the seventh day" (Exod. 20:11). But note that this commandment does not depend on the length of the day as much as the pattern established in the creation account. Other obligations among the Hebrews followed the same pattern and had an obvious independence from 24-hour periods. For instance, they were to sow their fields for six years and then grant the land a "Sabbath rest" on the seventh year (Lev. 25:3–4). Likewise, Hebrew slaves were to serve for six years and be released on the seventh (Exod. 21:2). In each case the practice is patterned after God's creative workweek but has no dependence whatsoever on the length of the creation days.

## *Objections to the Recent Creation View*

**Conflicts with General Revelation:** The weight of evidence across all scientific disciplines indicates that the earth and the heavens are considerably older than seven to ten thousand years. For instance, the presence of long-lived radioactive isotopes contrasted with the absence of short-lived isotopes, thick sedimentary layers with fossils that are embedded and eroded, weathering and cratering on planets and moons, plus the immense travel time for distant starlight all argue for an ancient creation. Moreover, there are no scientific evidences that conclusively point to a recent creation.

***Recent Creation Response:*** The fall and the flood produced all of the evidence that is mistakenly interpreted as an indicator of long ages. In particular, all of the fossils and geological formations were formed during the flood.

**Heavenly Bodies on Day Four:** Some argue that the Recent Creation view undercuts itself since it holds that the sun, moon, planets, and stars were not created until Day Four. How could the first three days be solar days if no sun existed? This has been considered a weighty question since the earliest era of the church and Christian scholarship. Modern science seconds this difficulty by noting that the sun provides much more than light alone. Solar radiation is needed to sustain Earth's biodiversity, and the mass of the sun sustains the orbits of Earth and other planets. Finally, Genesis never says a temporary pseudo-sun was created or that the current laws of gravity and electromagnetism did not apply during the first three days of creation. The Ancient Creation view avoids these difficulties because it holds that the sun was created in Genesis 1:1.

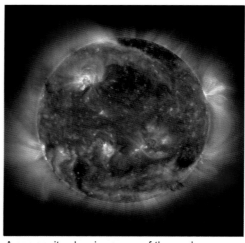

A composite showing many of the sun's properties. Photo NASA/JPL.

*Recent Creation Response:* God could have miraculously sustained His creation using a temporary source of illumination that would ebb and flow in the day-night cycle and manifest other sun like characteristics.

**Inferred Miracles:** The Solar Day view presumes miracles occurred even where the Bible leaves them unmentioned. One example is in Genesis 2, where we are told that God "planted" the garden and caused it to grow. We are not told this was a miraculous, instantaneous creation, but Recent Creation advocates assume that it was. Why assume this when nonmiraculous avenues for creation would glorify God just as much? In another example, the 24-hour reading of Day Six implies that God performed many miracles to enable Adam to fit so many events into a single day. Genesis 2:4-6 reads:

> This is the account of the heavens and the earth when they were created, in the day that the Lord God made earth and heaven. Now no shrub of the field was yet in the earth, and no plant of the field had yet sprouted, for the Lord God had not sent rain upon the earth, and there was no man to cultivate the ground. But a mist used to rise from the earth and water the whole surface of the ground (NASB).

In this text, notice terms like *now . . . was yet . . . no plant had yet . . . had not sent . . . there was no man to.* Each of these terms is a delimiter that points to the persistence of a long-term condition that required man's presence to correct. This text would be awkward if in fact each of these conditions had only existed for just a few hours, say from the early morning into the late afternoon of one single 24-hour day. So when we read this introduction to the creation of man, we get a sense of a long-term situation that was "at last" about to change for the better. The second chapter actually closes with this very idea as Adam exclaims "at last" when he meets Eve, his newly made companion. He has been waiting for this moment for a long time. Now his long loneliness is resolved, and he expresses his relief.

*When we read this introduction to the creation of man, we get a sense of a long-term situation that was "at last" about to change for the better.*

**Recent Creation Response:** Proponents of the 24-hour day view assert that it is not incorrect to presume that supernatural intervention was the norm, not the exception, during something as extraordinary as the creation week.

## Worldview Implications of the Recent Creation View

**1. A Perfect Creation:** At the core of this view is the notion that a "very good" creation would have been perfect, which means suffering and death were impossible. Death of humans and animals entered creation as a consequence of sin.

**2. Edenic Restoration:** Because advocates of recent creation hold that Eden represented God's ideal intent,

Would creatures such as this built-for-combat scorpion have had a place in Eden?

where death and violence were impossible, they say the future millennial kingdom will resemble Earth's original condition. Hence animals will supposedly once again become vegetarian (Is. 11:6–9 and 65:25). However, this may be a misreading of the millennial texts, which use vivid imagery that may not be intended as strictly literal. Further, this view implies that animals will be radically redesigned (digestive tracts, claws,

fangs, etc.) in the millennium to convert them from carnivores to herbivores. This reverses the changes that supposedly happened after the fall. But keep in mind that the Bible never says animals underwent such radical redesigns after Adam's sin. Further, this Edenic-per-

When did plants such as the *Acacia collinsii* develop thorns? Before the fall or afterwards?

fection view of the millennial kingdom seems to overlook the fact that humans will still be mortal at that time.

***3. Animal Death and God's Character:*** The Recent Creation view holds that all animals were originally vegetarians. To become carnivorous after the fall and after Noah's flood, animals would have to have been *radically* transformed. Plants would have had to change just as much, for the defenses they have today would not have been present if God's original intention was that all animal life would eat plants alone. The Bible never mentions these wholesale changes. But the Recent Creation view is about far more than biology. At base, this view maintains that the Ancient Creation view is inconsistent with God's loving, holy character since it entails that countless generations and species of animals suffered, died, and went extinct before Adam and Eve sinned.

***4. Accidents:*** For Eden to be perfect, as Recent Creation advocates maintain, God would have needed to supernaturally intervene at every moment to keep all of His creatures from coming to harm. After all, people and animals slip, fall, choke, and drown even in the best of conditions. But again, the Bible gives no indication that Eden was really like this.

## *Summary Assessment*

The strongest argument for the Solar Day view is that it has been regarded as the most straightforward view throughout church history. The greatest objection to this view is that it conflicts with impressive scientific evidence, thus requiring one to regard virtually all of modern science as fundamentally mistaken not just about the age of Earth but about most of the findings and principles that have made modern technologies possible.

## *Note*

1. Hugh Ross, *A Matter of Days: Resolving a Creation Controversy* (Colorado Springs: Nav Press, 2004). See chapter 4, "Wisdom of the Ages."

# Chapter 21
# The Day-Age View

Another broadly held interpretation of the days of Genesis is the Day-Age view, which holds that the days should be read literally as long periods of time. This perspective considers the days of Genesis to be consistent with astronomical and geological evidences for an ancient creation. Advocates say God created the entire universe (mass, energy, space, and time) from nothing at the beginning and providentially guided its development over eons of time,

*Progressive Creationists believe that God miraculously and progressively created life as described in Genesis 1.*

with the ultimate aim of preparing Earth for life. Emphasis is placed on the fact that, when the days are read as long creation periods, the sequence of events during the creation week closely resembles the best-attested scientific theories of early Earth development. As described in Genesis

Both Genesis and modern science say that the planet was previously covered by ocean.

1, the planet was covered with water; then dry land appeared, and plants sprung up on it; then the sun, moon, and stars appeared in the sky (became visible from the surface of Earth); then the waters teemed with living creatures; birds filled the sky; the earth brought forth living creatures; and finally God made humans in His image.

Some people criticize the Day-Age view by equating it with the theory of evolution. They do this because both of these viewpoints agree that Earth is old. However, while evolutionists and other advocates of ancient creation (such  as progressive creationists) agree that Earth is old, they fundamentally disagree over the ultimate "how" of creation.

Perhaps some of the confusion stems from the fact that some Day-Age advocates espouse a form of evolution called Theistic Evolution. In this view evolution was the primary or only mechanism God used to create life. Most Day-Age advocates hold to Progressive Creation, a view which is seen as more consistent with conservative theology. Progressive Creation differs with the Recent Creation view primarily in the duration of the creation week, and it differs with theistic evolution primarily in the means by which God created. Progressive Creationists believe that God miraculously and progressively created life as described in Genesis 1 through long ages of time. At providentially determined times, God spoke the "kinds" into existence. Because the Progressive Creationist view upholds biblical inerrancy and considers Genesis to be a historical narrative, we will focus on this version of the Day-Age view.

*Progressive Creation differs with the Recent Creation view primarily in the duration of the creation week, and it differs with theistic evolution primarily in the means by which God created.*

## Arguments for the Day-Age View

**Multiple Meanings of "Day":** Like our English word for "day," the Hebrew word *yom* has multiple meanings. It is primarily used in the Old Testament to indicate a 24-hour period, but it is sometimes used as a shorter period when contrasting day and night. Both uses are found in Genesis 1:5. It also can indicate a long period of unspecified length such as "the day of the Lord." This sense is used in Genesis 2:4 where *yom* refers to the entire six-day creation week as if it were merely one day. Thus *yom* can be interpreted literally as 24 hours, a portion of the day, or an unspecified period of time such as an age. Day-Age advocates understand *yom* to indicate long ages of creation.

*Critique:* Though it does not rise to the level of being a grammatical rule, Solar Day advocates argue that the use of an ordinal with *yom* necessitates the 24-hour meaning.

**God's Perspective on Time:** Scripture itself speaks of an ancient Earth. Habakkuk 3:6 says "He stands and shakes the earth; He looks and startles the nations. The age-old mountains break

*Psalm 90:2 uses the antiquity of the mountains to illustrate the eternality of God's existence.*

apart; the ancient hills sink down. His pathways are ancient." Had the mountains formed during Noah's flood or during a recent creation a mere 2,000 years before Habakkuk's time, the mountains would have not seemed "age-old" or "ancient." Keep in mind that the Bible says the earliest generations of humans often lived to be nearly 1,000 years old. Habakkuk's words seem to be an apt description of God's sovereign control over the geological processes that gradually built and tore down the mountains. Psalm 90:2 uses the antiquity of the mountains to illustrate the eternality of God's existence.

Psalm 90:2 uses the antiquity of the mountains to illustrate the eternality of God's existence.

Thousand-year-old mountains hardly seem suitable as a metaphor for eternity. The passage continues to explicitly say that God does not measure time as we do: "For in Your sight a thousand years are like yesterday that passes by, like a few hours of the night" (Ps. 90:4). This perspective is repeated in 2 Peter 3:5, which says that "long ago the heavens and the earth" were created.

*Critique:* Scientific Creationists argue that terms like "ancient" are relative, and thousands of years can indeed seem ancient when compared to the normal human life span which most biblical figures lived.

**Most Consistent Meaning:** It is important to make our interpretation match the intention of Genesis. Day-Age interpreters discern that Moses mentions both normal providence and miracles as the means God used to create the universe. Rather than try to read miracles into texts that do not mention them, it is best to settle on the natural interpretation.

Day-Age advocates believe defenders of recent creation fail to do this. For example, the sun was not created until Day Four according to the Recent Creation view. Proponents of that view presume the existence of a pseudo-sun for the first three days. This pseudo-sun was then replaced by the real sun on Day Four (along with the moon, planets, and stars).

*Day-Age interpreters discern that Moses mentions both normal providence and miracles as the means God used to create the universe.*

But the Bible does not teach this. It merely says that on Day Four, "God placed them in the expanse of the sky" (Gen 1:17). Here the Hebrew verb *nathan*, translated as "placed," has a range of possible meanings which include: "set, place, bring forth, make, or constitute." Hence, it does not necessarily mean "create." The most consistent option here is the one the translators have chosen: placed. This seems to indicate that on Day Four the heavenly bodies became visible in the sky and could therefore serve as markers for time, seasons, and direction. This resembles the usage of *nathan* found in Genesis 9:13, where God said, "I have placed My bow in the clouds, and it will be a sign of the covenant between Me and the earth."

The Day-Age view says that Day Four corresponds with the period in Earth's early history when the atmosphere switched from translucent (due to carbon dioxide, clouds, and dust) to transparent, as it is today. This was the first time in history that the sun, moon, and stars could be seen distinctly from Earth's surface. Thus

Artist's impression of a young planetary system filled with a thick disc of dust. Photo: NASA/JLP.

in the Day-Age view, there is no need to imagine that the sun did not exist during the first three "days" of creation. Some scholars point out that the Ancient Creation view is the most consistent harmonization between the two creation accounts of Genesis 1 and 2. Gleason Archer has stated the opinion that biblical inerrancy demands long creation days since "the more serious difficulty with the twenty-four hour theory is that it gives rise to an insoluble contradiction with Genesis 2."[1] Archer is referring to the apparent

*Some scholars point out that the Ancient Creation view is the most consistent harmonization between the two creation accounts of Genesis 1 and 2.*

conflict between the numerous time-consuming activities of Day Six spelled out in Genesis 2 and the twenty-four-hour duration supposedly mandated in Genesis 1. In his words,

As we compare Scripture with Scripture (Gen. 1:27 with 2:15–22), it has become very apparent that Genesis 1 was never intended to teach that the sixth creative day, when Adam and Eve were *both* created, lasted a mere twenty-four hours. In view of the long interval of time between these two, it would seem to border on sheer irrationality to insist that all of Adam's experiences in Genesis 2:15-22 could have been crowded into the last hour or two of a literal twenty-four-hour day.[2]

Rather than appealing to miracles the Bible never mentions, Day-Age proponents simply acknowledge that all of these things could not have been done in one day. Further, they note that several elements of the passage lose their significance if Day Six were

> *The underlying truth revealed in nature must be consistent with the truth revealed in the Bible.*

merely 24-hours long. The chief example is Adam's exultation ("at last!") in finally meeting his partner in Genesis 2:23. If he had been waiting only a few hours, it is hard to understand his pent-up excitement as he meets Eve.

*Critique:* Proponents of recent creation argue that if God instantaneously created the land animals and Adam early on Day Six, much of the day would have remained for Adam's

activities. It would not take long for Adam to name the animals if he only named the larger groups such as families instead of each individual species. In other words, perhaps he named canines as a family but not coyotes, wolves, foxes, and cocker spaniels specifically.

**Harmonizes Special and General Revelation:** The Apostle Paul says no one has an excuse for denying the existence of the Creator. "From the creation of the world His invisible attributes, that is, His eternal power and divine nature, have been clearly seen, being understood through what He has made" (Rom. 1:20). But if God has so revealed Himself through His creation, this general revelation cannot be misleading. Moreover, since there can be no conflict between

Interacting spiral galaxies. Photo: NASA, ESA, and The Hubble Heritage Team (STScI).

statements of truth, the underlying truth revealed in nature must be consistent with the truth revealed in the Bible. In fact, conflicts between our interpretation of the revelation in nature (science) and our interpretation of the revelation in the Bible (theology) actually show us places where we have more to learn in one or both areas. A chief strength of the Ancient Creation view is that it harmonizes the inerrant truth of Scripture with well-established scientific gleanings from general revelation. Instead of seeking to deconstruct and disprove all scientific findings that are inconsistent with recent creation, it points out the many consistencies between Genesis and proven science.

*Critique:* Many recent creation advocates say

> *A chief strength of the Ancient Creation view is that it harmonizes the inerrant truth of Scripture with well-established scientific gleanings from general revelation.*

the immutable truth of Scripture should not be wedded to scientific theories that change with time. Moreover, some argue that the truth revealed in nature was corrupted at the fall of humankind.

**The Seventh Day:** Each of the first six days in Genesis 1 end with the phrase: "Evening came, and then morning: the _____ day." Day Seven is different. "By the seventh day, God completed His work that He had done, and He rested on the seventh day from all His work that He had done" (Gen. 2:2). Because the familiar "evening/morning" phrase is not repeated and there is no end stated for this day, many scholars argue that the seventh day continues even now.

*Instead of seeking to deconstruct or disprove all scientific findings that are inconsistent with recent creation, Day-Age advocates point out the many consistencies between Genesis and proven science.*

*Critique:* This argument is in large part an argument from silence, based on the absence of the "evening/morning" refrain on Day Seven.

## Objections to the Ancient-Creation View

**Violates Perspicuity of Scripture:** The ancient Hebrew people had no knowledge of modern science and would likely have taken the Mosaic creation days to be regular calendar days. The same is true of the average believer today who can read and understand Scripture but has no training in the sciences. In this light, critics of the Ancient Creation view assert that it violates the perspicuity of Scripture (the principle that says

Do we see through a glass darkly, or is our vision crystal clear? Critics believe the Ancient Creation view implies that the Bible is hard to understand.

the central truths of the Bible are clear and understandable to all people in all generations). One should not be required to have knowledge of science, they say, to rightly understand the Bible.

***Day-Age Response:*** Protestant Reformers introduced the doctrine of perspicuity to counter the Roman Catholic idea that only priests were competent to interpret Scripture. However, this principle does not mean that all issues in the Bible are equally understandable. Peter makes this point when he says that some of Paul's writings are hard to understand (2 Pet. 3:16). Peter even said that neither angels nor the prophets fully understood what was prophesied about Christ (1 Pet. 1:10-12). Nor does perspicuity mitigate the need for scholarly study in order to accurately understand the Bible (2 Tim. 2:15). Old Testament theologian Walter C. Kaiser notes that this principle can be pressed too far:

*Properly understood, the principle of perspicuity does not mean that all issues in the Bible are equally understandable.*

> This principle may be overextended if it is used as an excuse against further investigation and strenuous study by believers who are not contemporaries of the prophets and apostles who first spoke the word of God. Scripture, in any faithful translation, is sufficiently perspicuous (clear) to show us our sinfulness, the basic facts of the gospel, what we must do if we are to be part of the family of God, and how to live for Christ. This does not mean, however, that in seeing (and even understanding) these truths we have exhausted the teaching of Scripture. Neither does it imply that the solution to every difficult question in Scripture or life is simple, much less simplistic. It only affirms that, despite the difficulties we find in Scripture, there is more than enough that is plainly taught to keep all believers well nourished.[3]

Also, the above objection based on perspicuity is influenced by a static view of biblical interpretation that denies (in practice if not in principle) the possibility that the church's interpretation of Scripture can improve over time. Yet clearly our understanding of the person and work of Jesus Christ is much richer today than it was for the first generations of the church. After all, the hard work and scholarly devotion of the early church fathers, the church councils, the Reformers, and modern scholars have surely not been in vain.

It also begs the question to assume that all early Hebrew readers would have interpreted the creation days to be literal solar days. We know that commentators have long recognized that the days of creation could have been longer or shorter than 24-hours and that the first three days in particular would not

*The objection based on perspicuity seems to depend on a static view of biblical interpretation that denies the possibility that the church's interpretation of Scripture can improve over time.*

have been normal solar days if you assume that the sun had not yet been created. Moreover the initial audience would have recognized that the activities of Day Six required more than a mere 24 hours for Adam to complete.

**Overlapping Days:** Although the Ancient Creation view attempts to reconcile the Bible with established scientific data, it does not do so exactly. For example, some plants (created on Day Three) appear after some fish (Day Five) in the fossil record.

*Day-Age Response:* One possible resolution is that Genesis marks the first creation of a "kind" or group of living things and does not imply that God created all species of that group on that day. Likewise, God did not fully populate the land on the day a particular kind was created. Rather, His commands to the animals to reproduce and

*"What kind of days these were it is extremely difficult, or perhaps impossible for us to conceive."*

St. Augustine, *The City of God*, XI.6.

fill the land were evidently executed over a long time frame. The apparent conflict of overlapping days can also be resolved by recognizing that the creation narrative is not exhaustive in detail. Genesis 1 succinctly states that God created various types of plants and animals in a particular order. It does not require that all plants and animals were created only on those particular days. Furthermore, some have suggested that if the days were of indefinite length, perhaps they could have overlapped, which would explain away the above objection.

**Death Before Sin:** One of the most significant implications of an ancient creation is that animal suffering and death occurred before the Fall. This means fossils represent animals that suffered and died before Adam's sin brought a curse on creation. But how could it be "very good" for the vast majority of species to suffer extinction? That seems to make God the author of death and suffering quite apart from the consequences of human sin.

*Day-Age Response:* The Bible does not teach that animals were originally immortal. Romans 5:12 and 1 Corinthians 15:21–22 are often said to indicate that physical death came to animals because of Adam's sin, but these passages refer only to death's spread to humanity. Nor does the Bible teach that all animals were originally herbivorous. Thus, the argument that no animals died before Adam's sin is entirely inferential. If God pronounced the creation "very good," so recent creation advocates say, it must have been perfect in every conceivable way. But that premise fails to recognize that God created this world according to an eternal purpose to bring glory to His name through the drama of fall and redemption. The goodness of creation can only be evaluated in light of the

*The goodness of creation can only be evaluated in light of the totality of God's purpose, not merely the state of man's existence in the garden of Eden.*

totality of God's purpose, not merely the state of man's existence in the garden of Eden. The original creation was "very good" not because of its pristine perfection but because it was perfectly suited as a stage on which the Creator's perfect purpose would begin to be achieved.

*The original creation was "very good" not because of its pristine perfection but because it was perfectly suited as a stage on which the Creator's perfect purpose would begin to be achieved.*

## Worldview Implications of the Ancient Creation View

1. ***Very Good Creation:*** Essentially, the distinction between the Day-Age and Solar Day views boils down to the type of world God would create and deem "very good."

2. ***Revelation:*** Ancient Creation advocates place a high priority on harmonizing the geological and astronomical data with the truth of Scripture. Some critics see this as a compromise of the Scriptures, but this harmonization is motivated by a pursuit of truth and a belief that God has revealed Himself truthfully through what has been made (Rom. 1:20).

3. ***The Big Picture:*** The Day-Age view is consistent with historical theology in recognizing that the creation week must be understood in light of God's eternal purpose. The garden of Eden was not an end in itself and it did not embody the fulfillment of the Creator's whole purpose. His eternal purpose has always been to glorify Himself, and His plan has always been to accomplish that purpose through His Son, our Savior Jesus Christ, in whom we were chosen before the foundation (creation) of the world (Eph. 1:4).

4. ***Genesis:*** Progressive Creationists believe that the Genesis creation account is an inerrant, historical narrative description of the Creator's divine work of creation. At providentially determined points, He brought the universe into existence, fashioned Earth for life, and miraculously created life.

## *Notes*

1. Gleason Archer, "A Response to The Trustworthiness of Scripture in Areas Relating to Natural Science," in E. Radmacher and Robert Preus, *Hermeneutics, Inerrancy, and the Bible* (Grand Rapids: Zondervan, 1984), 326–327.

2. Gleason Archer, *Encyclopedia of Bible Difficulties* (Grand Rapids: Zondervan, 1982), 60.

3. Walter C. Kaiser Jr., "Legitimate Hermeneutics," in *Inerrancy*, ed. Norman L. Geisler (Grand Rapids: Zondervan, 1980).

# Chapter 22
# The Analogical Days View

The Day-Age view and the Solar Day view both understand the days of Genesis to refer to literal periods of time, whether 24 hours or much longer. A third view, known as the Analogical Days view, takes a different tactic. God is not subject to time as we know it. Noting this, the Analogical Days view says the creation days are presented as ordinary days in Genesis because we can readily understand them when framed in that way, whereas God Himself experienced the time of creation in a completely different way, a way that cannot easily be expressed in human language. Maybe it was quicker than a normal workweek; maybe it was vastly longer. The Analogical Days view is not primarily concerned with that issue. Its main point is that the Bible often uses ordinary words and concepts of human experience to describe supernatural realities. Hence, God's workdays in Genesis are analogous (similar but not identical) to man's workdays. This analogy is the basis for the Creator's

REVEREND FUN ©GCI, INC.

YOUR EARTH WATCH WON'T WORK HERE ... WE ARE ON GOD TIME, WHERE ONE DAY IS THE SAME AS A THOUSAND YEARS command to work six days and rest on the Sabbath. Of course, the language of analogy does not imply that the Genesis creation narrative is mythical or allegorical. Even if God's divine workday is not identical to man's day of work, the Genesis narrative is an inerrant account of historical truth.

*Even if God's divine workday is not identical to man's day of work, the Genesis narrative is an inerrant account of historical truth.*

## Arguments for the Analogical Days View

**The Sabbath Day:** The Analogical Days view is inspired by the significance God placed on the six-day workweek and the seventh day of rest. In Exodus 20:8–11 man was commanded to work for six days and rest on the seventh because that was the pattern God established when He did His work of creation. It seems clear that God's chief aim here was to provide us

*Moses Breaking the Tables of the Law*, by Gustave Dore.

with a model for work and rest, not teach us the precise timetable for creation. After all, the six days of creation were unquestionably extraordinary days, and the Creator's work in Genesis is not identical to our work; it is *analogous* to our work. It shares points of similarity (the pattern), but it shares points of distinction as well (such as creating matter from nothing). Another interesting insight to the analogical nature of God's workweek is found in Exodus 31:17, which says that on the seventh day God "rested and was refreshed." Clearly God did not literally need to catch His breath after the creation week. This example of anthropomorphism further indicates that God's creation workweek is analogical rather than identical to a human workweek.

***Recent Creation Critique:*** Some suggest that the association between man's workweek and God's six workdays of creation in Exodus 20 requires a literal equivalence between man's days and God's days of creation. Certainly the most straightforward reading suggests this conclusion.

**Evenings and Mornings:**Elsewhere in the Old Testament, the phrase "evening came, and then morning" marks the beginning and ending of the *nighttime* (Num. 9:15–16) and thus refers only to the period of rest following each day's labor (as in Ps. 104:22–23). This is especially significant in the context of the analogy between God's workdays and man's since each day's refrain foreshadows the weekly Sabbath day of rest when the six days of work are complete. Hence, it seems that evening and morning are mentioned as a repeated foreshadowing of the seventh day of rest, not as literal notations of a 24-hour day.

This time clock measures time in the ordinary way. Does God measure time the same way?

***Recent Creation Critique:*** While this interpretation is possible, it is not the only option and is possibly not the best option.

**Markers for Nonliteral Days:** Several hints in the creation narrative indicate that the divine workdays were not normal days. First, as mentioned previously, strictly literal readings lead to the conclusion that solar days existed before the sun itself was created. Second, Day Seven is unique because it does not

*Several hints in the creation narrative indicate that the divine workdays were not normal days.*

conclude with the "evening/morning" refrain shared by the

## TO DO

Adam's to-do list for Day Six was overwhelming if that day was only 24 hours long.

six workdays of creation. New Testament passages such as John 5:17 and Hebrews 4:3–11 suggest that the Creator's day of rest did not cease after 24 hours. Even though He is at work *in* His creation, His rest from the work *of* creation continues. Third, it is difficult to compress the activities of Day Six into a regular day without either a loss of significance in the activities or an ad hoc appeal to miracles.

***Recent Creation Critique:*** It is not beyond the power of God to create a temporary sun for Days 1–3, and while the Bible does not mention a temporary sun, it may be reasonable to infer that one existed. The absence of the "evening/morning" refrain on Day Seven is an argument from silence. As for Day Six, Adam's pre-fall abilities were probably considerably greater than ours.

**Figures of Speech:** Throughout the Bible God appropriates common terminology and imagery to communicate sacred truths in a manner that is understandable. For instance, when we read that the Lord stretches out His hand or that His eyes range throughout the earth, we recognize that the Bible is employing anthropomorphic language, language that ascribes human qualities to God in order to convey truths that cannot be explained in a strictly literal sense. Similarly, the Bible often uses phenomenological language, language that explains events in a way that is familiar to human experience. Talk of the sun standing still is a prime example.

*Talk of the sun standing still is a prime example of phenomenological language.*

Given some of the nonliteral markers in Genesis 1 and 2, a strong case can be made that the "days" of creation week are analogous to, not identical with, the days we humans regularly experience. Analogy is useful for teaching important theological concepts.

*Recent Creation Critique:* Though the Bible certainly uses figures of speech, Genesis 1 and 2 have most often been interpreted literally throughout history.

**Structure of the Days:** Each of the six days is characterized by a repetitious structure consisting of a commencement, command, commentary, and closure. Focusing attention on the power of God's spoken word, each day begins with the phrase "Then God said." This structure, along with  the first use of the narrative verb tense in verse 3, indicates that the first day begins in verse 3 some *unspecified* time *after* the creation of the heavens and the earth spoken of in Genesis 1:1. Because the first two verses of Genesis 1 serve as a background to the six workdays when God fashions the earth and creates His image-bearers, attention is drawn to the pattern of the workweek rather than the length of time over which creation transpired.

*Recent Creation Critique:* Genesis 1:1–2 has typically been understood as an introduction to the creation account, not "background" for the creation week.

**Derived on Strictly Exegetical Grounds:** The Analogical Days view draws heavily on the literary structure of the creation account and is not driven by an attempt to harmonize the Bible with science.

*The Analogical Days view is not driven by an attempt to harmonize the Bible with science.*

*Recent Creation Critique:* While it draws heavily on the literary structure of Genesis 1–2, it reaches conclusions that are uncommon in the history of interpretation.

**Permits Either Recent or Ancient Creation:** Since the

Analogical Days view asserts that the text is silent on the actual length of God's workdays, it shares some of the strengths of the Recent Creation view as well as the Ancient Creation view. While allowing *yom* to be understood as a normal day (a strength of the Recent Creation view), this view also allows the actual length of God's workdays to be indefinite (a strength of the Day-Age view). Because natural revelation unambiguously and unanimously points to an ancient creation of Earth and the cosmos, the Analogical Days view readily harmonizes God's special and general revelations.

***Recent Creation and Ancient Creation Critique:*** Any view that equally permits either Ancient Creation or Recent Creation is an underdeveloped view. Creation is either young or ancient, not either/or. Besides, the reality is that most adherents to the Analogical Days view hold that creation is ancient, not young.

### *Samples of Phenomenological Language in the Bible*

| | |
|---|---|
| ***1 Chron. 16:30*** | Indeed, the world is firmly established, it will not be moved (NASB). |
| ***Psalm 104:5*** | He established the earth on its foundations; it will never be shaken. |
| ***Isaiah 11:12*** | He will collect the scattered of Judah from the four corners of the earth. |
| ***Ecclesiastes 1:5*** | The sun rises and the sun sets; panting, it returns to its place where it rises. |
| ***Job 38:4, 6*** | Where were you when I laid the foundation of the earth? . . . On what were its bases sunk? Or who laid its cornerstone (NASB). |

## *Does Anybody Really Know What Time It Is?*

One of the most intriguing discoveries in the history of science came when Albert Einstein formulated his theories of relativity. Scientists had long known something was missing in their theories of light and motion, but none could make the bold leap Einstein made: he reasoned that time (the rate at which processes operate) is not an absolute quality but is instead a dependent quality. Time is not the same throughout the universe because velocity and the strength of local gravity influences time itself. You and I will never travel fast enough to notice the difference, but time actually slows down dramatically as one approaches the speed of light.

*Time is not the same throughout the universe because velocity and the strength of local gravity influences time itself.*

A classic example of this "time dilation" is the twin paradox. Suppose two twins are born, and one is placed on a rocket ship traveling close to the speed of light while the other stays grounded on earth. When the rocket ship returns to earth decades later, the earthbound twin is old while the space-traveling twin is only a few years old! This is no science fiction tale; the effect has been measured and confirmed by ultra-precise atomic clocks traveling in high-speed spacecraft. This is the way the universe really is. The same effect is experienced on planets where the gravity is much stronger than Earth's.

In summary, there is no such thing as absolute time. This means views that suggest there is a difference in man's time and God's time are not guilty of special pleading or a literary bait and switch. Time here is not the same as time over there, and time for God is certainly different than it is for you and me.

Atomic clocks such as this one at the National Institute of Standards and Technology have measured time dilation at high speeds.

## Summary

In the Analogical Days view, the biblical words for day, evening, and morning are, on the surface, understood in their normal sense. Yet noting the common biblical use of non-literal elements such as figures of speech, anthropomorphism, and phenomenological language, advocates of the Analogical

Days view hold that the days of the creation week are ultimately analogies, for God's experience of time differs from ours. Commentators throughout history have recognized this. Additionally, it seems clear that Sabbath law is the ultimate basis for the analogy of days in the creation account. It is

*Advocates of the Analogical Days view hold that the days of the creation week are analogies, for God's experience of time differs from ours.*

important to stress that the Analogical Days view is based strictly on textual analysis, not appeal to science. For this reason it is science neutral and historically accurate.

# Chapter 23
# The Fiat Days View

It is natural when reading Genesis 1 to assume the days were regular days and that the acts of creation were instantaneously fulfilled, yet the vast preponderance of scientific evidence places the creation of Earth and the cosmos billions of years in the past. The Fiat Days view attempts to harmonize these disparate notions in a unique way. Simply stated, this view says God spoke the commands to create during the span of six 24-hour days, but the fulfillment of those commands took an indefinite period of time, perhaps billions of years. By distinguishing the pronouncement of the commands from the execution of the commands, the Fiat Days view allows interpreters to take the creation days to be literal while

Did God speak the commands in six literal days, then watch as they were fulfilled over many years?

preserving an extended time for the commands to be executed. Hence this view is essentially a hybrid between recent- and ancient-creation approaches.

## Arguments for the Fiat Days View

**Structure of the Genesis Text:** Advocates of the Fiat Days view believe the literary structure of the creation narrative places emphasis on God's commands, not the fulfillment of the commands. Note the elements of each creation day:

- Commencement
- Command
- Commentary (fulfillment, evaluation, and description)
- Closure

The text is unconcerned with how the creative processes actually occurred. Rather, its concern is to highlight the power of God's spoken command. For example, when we read "Let there be light, and there was light," the impression is that God speaks and is invariably obeyed. The words "and there was light" comprise a parenthetical statement (see "Command and Fulfillment" diagram below) that does not bother describing details about the process of light coming into existence. Hence, the way is open to suggesting that the commands were literally given over a week's time while the fulfillment took much longer.

*Critique:* While the literary structure of the creation account suggests the Fiat Days view is possible, it certainly does not necessitate it.

## Command and Fulfillment in the Creation Days
### Genesis 1:3–5 as an Example

| | |
|---|---|
| **Commencement** | "Then God said, |
| **Command** | 'Let there be light,' |
| **Commentary** (fulfillment, evaluation, description) | (and there was light. God saw that the light was good, and God separated the light from the darkness. God called the light 'day,' and He called the darkness 'night.') |
| **Closure** | Evening came, and then morning: the first day." |

**Other Scriptures affirm creation by fiat alone:** The Bible teaches in several places that the spoken command of God brought about creation. The psalmist affirms that fiat was the sole ultimate cause of creation when he writes, "for He commanded, and they were created" (148:5). Echoing the Genesis narrative, King David states that "the heavens were made by the word of the LORD, and all the stars, by the breath of His mouth. . . .For He spoke, and it came into being; He commanded, and it came into existence" (33:6, 9). Likewise, Hebrews 11:3 says "the universe was created by the word of God."

> *The Hebrew verbs used in the creation narrative allow for both natural processes as well as divine ex-nihilo action to be used in the Creator's work.*

*Critique:* The means by which the fiat commands are executed is left completely unspecified in the Fiat Days view. Whether the Creator instantiated new laws and new forms of inanimate and animate matter or worked within the laws to form Earth and life are completely unresolved in this view.

In response to this, Fiat Day advocates may ask if the modest claims of their view is really a weakness. After all, Scripture is silent as to the exact means whereby God brought about creation. Furthermore, the Hebrew verbs used in the creation narrative allow for both natural processes as well as divine ex-nihilo action to be used in the Creator's work.

**Genesis suggests fulfillment occurred *after* the creation days:** The text does not explicitly place the effects produced by God's commands on the same day the commands were uttered.

Furthermore, we have already noted that the activities of Day Six would require considerably more than 24 hours if they were to have any significance. Hence, nothing precludes the suggestion that fulfillment of the commands stretched well past the days on which they were uttered.

NASA, ESA, S. Beckwith (STScI) and the HUDF Team.

### Critique:

1. Recent Creation advocates say the chronological enumeration of the creation days implies that the days progressed in a consecutive order and that the fulfillment and close of one day necessarily preceded the beginning of the subsequent day.

In response to this critique, Fiat Day advocates say the precedence for overlapping days is illustrated by the successive links of genealogies in Genesis 5. There we see that the end of one patriarch's life is discussed before the beginning of the next is introduced even though their life spans largely coincided. In other words, a quick glance at the text leads one to believe the patriarchs did not live simultaneous to one another, whereas a closer examination shows they did. This is a strong precedent for the legitimacy of the Fiat Days view of overlapping days in Genesis 1.

> *Fiat Day advocates say the precedence for overlapping days is illustrated by the successive links of genealogies in Genesis.*

2. On the Ancient Creation view that Genesis 1:1–2 represents the creation of the heavens and earth, the Fiat Days view is refuted since fulfillment occurred before command.

But given the straightforward assertion in Genesis 1:1 that God created the heavens and the earth before Day One is introduced in 1:3, there seems to be no good reason to object to the idea that God began creating prior to Day One. Indeed, He created angels before the creation week (Job 38:7), and they are certainly part of our created world and everyday existence.

## Summary

The Fiat Days view is perhaps the most reserved of all the major views we are surveying. On one hand it takes the days of Genesis 1 to be literal, but on the other hand it does not attempt to force the fulfillment of the creation acts into six literal days. As for Genesis 2, which some take to be a separate creation account, the Fiat Days view says it is an inspired elaboration on the fiat events specifically related to humankind's genesis and role in God's creation. There are many pertinent creation details found here (and elsewhere, such as Job 38–39; Ps. 104; Isa. 40; John 1 and Deut. 4) that are lacking in chapter 1. Fiat Days advocates remind us that this serves as a strong caution against thinking Genesis 1 sets out to answer all the questions we could ask of it. Taking note of this, the Fiat Days view emphasizes the sovereign command of God rather than the means by which His creation commands were fulfilled or how long that fulfillment took.

> *The Fiat Days view emphasizes the sovereign command of God rather than the means by which His creation commands were fulfilled or how long that fulfillment took.*

From God's point of view, the work of creation was virtually completed as soon as He uttered His unstoppable fiats even though the actual fulfillment was yet future. God is sure of His Word and sure of His power to fulfill it.

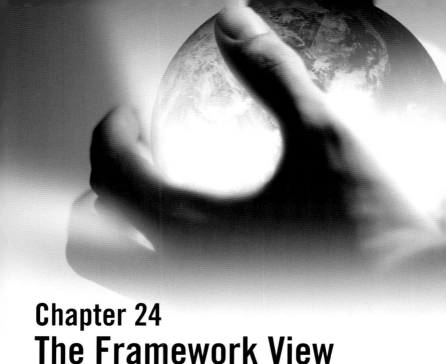

# Chapter 24
# The Framework View

Much like the Fiat Days view, the Framework view (or Framework Hypothesis) accepts the scientific evidence for an ancient creation while maintaining that the author of Genesis uses literal 24-hour days in his description of the creation week. To resolve this obvious tension, this view holds that the creation "days" as conveyed in Genesis are literary devices chosen by Moses (under God's inspiration) to frame various pictures of creation history. Each of the six days of creation is presented as a normal day, narrated in topical order, even though God's creative work (His commands and their fulfillment) did not actually occur within a literal week. The Bible is full of carefully crafted literary structures. Genesis 1 is just one among many examples.

> *The Framework view holds that the creation "days" as conveyed in Genesis are literary devices chosen by Moses (under God's inspiration) to frame various pictures of creation history.*

## Arguments for the Framework View

**Parallel Structure of the Days:** This view draws heavily on the literary structure of the six work days of creation. Noting that the account clearly seems crafted to present important truths in a topical fashion, Meredith Kline suggests that the six days form two parallel triads (see diagram) with the first dealing with *creation kingdoms* and the second with *creature kings*. For example, birds and sea creatures were created

Genesis says God made the sky on Day Two, and birds on Day Five. Hence, Day Five represents the filling of the domains created on Day Two.

on Day Five to rule over the sky and seas that were created on Day Two. This striking parallelism is clear evidence that Moses used a literary device to arrange his account topically, not chronologically.

### Critique:

- As with the Fiat Days view, literary structure alone is not sufficient to establish once for all that the days were nonsequential.

- This view risks presenting the Genesis account as non-historical.

- The Framework Hypothesis is difficult to understand and thus violates the doctrine of perspicuity, and it is doubtful that the Hebrew people for whom Moses wrote would have read the text in the manner the Framework view commends.

### Framework Response:

- Literary structures in the inerrant Bible are not accidental but purposeful. The Framework view takes seriously the task of understanding the kind of literature represented in Genesis 1.

The Framework view says Moses chose to frame God's creative activity in a readily understood concept: 24-hour days.

- Though it is admittedly awkward to affirm the historicity of Genesis 1 when the time markers are taken to be completely figurative, Framework advocates *insist* that Genesis describes historical events.

- One of the key points of the Framework view is that the essential message of the creation week is easily accessible to all readers. Proponents of this view assert that it is not necessary to understand the complex literary framework itself, for the central, readily understood message of "God is Creator of all" is the main thing Moses is trying to convey.

> *Framework advocates assert that it is not necessary to understand the complex literary framework itself, for the central, readily understood message of "God is Creator of all" is the main thing Moses is trying to convey.*

## Two Triads of Creation Days

| Creation Kingdoms | Creation Kings |
|---|---|
| **Day 1** - Light | **Day 4** - Luminaries |
| **Day 2** - Sky and seas | **Day 5** - Sea creatures and birds |
| **Day 3** - Dry land and vegetation | **Day 6** - Land animals and humans |
| **The Creator King** | |
| **Day 7** - Sabbath | |

**Resolves Inconsistencies of a Literal Week:** The Framework view avoids a difficulty more literal views suffer from, namely, that light was created three days before the sun. Working from the natural assumption that the creation of light corresponded with the creation of the sun and solar system, Framework advocates believe the creations God performed on Days One and Four actually *coincided* in time. This proposal is reinforced by the use of the same Hebrew verb for "separate" to indicate the common purpose of these two days. In keeping with Kline's observation above, the creation of light and the creation of the sun are assigned to different days in the creation account because Moses uses a literary approach that treats the creation of kingdoms and creation kings separately.

> *Framework advocates believe the creations God performed on Days One and Four actually coincided in time.*

*Critique:* Throughout history most interpreters have understood the events of Days One and Four to be distinct, with the initial creation of a light on Day One being independent of the sun's creation on Day Four. Others argue that the sun was not created on Day Four, but rather became visible from the surface of Earth at that time. In that case also, Days One and Four are distinct. The view that these days were simultaneous has very little historical support.

> *Critics point out that the view that the creation days were simultaneous has little historical support.*

**Consistent with Revealed Mode of Providence:** Regular, sequential creation days of 24-hour duration require the presumption of miraculous providence even where the Bible seems to presuppose normal providence. For example, Genesis 2:5 states that the explicit reasons there were no plants at that time was that "the Lord God had not made it rain on the land, and there was no man to work the ground." Rain is a work of normal providence as

There was no vegetation in the time before rain and human agricultural activities brought it forth, says Genesis 2:5.

nature functions according to God's design, and man's work of tilling and irrigating the ground is certainly not miraculous. Hence, Moses is saying that plants did not exist because vital natural factors were not yet in place. Furthermore, even if it had rained and man had been around to work the ground,

plants would not have appeared instantly, as would be required if all these things were really accomplished in the first five literal days of the creation week. (Notice that 2:7 says, "Then the LORD God formed the man out of the dust from the ground," which indicates that we are just entering Day Six of the creation account as Moses mentions the lack of vegetation on the earth.) Thus, Genesis 2:5 clearly appeals to *natural*, not supernatural, conditions to explain the absence of plants, and furthermore it presupposes nonliteral creation days, else it would not make sense to attribute the absence of plants to the absence of rain and tilling.

***Critique:*** Defenders of the Recent Creation view acknowledge that the Bible does not always say miracles were involved, but note that it seems fitting to assume that the creation of the world involved unparalleled supernaturalism. Framework advocates seem prepared to jump to the opposite conclusion: that no miracles occurred unless they are spelled out explicitly.

***Framework Response:*** It is best not to say more than the text of Scripture says. This conservative approach seems inevitably to lead to the conclusion that normal providence was often the means by which God carried out creation.

## Summary

The Framework view teaches that Genesis 1 is an inspired revelation of God's creative work. All of the core doctrines of creation are maintained in this view, such as the creation of creation are maintained in this view, such as the creation of all things from nothing, the special creation of Adam and Eve in God's image, and humanity's fall into sin. The Framework view says the events of the six creation days are arranged topically to demonstrate the creation of kingdoms and their filling with rulers in a manner that gives a pattern for our workweek and day of Sabbath rest.

*The Framework view says the events of the six creation days are arranged topically to demonstrate the creation of kingdoms and their filling with rulers in a manner that gives a pattern for our workweek and day of Sabbath rest.*

# Part VI

# Science and the Age of the Earth

# Chapter 25
# Science and a Young Earth

We have examined the major biblical views on the days of creation, but what does the record of nature say about the age of creation? Many Bible students are familiar with the scientific arguments commonly offered in support of a recent creation (within about 10,000 years), but they are often unfamiliar with evidence for an ancient creation (billions of years) and the critical evaluation of Young Earth arguments. To help you gain a fuller understanding of these issues, we will address the scientific evidences related to the time of creation in this chapter and the next three.

*What does the record of nature say about the age of creation?*

Our goal is to state briefly the primary arguments for and against each major viewpoint. We aim to be fair and balanced, though we must call it as we see it. By design our discussions are brief, but our hope is that they will enable Christians to be better informed and better able to defend the faith.

## *Young Earth Evidence from Astronomy*

**Short Period Comets:** Since comets lose material when they pass close to the sun, comets that frequently orbit the sun should have already disintegrated if the universe is ancient. The

Comet Hyakutake. Photo: NASA.

continued existence of these comets proves that the solar system was recently created.

*Critique:* Short-period comets do get used up as they repeatedly cycle past our sun, but new ones enter the inner solar system from a region beyond the orbit of Neptune known as the Kuiper Belt. Think of it as a vast parking area for icy and rocky objects that can become comets and asteroids if they are jostled in a way that sends them into the inner solar system. Since debris fields have been located around other stars, scientists believe that another such region, the Oort Cloud, exists in the outer reaches of our solar system. Thus the fact that short period comets still exist is no proof for a young universe.

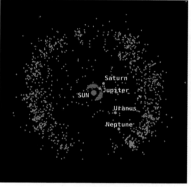

The green dots in this diagram of our solar system represent the clusters of rocky and icy debris in the Kuiper Belt, which replenishes the supply of short-period comets.

**Wind Up of Spiral Galaxies:** Spiral galaxies such as the Milky Way rotate around a central axis. Stars close to the center rotate faster than those in the outer reaches, and so it stands to reason that spiral galaxies should "wind up" within a few hundred million years and not have the spiral arrangement any longer. This has not happened,

Spiral Galaxy. Photo: NASA, ESA, S. Beckwith (STScI), and The Hubble Heritage Team (STScI/AURA).

and so the universe cannot be billions of years old.

*Critique:* The problem with this argument is that the spiral arrangement of galaxies is *not* due to the rotational motion of the material (stars, planets, etc.) in their arms. Backed by strong evidence, scientists theorize that spiral arms are instead formed by density waves that travel through the galactic disk much like sound waves travel through air. Several mechanisms may explain how these waves are generated, and the spontaneous development of spiral arms has been demonstrated in computer simulations.[1]

**Moon Dust:** Given the rate of accumulation, the thickness of dust on the surface of the moon would be much deeper if

Did NASA think the astronauts would sink into the moon dust? Photo: NASA.

the moon were billions of years old.

*Critique:* Actually, the depth of lunar dust is consistent with expectations for billions of years of accumulation. Initial thoughts to the contrary were based on results published in 1960 from an experiment conducted by Hans Pettersson on two mountaintops in Hawaii. Pettersson erroneously calculated that the moon, if it were billions of years old, would have a thick layer of dust. However, since 1963 it has been widely known that he overestimated the rate of cosmic dust influx. The actual rate proved to be a hundred times slower than he estimated. Some people claim that NASA believed Pettersson's original figures right up until the day the first astronaut walked on the moon in 1969 and that the agency was therefore worried that the astronauts might sink and be buried in the dust. But this story is a myth. NASA knew by then that the moon did not have as much dust as Pettersson had originally calculated.

## Young Earth Evidence from Anthropology

**Human Civilization:** Written records of human history date from about 4,000 to 5,000 years ago at most. This is consistent with a recent creation.

*Critique:* Humans were God's last act of creation. Thus, even the Ancient Creation view holds that humans have not been around

*Humans were God's last act of creation. Thus, even the Ancient Creation view holds that humans have not been around for long.*

for millions of years. The age of Earth is a different matter. God may have spent many ages preparing Earth for humanity. Thus, the brevity of human history does not imply recent creation. Further, it is to be expected that the earliest traces of human civilzation have been lost.

**Population Statistics:** Population growth rates average 0.5 percent annually. This indicates that the current global population would be achieved within a few thousand years of the creation of the first human couple.

*Critique:* Historical records indicate that the population growth rate during the twentieth century was much higher than at other times in the past. Human populations have not grown at a constant rate through history. In fact, there have been many periods of stasis and population decline due to wars, plagues, and famines.[2] More importantly, the antiquity of the human race is not directly tied to the age of Earth and the entire cosmos, and advocates for an old Earth maintain that humans were created late in Earth history.

## Young Earth Evidence from Earth Sciences

**Niagara Falls:** Current rates of erosion indicate that the Niagara Falls formed within the past 10,000 years, which is inconsistent with an ancient Earth.

Did Noah's flood create Niagara Falls?

*Critique:* According to geologists, Niagara Falls formed after the last Ice Age, which ended around 11,000 years ago. The age of Niagara can only limit the age of Earth if one supposes that Niagara was created when Earth itself was created. And even if the falls had been created in Noah's flood, that would not imply anything about the age of the entire Earth.

**Magnetic Field Decay and Reversals:** Measurements of Earth's magnetic field over the past two centuries indicate a steady decline in total energy. Originally this trend was

*The magnetic field has reversed many times in Earth's history.*

extrapolated back in time to show Earth could not be more than 10,000 years old. More recent data indicates that the field has actually reversed many times in the past, indicating that the present downward trend is not due to a constant, steady decline. Recent Creation advocates have introduced flood models which attempt to explain these reversals.

*Critique:* While Recent Creation advocates believe their flood models explain the magnetic field reversals better than conventional theories, it is important to note that the conventional theories are substantiated by multiple independent lines of evidence such as rates of seafloor spreading and dating of seafloor sediments and ice cores.

**Erosion and Seafloor Sediment:** Sediment continually accumulates on the ocean floor as material is eroded from the continents. If Earth were ancient, the amount of sediment on the ocean floor would be much greater.

*Critique:* The ocean floor does not just collect material that is eroded from the continents; it also *recycles* it back into the continents as the ocean floor slides under the continental plates in a well-documented process known as subduction. Though it is sometimes claimed that the rate of subduction is much less than the rate of erosion, which would mean sediment should pile up on the ocean floor faster than it is removed, careful comparisons reveal results that are consistent with conventional models of geology and an ancient creation.

**Not Enough Salt in the Oceans:** Salt accumulates in the oceans at a rate that, if permitted to continue for billions of years, would result in a much higher salinity than our oceans actually manifest. Thus, Earth cannot be billions of years old.

How much salt should be in the oceans if Earth is ancient?

*Critique:* Many processes remove salt from the ocean. Sea spray, chemical reactions at deep sea vents, deposition, and plate subduction are a few examples. In many respects we know more about the surface of the moon than the ocean floor, so there are likely other salt removal processes that we have not yet discovered. Besides, it is difficult to obtain measurements that are accurate enough to support the contention that an imbalance exists. The jury is still out on the exact rate of salt accumulation and removal in our oceans.

**Not Enough Helium in the Atmosphere:** It is sometimes claimed that our atmosphere would have much more helium if Earth were ancient.

Should the atmosphere have more helium?
Young Earth advocates believe so.

*Critique:* This argument fails to account for key processes that balance the production and loss of helium from the atmosphere. In addition to thermal-gravitational processes which heat helium high in the atmosphere, allowing it to achieve escape velocity (and thus leave Earth's atmosphere), helium is also photoionized, which allows it to escape along Earth's magnetic field lines.

## Methodology of Recent Creation Arguments

The Recent Creation arguments commonly take two forms. First, many of them rely on what could be called "incomplete solution" arguments which take some process and show that it cannot have persisted for millions or billions of years. Some observers say these kinds of arguments fail to take the whole picture into account. For instance, sources of replenishment are overlooked or assumed not to exist (as with short-period comets). Or in cases where accumulation processes are operative (e.g., the steady addition of salt to the sea), processes which cancel out the accumulation are ignored or underestimated.

*By its nature, science is the continued pursuit of understanding, and history shows that so-called mysteries are regularly explained as science advances.*

A second common tactic is the appeal to purported mysteries. This line of reasoning claims that because science has not yet fully explained an observation (such as spiral galaxy life cycles), no natural solution exists; hence, only miracles (recent ones at that) can explain the phenomena. However, this is a risky tactic. By its nature, science is the continued pursuit of understanding, and history shows that so-called mysteries are regularly explained as science advances.

## The Appearance of Age

One way to reconcile a recent creation with evidence for an ancient Earth is to presume that God created many things with an appearance of age. In other words, God made the creation to *appear* old even though it is not. For example, Genesis describes the newly created Adam as a fully grown adult. Thus, he had the appearance of age. Recent Creation advocates suggest that God made the whole world this way.

*Light from distant stars takes thousands, millions, or even billions of years to reach us.*

This is an appealing argument at first glance, but critics say it suffers from theological and conceptual problems. First, God cannot author a falsehood (Num. 23:19; Titus 1:2). Yet for God to create a world with a false appearance of age would seem to be deceptive. According to Romans 1:20, God reveals His nature through what has been made, and deceit is not His nature. Moreover, God holds people accountable for rejecting His self-revelation through the created world. Wouldn't it be unjust to hold people accountable for rejecting a false record?

Light Echo from Star V838 Monocerotis. Photo: NASA, ESA and H.E. Bond (STScI).

Another significant challenge to the Appearance of Age argument is distant starlight. Light from distant stars takes thousands, millions, or even billions of years to reach us. We can even watch the birth of stars as we essentially look backward in time through our telescopes. For instance, in February 1987 astronomers observed a supernova in a nearby galaxy called the Large Magellanic Cloud. One of the stars had

exploded, which is a normal event in the life cycle of large stars as they are depleted of fuel. This collection of stars is 168,000 light-years away from Earth. (A light-year is the distance light travels in one year at the speed of 186,000 miles per second.) So this explosion did not actually occur in 1987. Rather, it occurred 168,000 years before

Scattered Light from the Boomerang Nebula. Photo: NASA, ESA and The Hubble Heritage Team (STScI/AUR).

1987. It took the "pictures" of the event that long to travel from the exploding star to within the reach of our telescopes on Earth. Astronomers have been watching this explosion progress ever since 1987. By timing and measuring the motion of the expanding ring of gases around the dead star, they have been able to confirm the great distance to this star using the same geometric triangulation methods surveyors use to measure distance in your town.

If one believes the universe itself did not exist until just a few thousand years ago, then this star exploded before the universe was created. How is this dilemma resolved? The Appearance of Age argument says the whole picture show we're watching as we look at this supernova is a false history. God created the light in transit, thus making it look like a star existed there for the past 168,000 (nonexistent) years. The same holds true for the entire Large Magellanic Cloud. Furthermore, none of the stars in any of the other galaxies are projecting a true

*If one believes the universe itself did not exist until just a few thousand years ago, then this star exploded before the universe was created.*

history either. Essentially everything we watch in the night sky is a false picture show since, according to Recent Creation advocates, the universe isn't old enough for starlight to have traveled such great distances.

It is a little known fact that starlight carries markers that indicate how far it has traveled (i.e., spectral lines that broaden proportional to the distance traveled). If God had created starlight in transit rather than letting it dutifully travel the vast distance from "out there" to Earth, we would be able to identify this fact by the width of *The book of nature should be read, and believed, with care.* these spectral lines. But starlight *does* contain these broadened spectral lines, and they are broadened in proper proportion to the vast distance traveled. So either the starlight really did travel the full distance at the normal speed of light, or else God put highly specific yet falsified age and distance markers in starlight. But that does not fit with what we know about God's nature or His invitation for us to study creation and see

Geologic Time Spiral. Illustration by the U.S. Geological Survey.

evidences of Him in it. The book of nature should be read, and believed, with care.

## Can Science Tell Us Anything about Creation?

Scientific estimates of Earth's age have changed over the years. Noting this, advocates of recent creation conclude that the scientific evidence is inconclusive or untrustworthy. In *The Young Earth*, John Morris writes,

> It is true that the rocks and fossils *can be* interpreted within the old earth viewpoint, with some degree of success. They can be made to fit. In fact, the rocks can fit within any number of old-earth scenarios. This is obvious when one recognizes that the accepted age for Earth in 1900 was only about 100 million years, and now evolutionists date it 50 times as great! No matter what the evidence and what the 'politically correct' interpretation of the day may be, the rocks can be made to fit it.[3]

Morris goes on to say: "Neither the old-earth idea nor the young-earth idea can be scientifically proven by geologic observations, and, likewise, neither can be disproved."[4] In other words, Morris believes no scientific estimates of the age of the earth are reliable. On his view, the fall and Noah's flood altered nature, with the result that the present laws of nature cannot be extrapolated backward in time. The universe was so altered by these events that "any attempt to reconstruct history which denies these truths will surely fail." Morris concludes, "I am convinced, that when they are compared, the Creation/Flood/young-earth model will be found not only to fit the data quite well, it will fit the data much better than does the old-earth/evolutionary model."[5]

*Early estimates of the age of Earth were less accurate than modern estimates because theories have been refined or rejected as instruments and investigators improved their capacities.*

How should we assess Morris's position? His commitment

to Scripture is good, and we share that stance. As for his view of science, we believe there are some outstanding difficulties. For instance:

• Morris seems to dismiss centuries of scientific progress and draws improper conclusions from the history of science. Early estimates of the age of Earth were less accurate than modern estimates because theories have been refined or rejected as instruments and investigators improved their capacities. Scientists today have access to much different and better types of data than they did in former times. Past error does not prove current error.

• Proof is a relative term. A claim is proven when enough evidence is accumulated to be convincing. Clearly proof is in the eye of the beholder. Science never really proves anything in a strict logical or mathematical sense. What science does do, however, is continue

Science has advanced remarkably far since Michael Faraday (d.1867) worked in this laboratory. In fact, the rate of advance increases exponentially each year.

to incorporate observations into working models that seek to explain the data. As data accumulate, models are adjusted or confirmed beyond reasonable doubt.

• If God "restructured" nature (at the fall and/or flood) so drastically that we cannot reconstruct history, then science cannot be used in *any* way to estimate the age of Earth. And yet Recent Creation advocates regularly cite scientific evidence for a young Earth. This seems to be an inconsistency within that model.

• Biblical and scientific reasoning refutes the notion that God restructured the laws of nature at the fall and/or flood.

• Scripture teaches that God would never allow the laws of nature to be altered (Jer. 31:36; 33:19–26). They are immutable signs of His eternal, immutable nature and His unalterable covenants. In fact, this biblical conviction formed the basis for the development of science.

• Science is able to study the laws of physics in action at the earliest times of the universe by observing distant stars whose light takes many millions of years to reach us. These studies of the ancient universe consistently confirm that the laws of nature have not changed in any perceptible way since the very beginning.

## Conclusion

God established the laws of nature to regulate creation and also to teach us about Himself. In this light, science can be a tool to help us understand the "invisible attributes" of our Creator (Rom. 1:20). For these reasons we believe Christians can have confidence in the testimony of the natural realm even as our highest commitment is to God's revelation in the Bible.

*Christians can have confidence in the testimony of the natural realm even as our highest commitment is to God's revelation in the Bible.*

## Notes

1. Spiral arms do indicate "younger" galaxies, but young here means "about half the age of the universe." Galaxies that are older lose their spiral structure, as seen in very distant galaxies observed by the Hubble Telescope.

2. See the U.S. Census Bureau Web site, International Data Base, for helpful statistics on population growth in the past century and projected rates for the next half-century.

3. John Morris, *Young Earth: The Real History of the Earth—Past, Present, and Future* (Green Forest, AR: Master Books, 2007), 36.

4. Ibid.

5. Ibid, 36–7.

# Chapter 26
# Science and an Ancient Earth

How likely are you to mistake a ninety-year-old man for a twenty year old? Furrowed skin, breaking voice, white-topped or bald head, and unsteady movements—these are just some of the signs that tell you that you are not looking at a young man. After all, time leaves its mark on humans. So it is with all of creation. As time marches on, it steals away the newness that once marked all things. This is a direct consequence of one of the most firmly established rules of nature: the second law of thermodynamics, which states that all things decay over time. Fortunately, we are able to study this process and learn about how things work, how they age, and how old they are.

## *Evidence from Tree Rings*

The best known "age recorder" is the annual tree ring. Each year a tree adds a new ring to its trunk beneath the bark. The thickness and coloration of these rings encodes information about the weather conditions during a given year. For example, wet years leave larger rings than dry years. The Methuselah Bristlecone pine tree in Oasis, California, is over 4,700 years old. It is still growing. Timber from a bristlecone pine tree has been discovered in a 3,000-year-old structure in the western U. S. Counting the rings in these timbers reveals that the pine tree was over 5,000 years old when it was cut and used to construct the building. Hence, the tree lived 8,000 years before now.[1] This is evidence for a creation date that stretches farther into the past than many early Recent Creation advocates have allowed. For instance, Bishop Usher (1581–1656) calculated from biblical genealogies that creation occurred in 4004 BC.

Bristlecone pine trees are extremely hardy and can live for thousands of years.

## Evidence from Sedimentary Strata

Earth's surface is covered with layered sedimentary rock such as limestone, sandstone, and shale. Sedimentary rock is distinct from igneous or metamorphic rock. Igneous rocks are formed from molten magma, whereas metamorphic rocks are sedimentary or igneous rocks that have been remelted. Sedimentary rock is simply a layer of sediment that has hardened into stone as loose sediment is pressed down for long periods of time. The Grand Canyon is one of the most spectacular examples of sedimentary layering.

At a general level, here is how sedimentary rocks are formed. Soil and existing rock are eroded by the forces of weather. There is not much loose soil on the earth's surface, so most sediments come from the erosion of preexisting rock. This is a very slow process. Even fast-moving mountain streams produce a fairly small amount of sediment as the rocks slowly wear down. Once produced, sediments must be transported to a region where settling can occur. Often this is at the mouth of rivers, where sediments are deposited to form deltas. As water spreads out over the delta, it slows down and first deposits the

*Sedimentary rock strata are the cemeteries of the ongoing decay process of the earth's surface.*

largest rocks it has carried along the course of the river. These rocks form a layer of brecca or conglomerate sediment. Then as the water slows more, lighter debris settles out. The sand particles will fall out, forming a sand layer which eventually becomes sandstone. Next the lighter clay and lime particles settle out, forming shale and limestone layers. Finally, if the water is very still, the finest particles settle out to form layers that can become chalk. This entire process takes an enormous amount of time. Sedimentary rock strata are the cemeteries of the ongoing decay process of the earth's surface, and by "reading the headstones," we can determine how old Earth is.

## Evidence from Varves

Varves are a type of annual sediment deposit occurring in still water which contains fine clay particles. These deposits are usually associated with shallow inland lakes, where clay particles slowly settle and form a layer which will harden into shale or limestone. During the summer, pollens and other organic materials are deposited with the clay, giving the clay color and coarseness characteristics that differ from the clay layers laid down during winter. The winter layer is fine

*Varves are annual layers that resemble tree rings, except this is rock.*

and dark, the summer layer is coarse and lighter. Over time the sediment layers harden into layered shale or limestone.

So varves are annual layers that resemble tree rings, except this is rock. As with tree rings, you count the varves to tally up the years. The Green River Formation in the western U. S. contains varved shale deposits that exhibit thirteen million annual layers. This is clearly the work of many years of annual deposition, for this type of varving cannot occur during catastrophic events such as Noah's flood.

Corals grow slowly and leave behind evidence of their age. Photo: Dwayne Meadows, NOAA/NMFS/OPR.

## *Evidence from Coral*

Coral is a marine organism that builds colorful rock formations in the world's oceans. Hence the name "coral reef" for these rock structures. Corals live in large, shallow sea colonies, and the reef itself is made of the remains of deceased corals. This is possible because corals form a hard shell of calcium carbonate ($CaCO_3$) which they extract from seawater. Each year the coral itself "molts" or sheds the old carbonate casing and begins to form the next year's housing. Thus, layer by layer the abandoned coral remains build up a bank of layered $CaCO_3$ rock underneath the topmost living layer. This accumulating rock is termed a *reef*. The weight of the coral reef actually causes the reef to sink slowly into the seabed at approximately the same rate as it grows, keeping the top of the coral at a near constant distance just below the surface. In this way coral reefs can grow to enormous depths, recording a continuous history over time. Typical coral growth rates are between 0.1 and 1 millimeter per year, although in rare circumstances corals grow as much as 10 mm in an annual layer. Thus, coral reefs can be dated much the same way as trees and varves can be. The Grand Bahaman Bank is a solid bank of continuous limestone coral deposition over 18,000 feet thick. That equates to 5.5 million millimeters, or over 5 million years worth of accumulation if we assume it grew at an impressive average of 1 mm per year.

While it is easy to slow down the rate of coral growth, it is almost impossible to speed up its growth rate because it is limited by the concentration of $CaCO_3$ in seawater. Even in good times corals cannot grow much faster than 1 mm per year because there simply is not enough calcium available in seawater to beat this pace. Any way you look at it, coral reefs form slowly. Also, extreme storms such as typhoons and hurricanes can easily damage or kill reefs. Hence, a violent global flood roughly 6,000 years ago cannot be responsible for forming fragile coral reefs 18,000 feet thick.

*Corals cannot grow much faster than 1 mm per year because there simply is not enough calcium available in seawater to beat this pace.*

One final testimony from corals requires a small detour though the tides. Tides are caused by the gravitational pull of the moon against Earth. This friction slows down Earth's spin by a very small amount, with the result that Earth spins slower now than it did in the past. For instance, two million years ago the day would have been 20 seconds shorter because Earth was spinning faster. Four hundred million years ago the day would have been a whole 2 hours shorter. At that rate of spin, Earth would have gone through about 400 twenty-two hour days during the course of a year (measured

Photo: NOAA/Florida Keys National Marine Sanctuary staff.

as one full revolution around the sun). This is not just theory, but proven fact. We know this by examining rugose corals, for in addition to annual layers, these corals also formed a daily "ridge" on their living coral fronds. By counting these ridges, we can determine how many days were in a given year when the coral was still alive. Fossilized rugose corals estimated to be about 400 million years old have about four hundred of these daily ridges per annual layer, which means there were 400 days per year when it was still alive. Sound familiar? It matches the independent calculations for ancient Earth's rotation period and thus offers *very* strong confirmatory evidence for an ancient creation.

## Evidence from Salt Layers

Deep underground, large deposits of layered salt are often found in association with petroleum deposits. These layers formed in the past when a body of salty water evaporated. In other cases the salt deposit is on the surface, as with the great salt flats in Utah. Salt deposits are layered because different minerals settle at different rates as the water evaporates. First a layer of lime is deposited followed in turn by layers of gypsum and salt itself once over 90 percent of the water has evaporated. So the salt layers represent not necessarily annual layers, but one complete drying cycle which could span many years as the sea evaporated.

*The Castile Formation in west Texas contains a 1,300 meter thick layerd salt deposit with over 200,000 distinct layers, which means there have been 200,000 drying episodes in the history of that deposit.*

This cycle is repeated often as shallow sea beds alternatively fill up and dry out. The fact that salt deposits show repeated drying cycles indicates that Noah's one-time flood could not be the cause of these repetition-based phenomena. The Castile Formation in west Texas contains a 1,300-meter thick layered salt deposit with over 200,000 distinct layers, which means there have been 200,000 drying episodes in the

Guadalupe Peak (or El Capitan) in the Guadalupe Mountains of west Texas, part of the Castile formation.

history of that deposit. Further, this deposit is located between many other layers of overlying and underlying sedimentary rock which was formed by different processes under different conditions at an altogether different time. Clearly, salt formations tell a story of great antiquity.

## *Evidence from Ice Cores*

Artic and Antarctic ice fields are dated by counting the annual layers in ice core samples. Ice that accumulates during winter has a different composition and thickness than summer ice. These variations are measured with instruments that detect variations in levels of carbon dioxide, oxygen isotopes, soot, and pollen. In one test ice layers in Greenland measure 2,790 meters in depth and contain over 110,000 annual layers. This core was repeated 30 km away with nearly identical results. Similarly, studies of ice in Antarctica have found over 450,000 annual layers. This means that on 450,000 different occasions, ice was laid down during two distinct seasons: winter and summer. Again, Noah's flood could not account for this cyclical layering pattern.

This ice core sample, taken from another location on the Greenland Ice Sheet, clearly shows annual layers (summer and winter). This section of the sample gives evidence of 38 years. The toal sample, which is much too large to picture in this book, measures 1,838 meters long and, by evidence of its layers, tells us that the ice has been laid down over the course of 16,250 years. Photo: USGS (National Ice Core Laboratory division), Eric Cravens.

## *Evidence from Plate Tectonics*

Plate tectonics is the process that underlies (literally) much of the geological activity exhibited on Earth. As we mentioned previously, it is obvious when looking at a globe that our continents can be fitted together like the pieces of a puzzle. Alfred Wegner (1880–1930) proposed that the continents had once been joined, but over time drifted apart due to convection currents in the hot upwelling magma underneath earth's surface. By the 1970s his views were vindicated by the extensive mapping of the seafloor, plus evidence that fossils found on the coast of Africa match fossils found along the same zone on the South American coast. Furthermore, we now have hard evidence that the continents are still moving. For example, North America is moving westward away from the mid-Atlantic ridge at about four centimeters per year. Similarly, the European continent is being pushed east in the opposite direction. At this rate (and there is data that indicate the rate has not varied greatly over time), we can calculate that the continents separated about 160 million years ago.

> *North America is moving westward away from the mid-Atlantic ridge at about four centimeters per year.*

The Pacific plate is rotating in a counterclockwise fashion, resulting in almost continuous seismic and volcanic activity from South America to Alaska. This "ring of fire" continues all around the Pacific basin. As plates push and shove one another, continental crust tends to fold up on itself with the result that mountains are formed. For example, the Himalaya Mountains grow about two centimeters taller per year due to this process. This uplift-ing and folding of con-tinental plates also ex-plains why we often find sediment layers lying at odd angles rather than the horizontal orienta-tion in which they were originally deposited. Further, it explains how seafloors, replete with marine fossils, are found in places such as the top of Mount Everest. Origi-

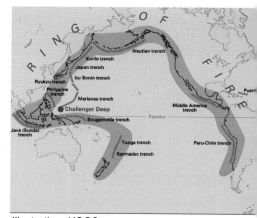

Illustration: USGS.

nally, it was a seabed! It moved from seafloor to nearly 30,000 feet in elevation at a creeping rate of less than one inch per year.

The 2004 tsunami in Indonesia was the result of the tectonic uplifting of marine layers. This happened when a mega earthquake (9+ on the Richter scale) shoved the earth's crust sideways about 50 feet over a zone stretching 60 x 240 miles. All of this happened about 30 km beneath the crust's surface as the India plate slid deeper under the Burma plate. As a result, the Burma plate was uplifted several meters. This remarkable action displaced about seven cubic miles of seawater above the slip zone, causing the fatal tsunami which killed about a quarter of million people. In this and other examples, massive geologic uplift is an ongoing process capable of lifting whole seabeds, creating new mountain ranges, and otherwise reshaping geology.

## Conclusion

These are just some of the many natural processes that reveal the antiquity of Earth. Current estimates for the age of Earth are about 4.5 billion years. None of these dating methods are biological, and so they are independent of evolutionary theory. Hence, they do not imply naturalism

*Observations of geological antiquity were made well before Darwin had even formed his ideas, so these are unbiased observations of God's natural revelation.*

or atheism in any way. Indeed, many of these observations of geological antiquity were made well before Darwin had even formed his ideas, so these are unbiased observations of God's natural revelation.

## Note

1. P. H. Armstrong, "Bristlecone pines tell an 8000-year story," in *Geographical Magazine* 44(9): 637–639.

# Chapter 27
# Geology and Noah's Flood

Noah's flood was a unique historical event where God judged the wickedness of humanity by destroying all humans except for righteous Noah and his family. Recent Creation advocates have developed a concept called "flood geology" to explain how Noah's flood shaped geography in such a way as to make our planet's surface features appear to be ancient. Flood geology is not a direct teaching of the Bible but is formulated as a science theory. Thus, flood geology must be critically evaluated on a scientific basis. Is it a credible and valid explanation of geological data?

*Flood geology is not a direct teaching of the Bible but is formulated as a science theory.*

It is understandable why many people think Noah's flood is responsible for the geological features observed in earth's surface layers. After all:

- Surface layers are usually sedimentary rock (sediments that settled out of water and hardened into rock as a layer), and floods are known to leave big sediment deposits.

- Fossils of plants and animals are found buried in

sedimentary layers all over the world, as if they were overwhelmed in a flood.

- Many fossils are found at high elevations, even on mountaintops, which seems consistent with a flood deep enough to cover the mountains.

So flood geology argues that these and other major geological features are the result of a global food rather than natural processes operating over eons.

## *History of Flood Geology*

Flood geology has its roots in the teachings of the Seventh Day Adventist prophetess Ellen G. White, who taught that Noah's global flood was responsible for the geological column and the fossil record. Her teachings were advanced by Harry Rimmer and George McReady Price. Both of these men were largely uneducated and had no advanced training in science, and yet they published books on flood geology that were readily embraced by many Christians.

Ellen G. White, whom Seventh Day Adventists regard as a prophetess.

Then theologian John C. Whitcomb collaborated with civil engineer Henry Morris in *The Genesis Flood: The Biblical Record and Its Scientific Implications*, published in 1961. In this book Whitcomb and Morris aim to give theological and scientific credibility to the concepts advanced by Rimmer and Price.

## *Just Doing What Floods Do*

One of the main aims of flood geology is to explain how a global flood could cause earth's *geological* features by standard flood processes. To do this, flood geologists must explain how the fossil record could be a record of the effects of a rapid deluge. Christians naturally find this approach attractive, for if the earth's geological features are a consequence of the flood, then the rocks themselves become physical validation for our biblical faith. But many observers believe the evidence is against flood geology. Scientific observations reveal four basic problems with the idea that Noah's flood shaped geography.

## Problem #1: Grinding Away at the Sediment

The average depth of fossil-bearing sediment rock layers on the continental crust is one mile. The formation of these sedimentary layers is one of the major topics studied by professional geologists. Flood geologists assume that all of this sediment (now turned to rock) came from the erosion of nonsedimentary rocks during Noah's flood. The only other option is to assume the sediments were formed by standard geological processes (freeze-thaw cycles, wind erosion, chemical reactions, wave action at shorelines) that take long periods of time. But can a global flood really account for these vast

*Deep water actually impedes the erosion process because it moves slower and is less likely to jostle rocks together.*

Deep water is not turbulent enough to cause aggressive erosion.

sediment deposits? For the most part floods do not extract new sediment material from rock; they simply redistribute existing sediment. Very fast- moving water, as in mountain streams, causes some erosion by banging rocks together, albeit slowly. Deep water actually impedes the erosion process because it moves slower and is less likely to jostle rocks together. In the global flood model, the whole earth was quickly covered by deep water. This kind of inundation actually prevents large-scale erosion of the area under water. Thus, no natural flood process, even if it were global, could produce the amounts of sediment needed to account for the earth's vast sedimentary rock formations. The scientific evidence, therefore, is in favor of the standard geological model in which the earth's sedimentary layers were successively laid down over long ages.

## What about Coal and Fossils?

Advocates of flood geology say all coal and fossil deposits are the result of plants and animals that were buried simultaneously during Noah's flood. But that would be too many plants and animals alive at once. Earth could not have sustained all of that life simultaneously. Hence, the multitude of plants and animals represented in coal and fossils come from many different ages of earth's long past.

## Problem #2: Laying Down the Layers

In spite of Problem #1, for the sake of argument, let's assume that the earth's sedimentary layers were all produced by Noah's flood. To form layers, sediments have to settle out of the water as the flood recedes. Two factors control the deposition of sediments: the *velocity* of the water carrying the sediment load and the *mass* of the sediment particulates. Fast-moving water holds heavier particulates in suspension. As the water slows, the heaviest particulates settle out first, then the next heaviest, etc. This means that water-borne sediments are sorted bottom-to-top according to size. For example, consider delta formations. In upstream delta regions, where water is moving fastest, only heavy rocks drop out of suspension. As the water spreads out at the mouth of the delta and slows down, lighter materials (gravels, sands, silts, etc.) drop out. These deposits harden into conglomerates, sandstones, mudstones, and so on over time.

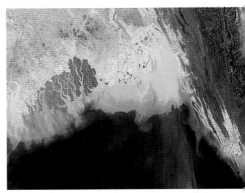

Ganges River delta. Heavy sediments fall out of suspension, then lighter sediments as the water slows. SeaWiFS, NASA/Goddard Space Flight Center, and ORBIMAGE.

Moreover, fine-grained particulates such as those that form limestone and chalks never settle out until the water completely stops moving. Such layers cannot form during flood conditions or during flood-water runoffs. This presents a problem for flood geology because the sorting processes described above would entail the neat, orderly deposition of all the earth's sedimentary layers if in fact all such layers were laid down in a single, worldwide flood. In fact, the earth's sedimentary layers are disorderly. As often as not, gravel and sandstone layers lie atop layers of muds and limestones, which is the reverse order of deposition. This indicates that many, many local floods have come and gone, as the ancient-earth model predicts.

*As often as not, gravel and sandstone layers lie atop layers of muds and limestones, which is the reverse order of deposition. This indicates that many, many local floods have come and gone, as the ancient-earth model predicts.*

## *The Grand Canyon as a Test Case*

Flood geologists believe a massive flood was required to carve out the Grand Canyon. They point to the aftermath of the Mount St. Helens eruption to show that sedimentary layers can form rapidly as floodwaters tear through a canyon. While it is true that layered deposits can form rapidly in some circumstances, it does not hold for all situations. And importantly, sedimentary rock layers are very different from layered ash deposits and cannot be formed in the same manner as the Mount St. Helens ash heaps.

Notice in the diagram that the Coconino Sandstone lies directly atop the Hermit shale. That's not the correct sequence if both layers were deposited in the same event. Hence, these layers were deposited by different events separated widely in time. Furthermore, the Coconino sandstone was not even deposited underwater, for it is a remnant of desert sands that were buried by the overlying marine sediments now forming the Toroweap formation and Kaibab limestone.

Another major problem for flood geology explanations of the Grand Canyon is the existence of several thin volcanic ash layers in between some of the canyon's layers. How could *airborne* layers of ash be inserted between sediment layers that were deposited *underwater* during a flood? Also, the top of the canyon's Redwall limestone layer is weatherworn, but this layer is buried under the Hermit shale and several other layers. How did it get so weatherworn on the top while being deposited under the water of Noah's flood? The only explanation for the layers of the Grand Canyon is regional inundations separated by long periods of drying, solidification and erosion of the deposits.

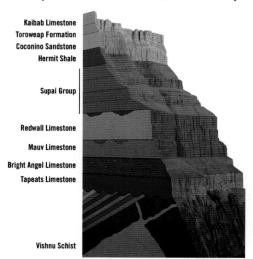

Kaibab Limestone
Toroweap Formation
Coconino Sandstone
Hermit Shale

Supai Group

Redwall Limestone

Mauv Limestone

Bright Angel Limestone
Tapeats Limestone

Vishnu Schist

## Problem #3: Lifting Up the Layers

Sediment layers are level (horizontal) when they form, so since many of the mountaintop sediment layers lie at steep angles, these layers had to have formed before the mountain was uplifted. For example, if you walk about a quarter of mile west on the trail from Clingman's Dome in the Smoky Mountains, you will be standing directly on top of sedimentary slate layers that have been thrust up at an angle of nearly 80 degrees, forming the top of the mountain ridge at 6,000 feet above sea level.

Author Hill Roberts and wife at the shale upthrust near Clingman's Dome.

Certainly such steeply inclined sediment layers could not have formed in place on the mountains during Noah's flood. After all, a sopping wet deposit of mud would not hold fast at a steep angle. Rather, it would drain down until it reached a low point and leveled out. Then it would harden in horizontal layers. But could the flood have deposited the layers horizontally, leaving other phenomena to push the layers into odd, non-horizontal angles? Yes, but the problem with that

is you are left with nothing but the gradual, noncatastrophic natural processes we have already discussed, and these do not act quickly enough to account for angled sedimentary layers that supposedly developed horizontally during Noah's flood only a few thousand years ago.

## Problem #4: Moving the Layers Around

Geological evidence indicates the continents spread apart slowly over very long periods of time due to the convective processes of plate tectonics. Flood geologists must offer an alternative mechanism that did not take millions of years.

One such suggestion is that when the "fountains of the great deep burst open" at the beginning of the flood, a crack opened up all around the earth and released a torrent of subterranean water which caused the shifting of the continents and hence the formation of mountains. Such rapid separation of the continental crusts during the flood is problematic,

Devastating earthquakes, such as the 1906 San Francisco quake, would be the norm if the continents broke apart and rapidly moved to their current positions merely a few thousand years ago.

however, for if the continents had moved thousands of miles so quickly, there would have been a buildup of such heat (from friction) that the rocks would have melted, and the water would have boiled away, filling the atmosphere with superheated steam. Noah's ark would have been boiled. Moreover, if such a violent shift happened only a few thousand years ago, earth's surface would still be reverberating today with devastating worldwide earthquakes, and the seas would still be boiling cauldrons as the seafloors continued to vent the tremendous heat built up deep within the earth.

> *Evidence indicates the continents spread apart slowly over very long periods of time due to the convective processes of plate tectonics.*

Another flood geology explanation, known as "runaway subduction," suggests that the continents shifted due to large portions of the earth's crust being quickly swallowed down into the mantle. But computer simulations using feasible values indicate that this simply cannot work.

## Conclusion: Points to Ponder

### Flood Geology and Biblical Faith

Flood geology is often portrayed as an indisputable, central truth of the Bible. Thus, to question it is paramount to rejecting biblical authority. However, the biblical account does not teach flood geology (or any science, for that matter). Flood geology is inferential Bible reading matched with speculative geology models that are not well respected among professional scientists.

> *Flood geology is not a teaching of the Bible but an inferential Bible reading matched to speculative geology models that are not well respected among professional scientists.*

### A Big Flood and Big Faith

Science shows that a single global flood cannot have produced the geological record found throughout the earth. In the face of this, flood geologists sometimes answer that they would rather have faith in the impossible than reject flood geology. Some even suggest that local-flood adherents lack faith. But remember, this is faith placed in a theory that is not taught in the Bible. Additionally, it does not take into account the "elbow room" found in the Genesis flood account itself (see chapter 8 of this book).

### A Miracle Flood

When natural explanations fail, sometimes miracle is the only recourse. Hence, some have suggested that the global flood was a miracle of God. This is a reasonable response, though it has consequences that are often missed. For instance, if Noah's flood was entirely a miracle, then it would likely be impossible to trace its effects today because nonnatural flooding would probably not leave traceable natural markers.

Photo: NASA/ SeaWiFS Project, NASA/Goddard Space Flight Center, and ORBIMAGE.

### A Radically New World

There is no indication in the Bible that the world Noah stepped back onto from the ark was much different from the world he lived in before the flood. The people and animals were gone, of course, but aside from that the Bible does not say it differed from its prior form. If flood geology were true, however, the post-flood world would have been like nothing Noah previously knew: the landscape would have been completely unrecognizable as huge layers of wet sediment covered everything; the landscape would have been completely denuded; mountains would dot the

*There is no indication in the Bible that the world Noah stepped back onto from the ark was much different from the world he lived in before the flood.*

land, and these would have been new phenomena to Noah; the continents would still be quivering and steaming in the aftermath of their epic journey. It is no exaggeration to say that, if flood geology were correct, Noah might as well have debarked onto a different planet. As the Bible does not suggest that Noah had any such impression, it seems best to assume things were not greatly altered geologically.

## Closing Thought

*"The truth of our faith becomes a matter of ridicule among the infidels if any [believer], not gifted with the necessary scientific learning, presents as dogma what scientific scrutiny shows to be false."—St. Thomas Aquinas[1]*

## Note

1. Thomas Aquinas, *On the Power of God*, 4:1.

# Chapter 28
# A Christian View of Radiometric Dating

You wouldn't know it to look at them, but rocks can actually tell us how old they are. They do so by using the "language" of radioactive decay. Minerals in some types of rock are radioactive, which means certain atoms in that mineral are unstable at their center (the atomic nucleus) and are thus prone to shooting off energy (radiation) in the form of particles or waves. This literally means the nucleus is giving away part of itself. As it does this, it takes on a new identity as its composition changes. The new product is called the daughter nuclide, while the former is referred to as the parent nuclide. Scientists use the term "decay" to refer to the incidents where atoms fire off their energy and convert from parent to daughter nuclide.

*Scientists use the term "decay" to refer to the incidents where atoms fire off their energy and convert from parent to daughter nuclide.*

Interestingly, the timing of decay events for individual atoms is impossible to predict with precision. At best, we can predict how much time it takes for half the atoms in a collection of radioactive atoms to undergo decay. This is referred to as the "half-life" of the radioactive element. For instance,

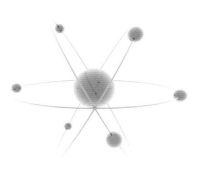

uranium-238 decays to lead-206. The half-life of uranium-238 is about 4.5 billion years. This means that in the course of 4.5 billion years, half of the uranium-238 atoms in a rock sample should have decayed to lead-206. The age of the rock is determined by figuring out just where the uranium-238 to lead-206 ratio stands. Furthermore, there are often numerous kinds of radioactive elements in a given rock, and all of them decay at different rates. In these cases scientists can test multiple elements as a means of cross-checking their results for the age of the rock.

## TYPICAL RADIOISOTOPES USED IN DATING

| PARENT RADIOISOTOPES | DAUGHTER RADIOISOTOPES | HALF-LIFE |
| --- | --- | --- |
| Potassium-40 | Argon-20 | 1.25 billion years |
| Rubidium-87 | Strontium-87 | 48.8 billion years |
| Samarium-147 | Neodimium-143 | 106 billion years |
| Leutecium-176 | Hafnium-176 | 35.9 billion years |
| Rhenium-187 | Osmium-187 | 43 billion years |
| Thorium-232 | Lead-208 | 14 billion years |
| Uranium-238 | Lead-206 | 4.47 billion years |
| Uranium-235 | Lead-207 | .704 billion years |

## Uranium-238 to Lead-206

Consider a rock sample which contains the mineral zircon. If the zircon is measured to contain equal amounts of uranium-238 and lead-206, this means one half-life of decay has passed since the rock was first formed. Hence, the rock is 4.5 billion years old. Interestingly, some meteorites found on Earth have been dated to 4.5 billion years in just this manner. Among rocks that are original to Earth, the oldest tested thus far have been dated to about 3.8 billion years. This indicates that approximately 3.8 billion years ago Earth cooled down enough to allow the rocks and surface features formed at that time to survive and persist unto our own day. All earlier rocks and geographical features were erased by the heat and chaos of early Earth. Conditions were different in space, where rocks formed and survived as long as 4.5 billion years ago. In all likelihood Earth itself began forming

*Scientists believe the early earth was too hot to sustain stable geological features. Only after it cooled down could such things as rocks and landscapes form and persist.*

at roughly the same time as the meteorites, but required an additional 700 million years to cool down and form stable features.

The figure on the right shows a pink granite rock collected by one of us (Roberts) from the Zoraster granite formation in the Grand Canyon. Also shown is the radiation spectrum measured by Roberts in his gamma spectroscopy laboratory. Notice that many of the members of all three decay series (U-238, U-235, and Th-232) are clearly identifiable

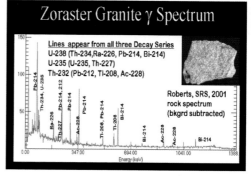

This shows the gamma radiation spectrum from the sample of pink granite from the Zoraster formation taken from near the bottom of the Grand Canyon. Members from all three of the uranium decay series are present. This rock could thus be dated using three independent decay clocks embedded in the granite's composite minerals. These formations have been dated by such means to about 1.6 million years before present (Roberts, 2001).

from this one sample. Probably the most widely used isotopic dating method is Potassium-Argon dating, due to the nearly ubiquitous presence of potassium in the rocks of the earth's crust. Potassium-40 decays to argon-40 with a half-life of 1.25 billion years. Thus about 3.6 half-lives worth of K-Ar decay in the same sample would be consistent with the U-Pb date, providing a cross-check on the age determination.

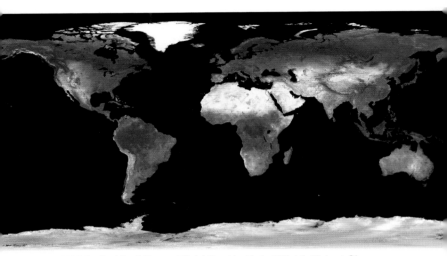

Photo: NASA, Goddard Space Flight Center, Reto Stöckli, Robert Simmon, MODIS, USGS Defense Meteorological Satellite Program.

## *Setting Boundaries for the Age of Earth*

Notice that the last three isotopes in the above chart (p. 258) all decay to an isotope of lead. Each of these decay processes involves several intermediate unstable isotopes, each with shorter half-lives than the parent isotope. All three of these decay series exist in natural ores, as would be expected if Earth is 4.5 billion years old. However, there is also a fourth decay series in this family. This is the neptunium-237 to bismuth-209 decay series, with a much shorter half-life of only 2 million years. There is no detectable neptunium-237, other than whatever is made by artificial means in nuclear reactors. However, the daughter product, bismuth-209, is abundant in natural ores. Why is this so? Apparently, all the neptunium-237 has already decayed to its daughter isotope, bismuth-209, due to its shorter half-life (short when compared to 4.5 billion years as for U-238 or the age of Earth). The existence of the bismuth-209 shows that neptunium-237 once existed in abundance but has now all decayed away. This helps us set up boundaries for the age of Earth. Earth must be much older than several neptunium-237 half-lives, else we would still find neptunium-237 in nature. Conversely, Earth cannot be much older than one uranium-238 half-life since it is still found in nature.

## Short-Lived Isotopes

The radiometric approach to judging Earth's age makes a broad examination of which decaying isotopes remain and which ones no longer exist. In fact, with a few exceptions to be explained momentarily, there are no original, naturally occurring, short-lived isotopes on the earth. The exceptions are those that are made during the decay of long-lived isotopes or those that are continuously replenished by some natural means. This absence of original short-lived isotopes is a clear indicator that Earth has existed long enough for all of these isotopes to decay out of existence.

Original, naturally occurring, short-lived isotopes are absent on the earth, but that does not mean short-lived isotopes are absent. For example, radon-222 has a half-life of only 3.825 days, yet it is fairly plentiful in some surface rocks—enough so that too much exposure to radon gas leaking into your house from below can be carcinogenic. So why is there so much radon-222 around if Earth

*The absence of original short-lived isotopes is a clear indicator that Earth has existed long enough for all of these isotopes to decay out of existence.*

is ancient? The answer is that radon-222 is one of several intermediate daughter isotopes in the decay chain that begins with uranium-238 and ends with lead-206. So, radon-222 is continuously replenished by the very slow decay of uranium-238, which is plentiful because it has a half-life of 4.5 billion years. Hence, while no *original* radon-222 exists today, plenty is being manufactured by the decay process.

In a somewhat similar manner, carbon-14 is abundant despite the fact that it has a half-life of only 5,730 years. It is still

*Nuclear decay rates are possibly the most constant phenomenon in nature.*

around because it is continually manufactured as cosmic rays strike nitrogen-14 atoms in the upper atmosphere, causing them to convert into carbon-14. This carbon-14 then decays back to nitrogen-14 at the characteristic half-life decay rate of 5,730 years.[1]

# Challenges to Radiometric Dating
## Nuclear Decay Rates Might Not Be Constant

Critics of radiometric dating say we cannot be certain that decay rates remain constant over time. However, the nucleus of every atom is mightily protected by an outer shield of electrons surrounding the nucleus. This protects the nucleus

from chemicals, heat, pressure, and electric fields. One implication is that nothing in the environment will tamper with the decay rate of the nucleus. This is why the decay rate is always the same for a given type of nucleus. This is true not just on Earth but throughout the universe. We know this not just because physics theory tells us so but because

Photo: NASA, ESA, and A. Nota (STScI/ESA).

observations of stellar spectra reveal that isotopic decay occurring in distant stars matches the rates measured here on Earth. In fact, nuclear decay rates are possibly the most constant phenomena in nature.

### Measuring Half-life

Clearly, no one has been observing the decay of uranium-238 for the past 4.47 billion years. So how can we be so sure that its half-life is really 4.47 billion years? Fortunately, we don't have to watch a uranium sample this long to measure its half-life. To determine an isotope's half-life, all that is required is a reading of its radioactivity in a given sample and an accurate measure of how much of the decay isotope is in that same sample. From that data a simple

*The nucleus of every atom is mightily protected by an outer shield of electrons surrounding the nucleus.*

calculation provides the half-life.

### Initial Conditions May Not Be Fully Known

Critics say radiometric testing assumes that all daughter isotopes are products of the decay process. Is it not possible, they ask, that a test sample might have had some daughter isotope in it to begin with (when the rock formed)? Would that not make the rock seem older than it really is? Fortunately, this confusion is overcome by the choice of decay isotope and minerals selected for the dating process. For example, zircon crystals are the mineral of choice for uranium-lead dating. A zircon crystal forms as molten magma cools to form igneous rocks. The chemical-physical processes that form the zircon also allow uranium to be incorporated into the zircon crystal but strictly exclude its daughter isotope (lead) from forming in the original crystal. Hence, any lead found in a zircon is guaranteed to have come from the decay of uranium in that mineral. Similarly, for the decay of potassium-40 to argon-40, any argon-40 found in the rock sample is mostly the product of radioactive decay because argon is an inert gas (which means it will escape rather than bond with anything). So, when the rock first formed as hot magma began to cool, any trapped argon would have dissipated before the rock finished the solidification process. Subsequent to that, decaying potassium-40 would release argon-40 into the crystallized interior of the rock, where it would be mostly trapped and available for us to measure. If some of the argon-40 manages to escape from the rock, the age of the sample will be *underestimated* rather than overestimated. It is also possible for some natural argon gas to migrate *into* a rock sample, especially during the hot formative period. In order to correct

When lava cools, zircon crystals form. Photo: USGS.

for this, a more accurate variant of K-Ar dating is used: argon-argon dating. This compares abundances of nonradiogenic argon isotopes (Ar-36 and Ar-38) to Ar-40 in a sample, thus eliminating this potential source of error.

### Errors in Dating Lava Flows

Critics point out that some lavas from Hawaiian volcanoes were dated by Potassium-Argon methods to be millions of years old when in fact the lavas were known to be merely 200 years old. Thus, they say, all radiometric dating is unreliable. However, these lavaflow tests were conducted in an attempt to understand cases where the Potassium-Argon dating method yields anomalous results. It was learned that in some types of lavas which cool underwater (known as pillow lavas), the rapid cooling forms a glassy "rind" on the exterior of the lava. This rind prevents the escape of the argon-40 that was originally in the molten lava. Hence, tests reveal heightened concentrations of argon-40, which makes it appear that the sample has undergone more decay than has actually occurred. For this reason scientists did *not* date these rocks to millions of years. In fact, when samples were taken from the interior of the lava, away from the rind area where argon-40 was trapped in the cooling process, scientists discovered that the lava's radiometric concentrations were consistent with their known recent origins.

Pillow lava. Photo: NOAA-OE.

### Coal and Carbon-14

Young Earth advocates have sought to show that radioactive decay is consistent with a young Earth. One recent effort is called R.A.T.E. (Radioisotopes and the Age of the Earth). This theory is based on the claim that some coal samples still contain C-14, a surprising fact if Earth is ancient. After all, C-

14 has a half-life of merely 5,730 years. The standard scientific view says Earth is a vastly older than that; science also says coal was formed millions of years ago as organic masses (plants and animals) decayed after burial. If both Earth and coal are so old, we would not expect to find any C-14 remaining in coal deposits. Since C-14 is found in some coal, Scientific Creationists say we have proof that coal could not have been formed millions of years ago.

Several points should be made in response to this theory. First, coal samples which are shown to contain C-14 contain only *trace amounts*. A great deal more C-14 ought to be present if coal was formed as recently as Young Earth advocates claim. Hence, C-14 in coal poses just as big (or bigger) a challenge to the Young Earth position as it does to the Ancient Earth position. In fact, if taken to be authentic and not an artifact, the trace amount of C-14 found indicates that the coal is more than 100,000 years old, a term which does not fit into the Young Earth timeline. To ward off this problem, some advocates of recent creation have argued that the decay rates have greatly accelerated during certain periods of the past, leaving coal short of the amount of carbon we would expect it to have if it were only a few thousand years old. But there is no evidence any such thing has ever happened. To the contrary, all evidence indicates that the radiometric decay rates are the most constant of all natural phenomena. The suggestion that they have changed in the past is motivated entirely by a questionable reading of the Bible, not physical data.

> *C-14 in coal poses just as big (or bigger) a challenge to the Young Earth position as it does to the Ancient Earth position.*

Second, scientists have suggested several plausible explanations for why trace amounts of C-14 can remain in

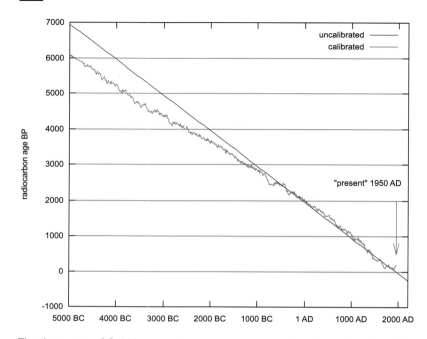

The decay rate of C-14 has remained extremely constant, which makes it useful for dating.

coal which was formed millions of years ago. For one, it is very possible that the coal samples were "contaminated" by C-14 from surrounding sources. After all, coal does not remain cordoned off from the rest of the environment. Dirt, water, and other minerals come into contact with coal deposits. Another possibility is that cosmic rays penetrate the ground and strike the coal seams, producing C-14 in the resulting chemical reactions. Finally, the decay of other isotopes can produce C-14, and this may account for the phenomena in question. Therefore, to maintain that C-14 in coal is proof for a recent creation, one must speculate that decay rates have varied over time, suggest that coal formed in a few short years as plants and animals were buried in the recent past, and deny several feasible theories on how coal has come to be contaminated with C-14.

## Conclusion

Radometric dating methods rely on one of the most constant phenomena in all of nature: the decay of radioactive nuclei. Based upon the abundances of long-lived isotopes and the absence of short-lived isotopes in rock samples from all over the world, scientists have determined that Earth is about 4.5 billion years old. Specifically, some terrestrial rocks have been dated to about 3.8 billion years, and some meteorites have been *Radiometric dating methods rely on one of the most consistent phenomena in all of nature: the decay of radioactive nuclei.* dated to about 4.5 billion years, which matches the age of our solar system as determined by the rate at which the sun is consuming its fuel.

## Note

1. The decay of C-14 is the basis of Frank Libby's Carbon dating process. Air breathing organisms incorporate C-14 into their cells along with stable C-12 in the same ratio as C-14 to C-12 is found in the atmosphere. But once the organism dies, no more carbon is taken into its cells. The C-14 slowly converts back to N-14 at the pace of the C-14 half-life of 5,730 years. The amount of C-12 remains unchanged since it does not decay. So properly measuring the ratio of C-14/C-12 gives a direct reading of the age since death of the organism. It has been calibrated on the basis of bristlecone pine tree rings back to about 8000 years. Beyond that the accuracy becomes less and less. The practical limits of this method are about 50,000 to 100,000 years, hence it is not relevant to the geological ages of most rocks but is very useful in archeology. The Dead Sea Scrolls were dated by this method to have been produced between the third century BC and AD 68.

# Part VII

# Six Impossible Things: Nature's Story of Creation

# Chapter 29
# Darwinism in a Nutshell

Nothing raises the hackles of Bible-believing Christians more quickly than Darwinism. After all, the term calls to mind such false ideologies as naturalism and atheism. For instance, the doctrine of naturalistic macroevolution, where life is said to have arisen by chance and then progressed from amoeba to man, is said to explain the existence of all life without God's involvement.

*Some of Darwin's key discoveries are well proven and offer no threat to the Christian worldview.*

Leaving aside naturalism and atheism, it is important to note that some of Darwin's key discoveries are well proven and offer no threat to the Christian worldview. For instance, natural selection is an observable, proven design that allows species to adapt to changing environments. In this chapter we will separate fact from fiction in evolutionary theory.

## Darwin

Charles Darwin published *The Origin of Species* in 1859. The book presented a tour de force of his research over the prior two decades, including his famous five-year world tour as the scientist aboard the *HMS Beagle*. Based on careful observations,

Darwin proposed that life forms are not fixed entities but rather that they change (evolve) over time. This now seems obvious to us. What is not so obvious was his proposal that all life is interconnected, stemming from a common family tree. This is typically referred to as common descent.

*The HMS Beagle*, on which Charles Darwin traveled and studied nature, by Owen Stanley.

Darwin was not as original as you might suppose. The fact is scientists had debated similar ideas in the century before *Origin* was published. What distinguished Darwin was the impressive evidence he collected from nature, plus his being the first to publish these ideas. His basic idea boiled down to four premises.

1. Natural populations of any organism exhibit a range of variable traits.

2. More offspring are produced in any such population than survive to produce offspring themselves.

3. Offspring that do survive will tend to be those whose mix of natural traits better suits them to overcoming environmental challenges.

4. Traits that give an organism a survival advantage will be differentially passed on to offspring, which means these traits will become increasingly prevalent at the expense of less beneficial traits.

Charles Darwin.

This overall process came to be called natural selection, where life conditions select which organisms are best equipped for survival and passing on their traits to offspring. This process results in changing life forms, known popularly as evolution. What Darwin provided was a logical mechanism for how this process occurs. Mostly, he got it right. Natural selection does occur at the species level due to exactly the four factors laid out by Darwin. It is a process farmers mimic in their artificial selection programs, and it is also well documented in the wild and in the laboratory. However, there was a "black box" of ignorance in Darwin's day: how exactly do organisms pass their traits on to their offspring? Darwin and his peers simply did not know the answer.

By Darwin's day Gregor Mendel had already worked out the basic principles of genetic inheritance, but his work was not published until 1866 and went largely unrecognized until about 1900. By the mid-twentieth century Darwin's

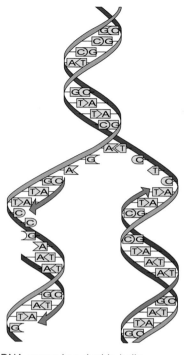

DNA comes in a double-helix configuration.

"black box" had been opened: scientists took Mendel's findings and joined them to new discoveries which enabled them to identify the biochemical basis of inherited traits. As the century progressed, electron microscopes began peering inside the cell; methods to amplify and sequence DNA were developed; and most recently the entire genomic maps of many organisms, including humans, have been developed. We are now in a better position than ever before to judge the feasibility of naturalistic evolution.

## Neo-Darwinism

Darwin's ideas have been updated to incorporate modern findings in genetics. This new hybrid theory is referred to as neo-Darwinism. This is further subdivided into two theories: the special theory (as in *specific* or *species*, not "special" as in "unique or good") and the general theory of organic evolution. The special theory of evolution deals with

*No one who properly understands microevolutionary theory will dispute it.*

changes that occur at the species level, whereas the general theory of organic evolution reaches farther by postulating that all life forms are interconnected by common ancestry and that even the first life forms emerged from non-living matter by natural processes. As you might have guessed by now, the special theory is also known as microevolution (a process of environmental adaptation at the species level), and the general theory is known as macroevolution (or evolution of all life from an original ancestral cell). We have on hand incontrovertible, overwhelming, repeatable, observable evidence for the truth of microevolution. No one who properly understands this theory will dispute it. Macroevolution, however, is much more controversial.

The finches on the Galapagos Islands are a classic example of a species adapting to its environment by the process of natural selection, but every species is capable of doing this. For instance, natural selection can make insect populations resistant to an insecticide and bacterial populations resistant to antibiotics. Natural selection also holds in check genetic defects, such as Downs Syndrome, so that they do not become the rule rather than the exception.

An illustration from John Gould's *The Zoology of the Voyage of H.M.S. Beagle. Part III: Birds.*

*Natural selection is actually a wonderful example of God's genius as Creator since it allows populations to adapt to changing environments.*

Far from detracting from God's glory, natural selection is actually a wonderful example of God's genius as Creator since it allows populations to adapt to changing environments, thus ensuring their survival in (and their contribution to) the larger ecosystem in which they live. If natural selection were impossible, life would be very fragile. Slight changes in environment could force extinction of every species. Microevolution, then, is a feature we should celebrate.

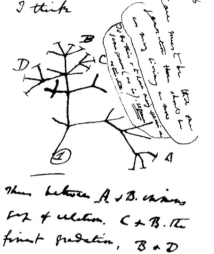

This 1837 sketch was Charles Darwin's first diagram of an evolutionary tree.

Natural selection is powerful and important, but it cannot create anything genuinely new. That's because the traits selected for survival and propagation must already exist in the gene pool of the population. At base, all natural selection does is adjust the relative frequency of a given gene's expression in a population. Far from morphing species into something unprecedented, Theodosious Dobzansky notes that it actually brings stability to a population. "It purges the gene pool of a population of deleterious genetic variants and thereby tends to keep the species constant."[1]

## Macroevolution: What the Experts Are Saying

While popular imagination holds that scientists have long since figured out how life arose, scientists themselves know better.

It is now approximately half a century since the neo-Darwinian synthesis was formulated. A great deal of research has been carried on within the paradigm it defines. Yet the successes of the theory are limited to minutiae of evolution, such as the adaptive change in coloration of moths; while it has remarkably little to say on the questions which interest us most, such as how there came to be moths in the first place.[2]

In other words, natural selection fails to explain amoeba-to-man evolution. While there is overwhelming evidence of microevolution, the case for naturalistic macroevolution suffers from a lack of support from the fossil record.

Paleontologist and evolutionary advocate Niles Eldredge says:

> [O]nce species appear in the fossil record, they tend not to change very much at all. Species remain imperturbably, implacably resistant to change as a matter of course — often for millions of years. . . . Species are fundamentally stable entities.[3]

At the heart of the matter here is the fact that genes won't accommodate the non-Darwinian fossil record of life on Earth. After all, genes are not inclined to change in the manner or rate required to support the macroevolutionary hypothesis.

Jerry Coyne (Department of Ecology and Evolution at the University of Chicago) writes: "We conclude—unexpectedly—that there is little evidence for the neo-Darwinian view: its theoretical foundations and the experimental evidence supporting it are weak."[4]

G. A Kerkut (University of Southhampton) has written a classic textbook called *The Implications of Evolution*. He wrote this for his incoming graduate students because he felt he needed to reeducate them concerning unanswered questions that litter the roadway of evolutionary theory. Having reviewed all the difficulties in the theory, and hence all the areas where graduate students might have a chance of scoring advances in science, Kerkut concludes: "In effect, much of the evolution of the major groups of animals has to be taken on trust. . . . The evidence that supports it is not sufficiently strong to allow us to consider it as anything more than a working hypothesis."[5]

In view of such candid statements, one may ask why naturalistic macroevolutionary theory has such a stranglehold on biology. Fundamentally, it is a matter of one's worldview. If you are predisposed to believe that something besides the physical world exists, then the

*If you are committed to the worldview of naturalism, then evolution of some form must be true even if the evidence is lacking.*

evidence for naturalistic macroevolution is admittedly weak. On the other hand, if you are committed to the worldview of naturalism, then evolution of some form *must* be true even if the evidence is lacking. Otherwise you have no theory for life's origins. One of the clearest, most candid statements of this fact was made by evolutionary proponent, Richard Lewontin.

> We take the side of science in spite of the patent absurdity of some of its constructs, in spite of its failure to fulfill many of its extravagant promises of health and life, in spite of the tolerance of the scientific community for unsubstantiated just-so stories, because we have a prior commitment, a commitment to materialism. It is not that the methods and institutions of science somehow compel us to accept a material explanation of the phenomenal world, but, on the contrary, that we are forced by our a priori adherence to material causes to create an apparatus of investigation and a set of concepts that produce material explanations, no matter how counterintuitive, no matter how mystifying to the uninitiated. Moreover, that materialism is absolute, for we cannot allow a Divine Foot in the door. . . . To appeal to an omnipotent deity is to allow that at any moment the regularities of nature may be ruptured, that miracles may happen.[6]

## Conclusion

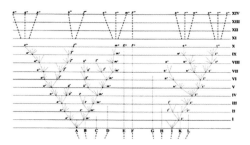

Darwin's evolutionary tree as it appeared in the 1859 edition of *On the Origin of Species*.

The phenomena of natural selection and microevolution (species adaptation) are true facts about the biological world God has designed. Christians should seek to understand these and celebrate them as evidences of God's glory as Creator. Naturalistic macroevolution, on the other hand, is an unwarranted extrapolation from microevolution.

## *Notes*

1. Theodosious Dobzansky, G. Ledyard Stebbins, Francisco Ayala, and James Valentine, *Evolution* (New York: W. H. Freeman, 1977), 107.

2. Brian Goodwin and Peter Saunders, eds., *Theoretical Biology: Epigenetic and Evolutionary Order from Complex Systems* (Edinburgh, UK: Edinburgh University Press, 1989), 78, 589.

3. Niles Eldredge, *Reinventing Darwin: The Great Debate at the High Table of Evolutionary Theory* (New York: Wiley, 1995), 3.

4. J. A. Coyne and H. A. Orr, "The Genetics of Adaptation: A Reassessment," *American Naturalist* 140 (1992): 726. Coyne has insisted that his quote should not be taken as evidence that the neo-Darwinian view is not scientifically viable, but many observers, including biochemist Michael Behe, have pointed out that his quote clearly does express doubt about the scientific status of the theory.

5. G. A. Kerkut, *Implications of Evolution* (New York: Pergamon, 1960), 154.

6. Richard Lewontin, "Billions and Billions of Demons," *New York Review of Books*, January 9, 1997.

# Chapter 30
# Intelligent Design in a Nutshell

### Natural Theology by Peter, Paul and Paley

Since the dawn of the church, Christians have sought to defend their faith through rational evidences. The apostle Peter provided the impetus when he instructed us to "sanctify Christ as Lord in your hearts, always being ready to make a defense to everyone who asks you to give an account for the hope that is in you, yet with gentleness and reverence" (1 Pet. 3:15). Our hope must be grounded in rational, objective truth rather than sentimental speculation or mere wishful thinking.

> *Our hope must be grounded in rational, objective truth rather than sentimental speculation or mere wishful thinking.*

Many Christians find a basis for a rational defense of the faith in the creation itself. Romans 1:20 establishes the feasibility of this approach when it says that "since the creation of the world His invisible attributes, His eternal power and divine nature, have been clearly seen, being understood through what has been made, so that they are without excuse." Some of the greatest theologians in history have believed that these in-built natural evidences can help us demonstrate the existence and nature of God. For instance, Augustine argued that nature provides an objective basis for understanding the existence and power of God. Thomas Aquinas built upon Augustine's work by developing a strong case for the existence of God through natural revelation. In his *Summa Theologica*, Aquinas laid out five arguments for the existence of God, the last one being that the complexity and order in the natural realm demands a designer.

*Martin Luther* by Lucas Cranach.

Luther and Calvin both held that nature is capable of proving God's existence and some elements of His nature. This "two books" (Bible and nature) view was endorsed in the 1561 Belgic Confession:

> We know him by two means: First, by the creation, preservation, and government of the universe, since that universe is before our eyes like a beautiful book in which all creatures, great and small, are as letters to make us ponder the invisible things of God: his eternal power and his divinity, as the apostle Paul says in Romans 1:20. All these things are enough to convict men and to leave them without excuse. Second, he makes himself known to us more openly by his holy and divine Word, as much as we need in this life, for his glory and for the salvation of his own.

Though nature unquestionably reveals God, theologians such as Aquinas and Calvin have stressed the need for special revelation (Scripture) to carry seekers from merely knowing God's existence to understanding and believing His redemptive plan. Others, such as Karl Barth, have actually rejected general revelation entirely

> *"Even wicked men are forced, by the mere view of the earth and sky, to rise to the Creator."*
> -*John Calvin*, **The Institutes of the Christian Religion,** *1:16:1*

*The Bible emphasizes that God has truthfully revealed Himself in many times and in many ways (Heb. 1:1-2) and in particular that He has revealed Himself through what He has made (Rom. 1:20; Ps. 19:1-2).*

because they fear it is useless or a possible distraction from the significance of God's special revelation in Jesus Christ. However, the Bible repeatedly emphasizes that God has truthfully revealed Himself in many times and in many ways (Heb. 1:1–2) and in particular that He has revealed Himself through what He has made (Rom. 1:20; Ps. 19:1,2).

## Defining Design

When I was in college, my classmates and I often passed by the campus art building on the way to our favorite burger place. The courtyard in front of the building typically had all manner of interesting art on display. Maybe it was just the engineer in me, but sometimes it was difficult to know whether someone's art project was on display or if the utilities crew was digging a new water line. Like beauty, art is in the eye of the beholder. Some say design is the same way: where one person finds evidence of design, another may find nothing but a chance collection of parts. But is it really so subjective?

Biochemist Michael Behe defines design as "the purposeful arrangement of parts."[1] He mostly had biological systems in mind, but we suggest that the concept of design can also include laws and natural processes which God has ordained to achieve His purposes. This broader conception sets up a number of possibilities. On one hand, perhaps God created the world and all living things by intervening in nature with fiat miracles of special creation. Or perhaps God does His work of creation by immanently working in and through the laws of nature, governing and shepherding them for His purposes. Or perhaps He operates in some combination of the above views. The point is design does not imply a particular method as much as intent. In summary, we would define design in the following way: Design involves an intelligent designer who intentionally creates and implements a plan to accomplish a purpose.

*Design involves an intelligent designer who intentionally creates and implements a plan to accomplish a purpose.*

## Detecting Design

William Paley

At its core the Intelligent Design (ID) hypothesis holds that it is possible to detect design in nature. William Paley based his *Natural Theology* (1802) on this belief. Paley argued that just as it is obvious that a pocket watch is the product of design, it is intuitively obvious that living systems are the result of a Designer. But two hundred years after Paley's argument, must we still rely on intuition when seeking to identify design in nature?

The modern ID movement replaces Paley's reliance on intuition with an objective approach to detecting design. In this approach, design detection begins with the observation that every pattern, event, or object is the result of one of three things: natural law, chance, or design. Detecting the difference between these three is the key. In *The Design Inference*,[2] William Dembski introduced the "design-detection filter" as a tool to systematically eliminate chance and natural law as contenders. Dembski's filter asks three

*"The elegant, coherent, functional systems upon which life depends are the result of deliberate intelligent design."*
—*Michael Behe, Ph.D.,* **The Edge of Evolution,** *166.*

questions:

1. Is the object in question an automatic result of some natural process? If so, it was a necessary outcome, not the result of design.

2. Is the object simple enough that its production is not highly unlikely? If so, it was a chance occurrence.

3. Does the object exhibit some type of specific pattern or function that is independent of the object itself? If so, then the object is the product of design.

To answer the first question, you must determine if the processes and conditions involved in producing the object

could have produced something different. If yes, the second question addresses how likely the actual outcome is compared to the alternative possibilities. Finally, question three determines if there is any specific meaning or significance to the actual outcome that is independent of the processes that produced it. This is important because unlikely events happen all

William Dembski. Photo: Laszlo Bencze.

the time. These are significant only when they manifest some specific pattern or meaning, as if they were intentional. In Dembski's terminology, such an event/object is characterized by *complexity* (too many possibilities to be likely) and *specificity* (there is significance that connotes meaning).

One way to assess the relative likelihood of chance events is to use probabilities. For example, when you flip a coin, the odds are 50 percent that you'll get heads and 50 percent that you'll get tails. To determine the likelihood of getting two heads in a row you would take the probability of getting heads on a single flip (50 percent) and multiply that against itself (50 percent x 50 percent, or, 0.5 x 0.5),

*The probability of a particular outcome diminishes as the specified complexity increases.*

which results in a probability of 25 percent. So the likelihood of an event depends on the number of possible outcomes (two in the case of a coin flip) and the specified complexity of the outcome (0.5 each time in the case of a coin flip). The probability of a particular outcome diminishes as the specified complexity is multiplied.

A simple example will illustrate how probabilities can help us distinguish between chance and design. Suppose you were given a deck of cards and the first card you take from the top is a spade and is the first number of your social security number (SSN). The second card happens to be the second number of your SSN, and it is in the same suit (spades) as the first card. You become increasingly amazed as you watch the nine digits of your SSN be drawn from the top of the deck in the correct order and in the same suit. What is the likelihood that you would draw your SSN  in spades by chance? The chance of drawing the first number of your SSN in spades is one out of fifty-two since there are fifty-two cards in the deck. The chance of drawing the second number in the same suit is one out of fifty-one (since one card has been removed), and so on. Finally, the chance of drawing the ninth number in the same suit is one out of forty-four.

*If you are ever dealt your SSN in spades, you'll know it's by design, not chance.*

Like the probabilities with coin flips, the probability of drawing your social security number is determined by multiplying all the probabilities together. In this case, it would be 1/52 x 1/51 x 1/50 x 1/49 x 1/48 x 1/47 x 1/46 x 1/45 x 1/44. You'll need a really good calculator to figure this up because the answer is one chance out of more than one million billion! Just how small is that probability? If a dealer were able to deal you a fresh set of nine cards every second, the probability is that it would take him 42 million years to deal out your SSN in spades. So if you are ever dealt your SSN in spades, you'll know it's by design, not chance. The deck has been stacked.

**CRIME SCENE DO NOT CROSS**

Dembski's design filter uses techniques similar to those used in forensic science.

## *Practical Examples of Design Detection*

Many scientific disciplines use something analogous to Dembski's design filter to detect intelligent causes. For example:

- Forensic science uses design detection to distinguish between accidents and murder. Circumstantial evidence can be used to demonstrate intelligent causation.

- Cryptography is the science of detecting complex patterns in a signal to break a code.

- Archaeologists distinguish between natural and man-made artifacts by detecting design.

- Arson investigators detect when a cause was accident or arson (design).

- The Search for Extraterrestrial Intelligence (SETI) distinguishes intelligent causes from undirected natural causes in interstellar radio transmissions.

Intelligent Design theory applies similar empirical methods to biology and the other domains of science that are related to origins.

## *Objections to Intelligent Design*

**It Undermines Scientific Research:** Opponents argue that ID invokes the supernatural to explain gaps in our knowledge and that this maneuver could hinder scientific research because people will give up looking for natural explanations. Critics support this objection by noting numerous occasions where science has discovered natural causes to something previously not understood.

*Response:* Essentially this objection mistakenly equates ID with the "god of the gaps" fallacy, in which anything not currently understood is attributed to God. ID proponents counter that they are arguing from evidence, not ignorance. After all, the purpose of the design filter is to identify things which require the design inference. For example, there is a particularly lovely vase sitting on my computer desk. I am impressed by its design and the skill of its creator. I assume the vase has a creator not because I find the origin of vases a mystery that leads me to posit a mystic vase maker. Rather, I assume the vase has a maker precisely because I understand the skill required to make a vase. Vases are complex and purposeful, and they don't exist by chance. Hence, by examining the vase, I can infer something about the nature of the vase's creator. So it is untrue that ID merely fills in our knowledge gaps with an appeal to divinity.

Nevertheless, this criticism of ID is helpful insomuch as it highlights a mistake that must be avoided. Also, we must

*Intelligent Design does not invoke design unless the potential for natural causes has been exhausted.*

not forget that God works in and through the natural order (e.g., natural law) to bring about His ends, and that these things cannot always be identified by ID theory as designs of God.

**It Undermines Faith:** This objection comes from Christians, and it argues similarly to the first objection that identifications of design in nature may someday be overturned. In such cases, the role of faith diminishes as gaps in our knowledge are filled in with natural explanations.

*Response:* First, promoting faith is not the primary aim of ID. Rather, it seeks to undermine naturalism. Second, ID does not invoke design unless the potential for natural causes appears to have been exhausted or is known on the basis of physical principles to be inadequate. Third, in the same way that science is not abandoned when one theory is discarded for another, ID will not be invalidated if some of its particular claims are overturned.

*In the same way that science is not abandoned when one theory is discarded for another, ID will not be invalidated if some of its particular claims are overturned.*

Nevertheless, this objection reminds us to be slow to conclude that we have detected design. If we jump the gun, subsequent discoveries in science might set aside the appearance of design and, for unbelievers, be taken as proof against God's existence.

**An Intelligent Designer Would Do Better Than This:** Critics say this world would be a better place if an all-powerful, all-good God designed it. Living systems are imperfect and suboptimal. Suffering, predation, and extinction could not be the work of an intelligent Creator.

*Response:* ID theory does not claim perfection or optimal design for any particular feature of creation. Rather, ID examines the effects of intel-

A sculpture in Nan Haizi Milu Park, China, commemorating extinct species.

ligent causes and identifies them as such. To argue that a Creator would fashion a better world than ours is to move beyond ID into the realms of theology and philosophy.

**Intelligent Design Is Not Scientific:** Science is restricted to natural causes and effects that can be repeatedly tested and potentially falsified. Because the action of a supernatural being is not subject to testing, it cannot be falsified and hence cannot be considered scientific.

*Response:* We basically agree with this objection. The power of science lies in the ability to formulate descriptions of the world that can be tested and potentially falsified. The identification of intelligent causation is beyond this scope and is not falsifiable. That does not mean it is worthless. It just means it is not science, strictly speaking. Yet some leading ID proponents argue that science should be expanded to include identification of intelligent agents,

*The power of science lies in the ability to formulate descriptions of the world that can be tested and potentially falsified.*

which would make ID a scientific theory of origins. This could be called the case for strong ID. Fortunately, the true power of ID does not depend on whether or not it gains admittance under the science tent. Rather, ID uses the tools of science and mathematics to investigate important philosophical issues

about origins. This form of ID could be called weak ID. It does not claim to be a science theory, but it uses the tools of science to point to causes beyond the natural realm.

ID theory uses the tools of math and science to investigate important issues about origins.

## The Proper Place for Intelligent Design

Strictly speaking, "proof" is a distinction reserved for mathematics and logic, and even in those fields one must presuppose (assume the existence and truthfulness of) key axioms. Step outside these zones, and scientists must temper their claims by using such words as well-established "theory" and "law." Basically, a law is a theory that scientists are tired of testing because it has repeatedly passed the test of falsification. But even then, the law is not regarded as "true" in the logical or mathematical sense.

*A law is a theory that scientists are tired of testing because it has repeatedly passed the test of falsification. But even then the law is not regarded as "true" in the logical or mathematical sense.*

Hence, science does not lead to inescapable conclusions, but to best explanations based on observed phenomena.

In this light a vital question arises: In what sense is it possible to prove the existence of an intelligent Designer? Does God leave incontrovertible evidence pointing to Himself?

*Ultimately, science can never prove either theism or atheism. In the final analysis, what you decide is a matter of faith—either in God or a chance universe.*

The Bible suggests that He does not, for in some sense He is a "God who hides Himself" (Isa. 45:15). Perhaps the Creator hides Himself because "without faith it is impossible to please Him" (Heb. 11:6 NASB). Furthermore, it is "by faith [that] we understand that the worlds were prepared by the word of God" (Heb. 11:3 NASB). Ultimately, then, science is incapable of strictly proving God's existence or the supernatural origin of the universe. Likewise, science can never prove naturalistic origins either. What you decide is a matter of faith—either in God or a chance universe.

But "proof" is often used in a less stringent sense than this. For instance, we speak of proof being good enough to warrant belief. In courtrooms jurors are told to seek proof that renders a verdict that is beyond a reasonable doubt. The evidence for God's existence and the supernatural origin of the universe meets and exceeds this kind of proof (recall Rom. 1:20, which says all people are without excuse for not believing). But ultimately it is up to each person to make a decision. Is the evidence sufficient to find God "guilty" of creating this world? Even nonbelieving scientists admit that the evidence is pretty good. For instance, staunch evolutionist Richard Dawkins says, "Biology is the study of complicated things that give the appearance of having been designed for a purpose."[3] Nobel laureate Francis Crick went so far as to say that "biologists must constantly keep in mind that what they see was not designed, but rather evolved."[4]

The next few chapters lay out some of the scientific evidences that lead such men as Dawkins and Crick to admit that the world seems to be designed. Tragically, both Dawkins and Crick look at the evidence and still end up rejecting knowledge of God. As you examine the forthcoming evidences, ask yourself:

### *Am I an accident of nature,*

or

### *have I been designed for a purpose?*

## Notes

1. Michael Behe, *The Edge of Evolution* (New York: Free Press, 2007), 68.

2. William Dembski, *The Design Inference: Eliminating Chance Through Small Probabilities* (Cambridge: Cambridge University Press, 1998), 36–66.

3. Richard Dawkins, *The Blind Watchmaker: Why the Evidence of Evolution Reveals a Universe Without a Designer* (New York: W. W. Norton & Company, 1996), 1.

4. Francis Crick, *What Mad Pursuit: A Personal View of Scientific Discovery* (London: Penguin, 1990), 138.

# Chapter 31
# The Adam Equation

God spoke through the prophets and challenged them to find a god that was His equal. He alone had measured the oceans, the heavens, and the mountains with His hand. He alone had conceived a design for the universe without the benefit of any consultants. All the power and wisdom of the combined generations of humanity are insignificant when compared to His greatness. Asking to whom they would liken Him, God said, "Look up and see: who created these?" (Isa. 40:26).

*To the surprise of some, we have learned that intelligent life may be unique in our tiny corner of the universe.*

Looking up today with modern telescopes, we are able

to see even more deeply and more clearly the One who has created these stars. For the first time in human history, we are beginning to understand what it takes for life to exist in the universe. It turns out that the conditions for life are extremely tenuous. The universe must be "just right" for life to exist. And to the surprise of some, we have learned that intelligent life may very well be unique in our tiny corner of the universe.

## Are We Alone?

Scientists started to seriously ponder the chances of finding life elsewhere in the universe when astronomer Frank Drake proposed a mathematical expression in 1961 that aims to answer the question, "Are we alone?" Specifically, Drake wanted to know how many intelligent, communicating civilizations might exist in our galaxy given the known physical characteristics of the stars and planets. As you will see below,

In this impossibly large universe, are we earthlings alone?

the Drake Equation bases the answer on factors such as the fraction of stars that have planets orbiting around them and the fraction of planets capable of sustaining life. We are only now beginning to have a good grasp on what these values should be.

## The Drake Equation

$$N = N^* \times f_p \times n_e \times f_l \times f_i \times f_c \times L$$

where

$N$ is the number of communicating civilizations in the galaxy.

$N^*$ represents the number of stars in the Milky Way Galaxy.

$f_p$ is the fraction of stars that have planets around them

$n_e$ is the number of planets per star that are capable of sustaining life.

$f_l$ is the fraction of planets in $n_e$ where life actually evolves.

$f_i$ is the fraction of planets in $f_l$ where intelligent life evolves.

$f_c$ is the fraction of planets in $f_i$ that are able to communicate through space.

$L$ is fraction of the planet's life during which the communicating civilizations live.

By the time you multiply all seven elements together, you will have arrived at a genuinely small number compared to the total number of star systems in our galaxy (estimates are as high as 300 billion). When Drake and his colleagues plugged in values

> *Based on known physical characteristics of our galaxy, the odds are decidedly against the existence of civilizations such as our own.*

they thought were reasonable, they arrived at an estimate of ten intelligent communities in our galaxy. Today that estimate is regarded as too optimistic by many observers. Common estimates for the Drake Equation now fall below one intelligent community in our galaxy. In other words, based on known physical characteristics of our galaxy, the odds are decidedly against the existence of civilizations such as our own.

But the Drake equation begins with a running start. What if instead of asking how many cosmic neighbors we have, we ask a much more fundamental question: If God had no role in the origin of life, what are the odds that any intelligent civilizations (including ours) would ever exist? In other words, what is the probability that intelligent life forms would arise through undirected processes? We can

No matter how we account for UFO sightings, such as this 1952 photo from Passoria, NJ, a strong scientific case can be made that life is very unlikely throughout the universe.

follow Drake's lead and use math to suggest an answer to this question. Let's call our equation the Adam Equation.

## The Adam Equation

$$F_{Adam} = f_U \times f_A \times f_P \times f_L \times f_C \times f_I$$

where

$F_{Adam}$ is the probability that intelligent living beings are here by chance.

$f_U$ is the probability that the universe would have begun without God.

$f_A$ is the probability that the right laws of nature result without God.

$f_P$ is the probability of obtaining a suitable planet without God.

$f_L$ is the probability that life arises from non-living material without God.

$f_C$ is the probability that complex life develops without God.

$f_I$ is the probability that intelligent, advanced life develops without God.

Just as is the case with the Drake Equation, the values one assigns for the elements in the Adam Equation are somewhat subjective. There are no sure, scientifically objective numbers for these elements. Rather, one must study all the variables for each element and then assign realistic probabilities. Many observers will decide that the only reasonable value for each element is zero. But even by more optimistic standards, the Adam Equation demonstrates that it takes far, far greater faith to disbelieve in a Creator than to believe in Him.

*It takes far, far greater faith to disbelieve in a Creator than to believe in Him.*

## Science in Wonderland

A. W. Tozer once calmed the nerves of an intimidated assistant by assuring him that we are all ignorant, we're just ignorant about different things. The same can be said of scientists when it comes to the question of origins. Scientists have particular areas of specialty, outside of which they must rely on other specialists. So it is not surprising for a scientist to be well aware of the challenges to naturalistic origins in their own field

*Every field of science presents serious challenges to the naturalistic origins theory.*

and yet share the public perception that all the problems are solved in other areas. For example, a geneticist knows very well how difficult it is to explain the chance assembly of DNA, but she is probably ignorant about the precise tuning of the universe and how physicists see this as a challenge to naturalism. Likewise, the physicist is aware of the challenges in his field but supposes the geneticists have pretty much sewn up the difficulties in genetics. The unavoidable fact, however, is that every field of science presents serious challenges to the naturalistic origins theory. Scientists who insist on a naturalistic origin of the universe remind one of the White Queen from Wonderland. When Alice told the Queen it was not possible to believe in impossible things, the Queen answered, "I daresay you haven't had much practice.

*Alice Before the Queen* illustrated by John Tenniel.

When I was your age, I always did it for half-an-hour a day. Why, sometimes I've believed as many as six impossible things before breakfast."[1]

To believe in naturalistic origins of life and the universe, one must join the White Queen and have faith in impossible things; six impossible things, in fact:

1. Impossibilities in Philosophy: The Origin of the Universe
2. Impossibilities in Physics: A Goldilocks Universe
3. Impossibilities in Astronomy: An Exceptional Earth
4. Impossibilities in Chemistry: The Origin of Life
5. Impossibilities in Biochemistry: The Complexity of Life
6. Impossibilities in Anthropology: The Image of God

Scientists are daily discovering that there are many, many factors, events, and circumstances that must be just right for intelligent life to exist. The idea that these things are all perfectly balanced in a naturalistic universe (where no God has created or guided events) is so wildly improbable that there is every reason to infer that the action of an "intelligent agent" was necessary. In the following chapters we will examine the creation story as told by the creation itself. As we do so, we will explore the six impossible things that must be believed if we are to accept the claims of naturalistic origins.[2]

> *Scientists are daily discovering that there are many, many factors, events, and circumstances that must be just right for intelligent life to exist.*

## Notes

1. Lewis Carroll, *Through the Looking Glass*, chapter 5.

2. Technically, by "impossible" we really mean "very highly improbable," so improbable that many observers agree that "impossible" is a reasonable synonym.

# Chapter 32
# Impossibilities in Philosophy: Origin of the Cosmos

Toward the end of the nineteenth century, German philosopher Friedrich Nietzsche announced the death of God. He did not mean that someone had killed God. Rather, as a citizen of an increasingly irreligious Europe, he was celebrating "the greatest recent event—that God is dead, that the belief in the Christian God has become unbelievable."[1]

He spoke too soon, for today more than ever before Christians are equipped to engage skeptics with confidence. Ted Cabal, professor of apologetics and general editor of *The Apologetics Study Bible*, says we are living in the golden era of Christian apologetics.[2] This is largely because modern scientific insights add

Friedrich Nietsche, the best-known atheist philosopher of all time.

greater weight to the arguments for God's existence. Not only is the Christian God believable, unbelief is more inexcusable than ever before.

## The Kalám Cosmological Argument

One of the oldest and yet most up-to-date arguments for God's existence is the cosmological argument. Taken from the Greek word *kosmos* (world), the various forms of the cosmological argument claim that the existence of the world requires the existence of God. William Lane Craig is the strongest contemporary advocate for this argument. He defends a particularly powerful version called the *kalám* cosmological argument (*kalám* is an Arabic term). Craig formulates this argument as follows:

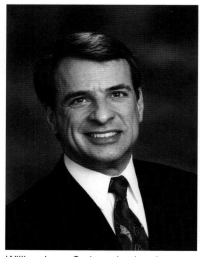

William Lane Craig revived and popularized the *kalám* cosmological argument.

1. Whatever begins to exist has a cause of its existence.
2. The universe began to exist.
3. Therefore, the universe has a cause of its existence.[3]

## Philosophical Basis of the Cosmological Argument

*Premise #1:* Whatever begins to exist has a cause. This premise is essentially intuitive, but experience backs it as well. After all, our experience proves that events, especially origins, never happen without a cause.

*Assessment:* Critics of the *kalám* argument reject the assumption that every effect must have a cause. It is not a proven violation of logic, they say, to think of something coming to exist without a cause. While that may be true, the principle of cause and effect is universally established by experience. In fact, the assumption that something cannot come from nothing seems to be a foundational principle for rational thought.

*The assumption that something cannot come from nothing seems to be a foundational principle for rational thought.*

***Premise #2:*** The universe began to exist. If you join the vast majority of thinking persons and affirm the first premise of the *kalám* cosmological argument, then your acceptance or rejection of the claim that the universe was caused to exist will hinge on this second premise. Defenders of the cosmological argument support this premise along two lines. First, they maintain that an actual infinite is impossible. An actual infinite would be a quantity (of anything) so large that its quantity does not change even if members are added to it or subtracted from it. Furthermore, all subsets of an actual infinite set would also be infinite. The majority of mathematicians take these things to be impossible, for the concept of actual infinity

incurs logical absurdities. For example, suppose you start with one and count on and on forever. If it were possible for you to reach actual infinity, by implication there would be an infinite number of even and odd numbers in the set, as well as an infinite number of prime numbers, an infinite number of multiples of six, and so on. See the absurdity here? Each of these is a subset of the actual infinite set, yet each subset is said to have as many members as the whole set. In other words, all the parts are as great as the whole. This is clearly absurd, and thus actual infinites are impossible. This means time itself cannot be infinite. And if the past is finite, the universe clearly began to exist at some point.

Second, defenders of the cosmological argument point out

that it is impossible to construct an actual infinite set through successively adding to a finite set. To illustrate this, imagine that Adam decided to count to infinity. He counted until his dying day, at which time he passed the task on to his son, Seth. Seth likewise counted till his death and gave the job off to Enosh. This continued down through history until your dad passed the job down to you. Did any of your forefathers reach infinity? No. Will you? No. Nor will any of your descendants even if the world never ends. Why? Because you can always add another number to your chain, and you can always start counting backwards with the expectation that one of your distant descendants will count all the way back down to zero, the place where Adam started. So long as you are able to do these things you have not reached actual infinity. At best you will have constructed a "potentially infinite set," a set that stretches toward but never reaches true infinity. So again, time

*Science has irrefutably proven that the universe is not eternal. Rather, it began to exist in the finite past.*

cannot stretch infinitely backwards. The universe, therefore, began to exist.

*Assessment:* Much like the first premise, it is difficult to build a good case against the premise that the universe began to exist. In past centuries many scientists and philosophers believed the universe was eternal and thus had no beginning. Albert Einstein, for instance, initially held that the universe is static and unchanging. But as new scientific findings kept piling up, this view became impossible to hold.

*Conclusion:* Therefore, the universe had a cause. If the universe had a beginning and whatever has a beginning has a cause, then it logically follows that the universe had a cause.

*Assessment:* As a last-ditch criticism, critics of the cosmological argument point out that the mere existence of a cause for the universe says nothing about what that cause might be. Christians identify the cause as the God of the Bible, but the cosmological argument merely entails that the universe has an external cause. This is a valid point. At most, the cosmological argument demonstrates the existence of a Creator. To prove that it is specifically the Christian God who caused it, we must make additional arguments.

## Scientific Support for the Cosmological Argument

### A Day Without Yesterday

As we mentioned above, the idea that the universe is eternal and static lost credibility as science progressed through the twentieth century. This shift began when men such as Edwin Hubble began noticing that remote galaxies are moving away from Earth. Though it took a while for it to sink in, these discoveries set in motion a scientific revolution. In 1927 Georges Lemaître applied Einstein's equations of general relativity to Hubble's observations and proved that the universe is expanding rather than static. This clearly implied a beginning and a Beginner. Upon hearing Lemaître explain

his theory that the universe began from a "primeval atom" on "a day without yesterday," Einstein reportedly remarked, "This is the most beautiful and satisfactory explanation of creation to which I have ever listened."

Changes in opinion often come slowly in science, especially when serious philosophical and theological implications are on the line. Up through the 1950s, many scientists resisted evidence for an expanding universe be-

The parts of the telescope at the Mount Wilson Observatory had to be hauled up the hill one at a time on trucks in 1917. Later, Edwin Hubble would use this telescope to send astronomy into a whole new direction.

cause it invoked God-talk. For this reason steady-state advocate Sir Fred Hoyle derisively coined the phrase "big bang" to refer to the expansion theory. He regarded the theory as a joke that would soon pass, but the evidence for the big bang soon

This space probe image reveals temperature fluctuations (shown as color differences) that eventually became galaxies in the expanding universe. Photo: NASA/WMAP.

won out. Ironically, it took two scientists working to eliminate noise pollution from antennae at Bell Labs to nail the coffin shut on steady state models. (And even more ironically, one of these scientists was a staunch supporter of the steady state model he inadvertently helped overturn!) Theorists had suggested that if the big bang really happened, there should be an "afterglow" of radiation in far-off space. This background radiation was discovered in 1965 when Arno Penzias and Robert Wilson were hunting for the source of the abovementioned interference and instead discovered signals coming uniformly from every direction outside our galaxy. This discovery fit the profile predicted by big bang theories. Penzias and Wilson, it turns out, were listening to echoes from the creation of the universe. They were awarded the 1978 Nobel Prize in physics for one of the century's key scientific advances. Since that time the weight of evidence has continued to grow. Recent images of the cosmic microwave background radiation offer undeniable proof that the universe had a beginning.

*Recent images of the cosmic microwave background radiation offer undeniable proof that the universe had a beginning.*

## A Universe Winding Down

The second law of thermodynamics also argues for a finite universe, for it says that the amount of thermal energy available to do work decreases with time in a closed system (a system that does not have energy entering it from outside). Thus given enough time, the universe (which is by definition a closed system) will run out of energy. If the universe were eternal, it would have run out of energy long, long ago since its past stretches back infinitely far. Further, if the universe continues to expand forever, the same thing will occur. Clearly, our universe has not always existed and it cannot go on existing forever. It had a beginning and will someday have an end.

If the universe were eternal, it would have "wound down" an eternity ago. In other words, it would have run out of usable energy.

To avoid this conclusion, some suggest that the universe eternally expands and contracts like an accordion, beginning and ending over and over again. But this does not work for two reasons. First, it implies an actually infinite number of past cycles, but as we have seen, actual infinity is impossible. Second, the second law of thermodynamics eliminates this option because with each cycle of expansion and contraction, the amount of thermal energy available to do the work of universe building decreases. One consequence of this is that the diameter of the universe increases with each cycle, which means that even a cyclic universe with an infinite future must have had a beginning since the diameter of each previous cycle decreases toward nothingness. Hence, the second law of thermodynamics says that the universe had a beginning.

## *Conclusion*

Philosophy and modern science both affirm that the universe had a beginning and was caused to exist by an outside force. Now more than ever before, Genesis stands as the one true account of the universe's origin.

## *Notes*

1. Friedrich Nietzsche, *The Gay Science*, 2nd ed., section 343 (1887).

2. *The Apologetics Study Bible* has more than one hundred apologetics essays focusing on common challenges launched against Christianity. More than 100 leading scholars contributed to this project. We recommend this as a study tool.

3. For Craig's exposition and defense of the cosmological argument, see "In Defense of the Kalám Cosmological Argument" *Faith and Philosophy* 14 (1997): 236-47.

# Chapter 33
# Impossibilities in Physics:
# A Goldilocks Universe

Did you know that the laws of nature seem to have been written with you in mind? The fact is that they must have been precisely fine-tuned in order for life to even be possible. As Goldilocks would say, the universe is "just right" for life to exist.

To assess the first of six impossible things that have to be true if the universe arose naturalistically, in the previous chapter we had to delve into philosophy and the cosmological argument. An examination of the five remaining impossible things brings us squarely into the realm of science. In this chapter we will explore the teleological argument

An early diagram of the geocentric model.

(from the Greek word *teleos,* meaning "end"). This argument says that the universe appears to have been designed with some purpose in mind. Scientific evidence for design in the laws of nature clearly points to the existence of a Designer.

Prior to the sixteenth century, scientists held that Earth was fixed at the center of the universe. This seemed fitting, for humans are made in the image of God, and Earth is our home. But then Copernicus showed that Earth orbits the Sun. Suddenly, humankind's significance in the cosmos was called into question.

*Coversation with God,* a portrait of Copernicus by Jan Matejko. Nicolaus Copernicus (1473–1543) was a pivotal figure in the heliocentric revolution in science.

Scientists began to think of Earth as an average planet orbiting an average star in an average galaxy. Maybe humans really are not so special after all. For centuries to come this "principle of mediocrity" would dictate secular man's view of his place in the cosmos.

During the latter half of the twentieth century, the pendulum began to swing back the other way as scientists learned that the laws of nature are not arbitrary but highly tuned to permit life as we know it.

## Basis for the Design Inference

Instead of the principle of mediocrity, scientists now speak of the "the anthropic principle," which essentially states that the universe is precisely tuned so that we can be here. Life is highly sensitive to finely tuned physical quantities,

*Life is highly sensitive to finely tuned physical quantities, so much so that if these quantities were to differ slightly, life would not be possible anywhere in the universe.*

so much so that if these quantities were to differ slightly, life would not be possible anywhere in the universe. As one scientist put it, "It seems as though somebody has fine-tuned nature's numbers to make the Universe. . . . The impression of design is overwhelming."[1]

## Life in a Fishbowl

A few years back our kids were pestering us to get a puppy. The lovely Mrs. Whorton and I said it would be another year before we were ready for a dog. So while I was away on business, my wife tried to appease the kids by buying a fishbowl and some fish. One would think that fish are easy to care for. After all, they get by just fine in oceans, rivers, lakes, and even large

mud puddles. Three weeks and ten dead fish later, we knew better. My wife diligently researched the care and feeding of fish. She dutifully maintained the proper pH balance in the tank. She did her best to keep ammonia in check. She stressed over nitrites and nitrates. Water temperature, water hardness, and everything we

Even goldfish require just the right balance of conditions, or else life is impossible.

could think of was kept in balance, but it just wasn't good enough. We found out the hard way that the conditions have to be just right, else fish go belly up.

Life in general is like that. Eminent physicist Sir Martin Rees says the existence of life in the universe is absolutely dependent on six precise quantities in nature.[2] Astrophysicist and pastor Hugh Ross keeps a running list of properties and initial conditions that must be precisely balanced for life to exist. That list now numbers into the hundreds.[3] Following are several examples of the "just right" values of our universe.

## Gravity Is Just Right

Sir Isaac Newton formulated the law of universal gravitation, which says that any two objects will be attracted to each other by a force that depends on the masses of the objects and the distance between them. This force of attraction is called gravity. It does far more than just make apples fall to the ground. It holds the universe together and makes life possible. Importantly, the amazingly precise gravitational constant ($6.672 \times 10^{-11}$) is apparently the same everywhere in the universe. We do not know why this is so. There is no known

*If the gravitational constant were even a fraction stronger, stars would be too massive and burn too quickly for life to exist.*

mechanism of nature that could cause it to be precisely this value. It seems simply to be a given attribute of the universe. What we *do* know is that if the gravitational constant were even a fraction stronger, stars would be too massive and burn too quickly for life to exist. Conversely, if it were a fraction weaker, stars would be too cool for nuclear fusion. This would mean key heavy elements (such as iron) would not be produced, rendering life impossible.

Newton's Law of Gravity descries the force that causes the astronaut to orbit Earth. Photo: Spacewalk from the Gemini 4 mission. NASA.

## Electromagnetism Is Just Right

Magnetism is one of the most vital forces of nature. We use its power to run electric motors and hang our children's artwork on the refrigerator. However, magnetism would rip whole worlds apart if an electrical imbalance developed in the universe. That's because electromagnetism is 36 orders of magnitude (1,000,000,000,000,

000,000,000,000,000,000,000,000) stronger than gravity. Fortunately for us, the universe is electrically neutral. This means the number of positively charged particles (protons) in the universe is equal to the number of negatively charged particles (electrons). How precise is this balance? Amazingly, it is better than one part in 10 with 36 zeros!

## Nuclear Forces Are Just Right

In addition to gravity and electromagnetism, there are two other fundamental forces in nature: the strong nuclear force and the weak nuclear force. The strongest of the four forces is the strong nuclear force. It overcomes the

*"The universe is unlikely. Very unlikely. Deeply, shockingly unlikely."*
— **Brad Lemley, "Why Is There Life?" Discover,** *November 2002.*

electromagnetic force, which causes particles of like charge to repel each other (e.g., a proton will try to flee the presence of another proton). Hence, the strong nuclear force binds protons together "against their will" in the nucleus of the atom. The weak nuclear force is a billion times weaker and is involved in radioactive decay and the interaction between subatomic particles. Together these two finely balanced forces control how stars operate. If the strong force were 5 percent stronger or weaker, we would not have stable stars or the basic chemistry on which life depends. Similarly, life would be impossible if the weak force were different.

*"A commonsense interpretation of the facts suggests that a superintellect has monkeyed with physics, as well as with chemistry and biology."*
— **Fred Hoyle, "The Universe: Past and Present Reflections," Engineering and Science,** *November 1981. Cited in* **The World Treasury of Physics,** *ed. Timothy Ferris, 1991, p. 392.*

## Expansion Rate Was Just Right

The expansion rate of the universe immediately after the big bang is one of the most impressive illustrations of how highly specific certain conditions of the universe must be to support life. If the balance between gravity and the expansion rate were altered even by one part in one million, billion, billion, billion, billion, billion, billion there would be no galaxies, stars, planets, or life. How delicate a balance is this? If the initial mass of the universe varied by as much as plus or minus one grain of common table salt, there would be no universe. Plus one grain and the universe would not have expanded; minus one grain and the universe would have expanded so rapidly that it would have spread out to nothingness in less than a second. Such facts come as no surprise to people of faith, but secular scientists are regularly surprised at how "just right" our universe is for life. Truly, the heavens are declaring the glories of God.

| *Parameter* | *Precision Necessary for Life* |
|---|---|
| *Gravity* | *1 part in $10^{40}$* |
| *Electromagnetic Force* | *1 part in $10^{40}$* |
| *Strong Nuclear Force* | *1 part in 20* |
| *Ratio of Strong Force to Electromagnetic Force* | *1 part in 100* |
| *Ratio of Protons to Electrons* | *1 part in $10^{36}$* |
| *Initial Mass Density and Expansion Rate* | *1 part in $10^{60}$* |

# Hugh Ross's Examples of Fine-Tuning of the Universe [4]

*Strong nuclear force constant:*

*If it were larger*, no hydrogen; unstable nuclei in other atoms.

*If it were smaller*, no elements other than hydrogen.

*Weak nuclear force constant:*

*If it were larger*, too much hydrogen converted to helium in big bang, hence too much heavy element material made by star burning; no expulsion of heavy elements from stars.

*If it were smaller*, too little helium produced from big

bang, hence too little heavy element material made by star burning; no expulsion of heavy elements from stars.

**Gravitational force constant:**

*If it were larger*, stars would be too hot and would burn up quickly and unevenly.

*If it were smaller*, stars would be so cool that nuclear fusion would not ignite, thus no heavy element production.

**Electromagnetic force constant:**

*If it were larger*, insufficient chemical bonding; elements more massive than boron would be unstable.

*If it were smaller*, insufficient chemical bonding.

**Ratio of electromagnetic force constant to gravitational force constant:**

*If it were larger,* no stars less than 1.4 solar masses, hence short and uneven stellar burning.

*If it were smaller,* no stars more than 0.8 solar masses, hence no heavy element production.

**Ratio of electron to proton mass:**

*If it were larger*, insufficient chemical bonding.

*If it were smaller*, insufficient chemical bonding.

**Expansion rate of the universe:**

*If it were larger*, no galaxy formation.

*If it were smaller*, universe collapses prior to star formation.

**Mass density of the universe:**

*If it were larger*, too much deuterium and stars burn too rapidly.

*If it were smaller*, too few heavy elements forming.

## Alternatives to the Supernatural Creation

Scientists who acknowledge the fine tuning of the universe but do not wish to invoke God generally chose one of two alternative arguments: either that some unknown natural law creates the delicate balance for life or that a vast number of universes exist and we are just lucky to be in one suited to life. Let's take a closer look at these arguments.

### Unknown Natural Law

This option is based on the hope that we will someday discover proof that the wished-for Grand Unification Theory (GUT) is really true. The GUT would explain in physical terms why all the initial conditions and constants of nature have the precise values that make parts of the universe habitable. But such a theory would not eliminate design

If scientists ever discover a superlaw, it would by no means be a proof against God's existence. To the contrary, it would be an even greater proof of the giant intellect that caused the universe to exist.

in the universe. Rather, it would push the design inference back one step and likely make it more compelling than before. After all, a superlaw that precisely fixes all other natural laws in a highly ordered way that permits life surely implies the existence of an indescribably ingenious Designer.

### Multiple Universes

Rather than acknowledging a Designer, some scientists prefer to speculate that an infinite number of universes exist and that all of them have random values for their natural laws and physical constants. If this is so, they say, it's no real surprise that at least one universe got lucky and came up with the laws leading to life. Known as the multiverse hypothesis, this theory aims to satisfy the secular hope that our universe is just a random occurrence and is not the product of design. The multiverse hypothesis originally developed from an interpretation of odd features in quantum mechanics. Quantum mechanics is

*The multiverse theory is a science fiction made possible only by our radically incomplete understanding of quantum physics.*

the study of things the size of atoms or smaller, where the normal laws of physics seem lost. One theory holds that normal cause-and-effect rules are inapplicable in quantum events, and that scientists actually cause quantum events simply by observing them. To avoid this odd conclusion, some have suggested that the observing scientist has not caused anything, but has only witnessed one of

Which came first, the quantum reality or the scientific observation of quantum reality? Amazingly, some scientists think we create quantum reality by measuring it.

an infinite number of outcomes that occur simultaneously. In that case, all possibilities are actualized, though we only have access to the one possibility which is actualized *in our universe*. The idea is that if an infinite number of universes exist, it does not seem so far-fetched that ours beat the odds by having the right values for life. It's an interesting idea, but of course it is sheer speculation since there is no possible way to access the hypothesized alternative universes. In the end the multiverse theory is a science fiction made possible only by our radically incomplete understanding of quantum physics.

## Conclusion

The Creator is an expert marksman. He targeted you and me and the fine-tuned conditions necessary for life when He designed the universe.

Imagine that you are standing blindfolded in front of a firing squad composed of twenty-five expert marksmen. On command they aim and fire. You hear the shots ring out in unison, and then you realize you are still standing! Could all twenty five marksmen have accidentally missed? No way. It's clear that you are alive because they meant for you to live. The same can be said for life in the universe. In this case the marksmanship is right on target. To a degree of precision that defies comprehension, the natural laws and starting conditions of our universe had to be "just so" in order for life to exist. Life is a gift to be treasured, and the Giver of that gift is worthy of all honor.[5]

## Notes

1. Paul Davies, *The Cosmic Blueprint: New Discoveries in Nature's Creative Ability to Order the Universe* (New York: Simon and Schuster, 1988), 203.

2. Martin J. Rees, *Just Six Numbers: The Deep Forces That Shape the Universe* (New York: HarperCollins, 1999).

3. Hugh Ross points interested readers to a Web site which maintains an updated listing of evidences for fine-tuning: www.designevidences.org

4. Adapted from Hugh Ross, *The Creator and the Cosmos*, 2d ed. (Colorado Springs: NavPress, 1995), 118–21.

5. This firing squad illustration was inspired by John Leslie, a Canadian philosopher and author of *Universes* (London: Routledge, 1996).

# Chapter 34
# Impossibilities in Astronomy: An Exceptional Earth

Gazing at the night sky, one naturally wonders if we are alone in this vast universe. Three centuries before Christ, two great philosophers staked claims on this very question. Aristotle said Earth is unique because, as popular opinion held, it resides at the center of the universe. Epicurus disagreed. He said the universe was infinite and thus filled with an infinite number of worlds. The debate goes on today, only now it is not just a philosophical question but a *science* question as well.

Modern technology has given us clear evidence of planets around other stars. In October 1995 Geoffrey Marcy and Paul Butler became the first scientists to detect the existence of a planet

Exoplanets are those which are located outside our solar system. With advances in technology, scientists will discover an ever-greater number of these. Will any of them be similar to Earth? Photo: Artist's conception of Terrestrial Planet Finder observatories, NASA.

orbiting a star outside our solar system. They did this indirectly by noticing that the star was wobbling slightly, a sign that an orbiting planet is tugging against it. Over the next four years they discovered indirect proof for another 28 extra-solar planets. Finally, on November 7, 1999 their colleague Greg Henry trained his telescopes on one of the wobbling stars and saw the starlight dim ever so slightly as a planet skimmed across its path. For the first time in history, humans had detected a planet outside our solar system.

Aristotle taught that Earth is unique, but his reasoning is insupportable today. Nevertheless, Earth may be unique after all. Only time will tell.

Since then over 260 extrasolar planets have been discovered. Although these planets are far from Earthlike, new instruments and more sophisticated search methods will enable us to discover countless new planets. As the list grows, the age-old question will only grow in importance: Are we alone? We may find that both Epicurus and Aristotle were partly right. Perhaps the universe is filled with planets as Epicurus supposed, but maybe the vast majority of them are lifeless. Evidence increasingly leads to the conclusion that Earth is unique.

## Bases for the Design Inference

As the following survey shows, an amazing number of factors have to be just right to make a planet suitable for advanced life.

### A Just Right Location

I once asked my wife [Mrs. Whorton] if she was thankful that she was not born into an irregular galaxy. "No," she said, "but being married to you makes me feel like I was." Sometimes we just don't know how blessed we are.

Our Milky Way is a large spiral galaxy with 100,000,000,000 or more stars. As far as we can tell, there are about that same number of galaxies in the entire visible universe. Assuming that other galaxies have on average roughly the same number of stars as the Milky Way, there are 100,000,000,000 × 100,000,000,000 stars (suns) in the universe. At first glance that may seem to indicate that life may be everywhere, but all galaxies are not created equally. Approximately 75 percent of galaxies are spiral while about 20 percent are elliptical in shape and 5 percent are irregularly shaped. When it comes to galaxies and their suitability to life, shape is everything. Elliptical galaxies lack sufficient supplies of dust and gas for building a large quantity of stars. Thus, not enough stars are produced to churn out the heavy elements (iron, etc.) that are vital to planet formation. Large irregular galaxies tend to be immersed in radiation (which would sterilize any planet) and smaller irregulars lack the heavy elements to form habitable rocky planets. Hence, spiral galaxies have the best shot at producing habitable planets.

> *"The universe is fundamentally hostile to life. Most planets and other places in the universe clearly could not support any type of Earth-like creatures."*
> —*Donald Brownlee*

But it takes more than just any ole spiral galaxy to produce conditions necessary for advanced life. Research suggests that complex life is only possible within the Galactic Habitable Zone. Stars too close to the galactic center do not produce life because of large radiation doses. Those too far out suffer from lack of the heavy elements required to form rocky planets. Furthermore, most stars are located either in the central bulge or in

Spiral Galaxy. Photo: NASA.

the spiral arms of the galaxy, where the gravitational attraction between the closely packed stars severely disrupts planetary orbits. We are fortunate that our solar system is located in a "sweet spot" between spiral arms where the density of elements is high enough for rocky planets to form but where stellar neighbors are relatively sparse, thus minimizing lethal radiation emission. Moreover, not only is our solar system well positioned, but Earth is also at just the right location within our solar system. Look

*Not only is our solar system well positioned, but Earth is also at just the right location within our solar system.*

at Venus and Mars, and you will see what could have happened to us. If Earth were 5 percent nearer to the sun, it would be baked like Venus. On the other hand, put us 15 percent farther out, and we would go cold and barren like Mars.

Even more profound is that our location is especially suited not just for advanced life but also for intelligent, observant creatures. Our vantage point between spiral arms allows us not only to appreciate the rich bounty of stars and galaxies in our universe, but also provides a clear path for observing that our universe is expanding from a finely tuned beginning in the not-too-distant past. We are at just the right spot to see that the heavens declare the glory of God.

Galaxies are composed of many, many stars. If this were an image of the Milky Way, our sun would be indistinguishable from the others. The lights are clusters of many different stars. Photo: NASA.

### A Just Right Star

If our sun was as small as 95 percent of all stars are, Earth would not be fit for life. That's because planets orbiting a smallish sun have to orbit close to the sun, else they won't

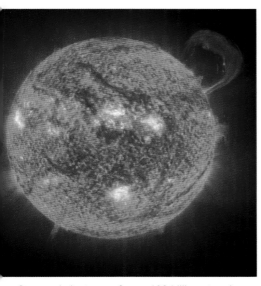

Our sun is just one of over 100 billion stars in the Milky Way Galaxy. Photo: NASA.

have enough heat to support life. However, such close orbits are gravity locked, like the moon is to the Earth. In these cases the orbiting body does not rotate. This means Earth would be baked on one side and frozen on the other.

Life on Earth would not be possible if the sun were much larger, either, for in that case it would burn too rapidly and would not have the long period of stability required for advanced life. Finally, our sun is alone, and that's a good thing. Most stars in the universe have companions, which forces orbiting planets into irregular orbits which disallow the formation of stable climates and ecosystems.

### Just Right Neighbors

Perhaps the most intriguing bit of "good luck" for Earth is its moon. While all other planets in our solar system have comparatively small moons, ours is over a quarter of the size of Earth. Consequently, its large mass places a gravitational grip on our planet that stabilizes Earth's spin axis and enables long-term, stable climates and beneficial tides that are conducive to life. Since such a large moon is an anomaly, how do we explain its origin? Evidence seems to indicate that

Limb of Copernicus Impact Crater on the Moon. Photo: NASA/JPL.

the moon formed during the early, cataclysmic period of our solar system. It appears that a Mars-sized object smashed into Earth, ejecting debris into space which eventually coalesced to form the moon.

*The moon, along with Jupiter, Saturn, and Neptune, serves to block asteroids from smashing into Earth.*

The moon has protected Earth from many large asteroid impacts. Similarly, we are protected by the giant planets Jupiter, Saturn, and Neptune. The gravitational attraction of these massive planets acts like a cosmic vacuum cleaner, sweeping the inner solar system virtually clean of marauding interlopers which, in a single destructive blow, could eliminate all life on our planet.

### A Just Right Planet

Life depends on a precise chemical balance. Too much or too little of the key chemicals renders life impossible. In addition to this, a home planet must have the right mass, atmosphere, crust characteristics, and water quantities for life to exist. Strangely enough, Earth meets these conditions in part due to the molten, tempestuous material below our thin crust which drives the

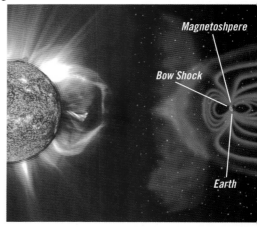

Earth enjoys many life-supporting benefits due to its position and features. Illustration: NASA Marshall Space Flight Center (Labels added).

plate tectonics, earthquakes, and volcanoes that continually recycle Earth's most vital elements. Take the carbon cycle for example. It is a coupled feedback control system where plants, animals, the oceans, the atmosphere, and rocks maintain a stable and hospitable global ecosystem. The spinning fluid below earth's crust also drives our magnetic field, which protects us from the lethal inundation of solar radiation. When all the rare factors and circumstances that make life possible on our planet are taken together, it becomes highly improbable that advanced life is common in the universe. Even to many naturalistic and atheistic scientists, it looks like we may be alone.

## Alternatives to Supernatural Creation

Atheistic theories of life's origins take two main forms: either there are more inhabitable planets than we suspect (which helps the odds) or life elsewhere doesn't depend on Earthlike conditions. It is unlikely that we will ever know how many planets exist, so hopeful atheists can always play the odds that there are enough life-friendly planets *It's carbon or nothing when it comes to building blocks for life.* out there to make life somewhat probable apart from God's involvement. The second option tries to avoid the problem presented by the universe's shortage of Earthlike planets by postulating that life elsewhere can be based on elements or conditions that, in our limited experience, do not support life. For instance, they say carbon (which is requisite for life as we

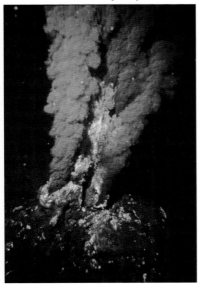

Rudimentary life forms live at deep ocean thermal vents. Could higher life forms live in such places? Most experts doubt it. Photo: OAR/National Undersea Research Program (NURP); NOAA.

know it) may *not* be required for life elsewhere. Perhaps advanced life can be based on elements such as silicon. However, silicon is not nearly as capable as carbon. Silicon-based life, if ever it could exist, would be very rudimentary. No other half-decent options exist on the periodic table of elements. In truth, it's carbon or nothing when it comes to building blocks for life.

Another avenue is to suggest that life elsewhere in the universe might indeed be carbon based but not require conditions similar to those found on Earth. Advocates of this option cite species which live deep down in ocean trenches and shafts where thermal vents give off heat, pressure, and poison in a zero-light environment. These species, known as extremophiles, give scientists hope that life can exist in unexpected places. But there is a huge difference between simple microscopic single-celled life forms and complex living creatures like you and me. Even if the universe were filled with robust extremophiles, we humans would almost certainly be alone in the halls of intelligence.

## Conclusion

Even though Copernicus shifted attention away from Earth and humanity as the center of the universe, the pendulum is swinging back to an emphasis on the special status of both based on the strength of modern scientific learning. We now know that life is an unimaginably complex orchestra of finely tuned factors and concentrations. That even one planet in this universe

*A reasonable accounting of the evidence indicates that Earth was providentially crafted to be the stage on which the Creator's drama of creation, fall, and redemption would unfold.*

should have life is inexplicable apart from the work of a Creator. A reasonable accounting of the evidence indicates that Earth was providentially crafted to be the stage on which the Creator's drama of creation, fall, and redemption would unfold.

# Chapter 35
# Impossibilities in Chemistry: The Origin of Life

Charles Darwin thought that cells were essentially little sacks of simple gel-like substance called protoplasm. Ernst Haeckel and T. H. Huxley proposed (circa. 1880) a two-step process called autogeny, where protoplasm (and life) would spontaneously form through chemical reactions when the right chemicals were combined. In the 1920s, biochemist Aleksandr Oparin and geneticist J. B. S. Haldane each suggested that life would spontaneously form over a very long period of time as biochemical molecules formed and interacted, becoming evermore complex. Known as the Oparin-Haldane Hypothesis, this theory was put to the test in 1952 by Stanley Miller and Harold Urey. In what came

In apparatuses such as this one, experimenters have long attempted to "create" life by mimicking conditions that are thought to resemble early Earth. Photo: NASA.

to be known as the Miller-Urey experiment, Miller success-fully formed a few amino acids (the building blocks that form protein molecules) by applying electrical charges to a chemi-cal mixture that supposedly simulated primitive Earth's atmo-sphere. Many people thought this confirmed Darwin's idea that life formed naturally in some "warm little pond," but this confidence was later tempered when it became known that Miller's test did not simulate the genuine conditions of early Earth. Nevertheless, scientists kept up their belief in a natural ori-gin of life as more and more basic building blocks were manufac-tured in test tubes. In the late mid-twentieth century, for instance,

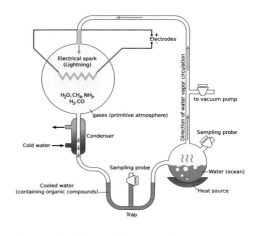

Diagram of the Miller-Urey experiment. Illustration by Yassine Mrabet.

biologist Dean Kenyon wrote in his widely read textbook *Bio-logical Predestination* that abiogenesis (the theorized natural assembly of life from nonliving chemicals) could explain the origin of life. Like many of his colleagues, Kenyon did not believe nature needed a God. However, Kenyon changed his mind as scientists discovered how complex the information storage and processing systems are in even the simplest cells. In his words, this is "the most compelling evidence of design on the earth."[1]

## Bases for the Design Inference
### Complex Information

The discovery of DNA's structure in 1953 revealed that life at the cellular level is remarkably complex. In a revelation that surprised and enthralled the world, DNA was shown to be composed of two strands that are connected like rungs in a twisted ladder. The rungs are formed by base-pairs made of four nucleotides: adenine (A), guanine (G), thymine (T), and cytosine (C). These four bases are uniquely paired together (A always with T and G always with C) to create a language so rich that a single cell contains enough information to fill one thousand encyclopedias. If the DNA within one human cell were stretched out, it would be a thin thread about three meters in length. All of the DNA in an adult human strung together would stretch from Earth to the sun and back almost 70 times.

*If the DNA within one human cell were stretched out, it would be a thin thread about three meters in length. All of the DNA in an adult human strung together would stretch from Earth to the sun and back almost 70 times.*

### Protein Sequence

One of the earliest challenges to chemical evolution was the discovery of protein structure. Proteins are the chemical workhorses in a cell, serving in many capacities, such as structural components of the cell and catalysts for metabolic reactions. Approximately 100,000 human proteins are formed by a combination of 20 amino acids. Amino acids are like 20 "letters" of an alphabet. The resulting protein molecule is like a "word" formed by the amino acid letters. A typical protein molecule consists of around 500 amino acids in a highly specific sequence. Just like letters in a word, each amino acid must be in the proper place for the correct protein to form. If the amino acid sequence is wrong, the protein will be misshapen and typically will not perform its intended function. In some cases the result is detrimental to the organism. Sickle-cell anemia, for example, is a genetic disorder where one wrong amino acid is inserted in the protein chain because of the mutation of a single nucleotide.

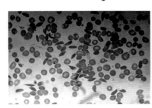
Sickle cells mingling with normal blood cells. Photo: NIH.

### Cracking the Code

Computers store information in a long series of ones and zeros. By itself this information is useless. It takes a code to translate the pattern into meaningful data, such as the sentence you just read. Likewise, the sequence of *A, G, T,* and *C* stored along the backbone of a DNA molecule must be translated into meaningful information that can be used to produce proteins. The genetic code satisfies this need as it translates the pattern of bases *A, G, C,* and *T,* as instructions for manufacturing proteins. The exact sequence of letters defines the step-by-step sequence of amino acids that combine to form protein molecules. This fantastically precise and complex system is present in even the very "simplest" single-cell organisms and points definitively to design, not chance.

### Chicken or the Egg?

In the early twentieth century, Henry Ford revolutionized manufacturing by introducing the assembly line. However, it turns out that biology beat him to the punch, for each cell houses a miniature assembly line. The design specifications for each subsystem in the cell is copied from the DNA; supply workers then read this blueprint and couriers fetch the right parts and bring them to the assembly line; assembly workers systematically add the pieces together according to the directions until the assembly is complete; quality control workers

*Each cell houses a miniature assembly line.*

inspect the completed product, and finally a delivery worker transports the finished product to its destination. This is not merely an analogy, this is exactly the process by which the cell operates. DNA provides the design specifications for the cellular components; molecules known as messenger RNA copy

Part of a 1913 assembly line at a Ford plant.

a specific segment of the assembly instructions; transfer RNA then translates the information coded in DNA into the specific sequence of amino acids; and finally ribosomal RNA assembles the amino acids into the proper sequence to form the specified protein molecule.

## The Mystery of Life

So cells need both DNA and RNA to fabricate proteins, but the information in DNA and RNA cannot be processed without proteins. So which came first? Proteins or nucleic acids (DNA and RNA)? This is a difficult question for the origins of life. Could this whole complex of information and cellular machinery have arisen all at once and by chance? Let Nobel Laureate Harold Urey answer that for you. "We all believe, as an article of faith, that life evolved from dead matter on this planet. It is just that its complexity is so great, it is hard to imagine that it did."[2]

## Rolling the Dice for Life

Just like jet aircraft production, assembling amino acids into the sequence required to produce a functioning protein is no easy task. What are the odds that  this can happen by accident? Let's assume we have equal quantities of all the amino acids in a huge barrel, and we want to calculate the odds of drawing out amino acids in a sequence that results in a functioning protein. Twenty different amino acids are used to make proteins, and nineteen of these come in two varieties: left- or right-handed. Only the left-handed ones are useful for making proteins. This means there are a total of 39 different kinds of amino acids in the barrel, but only twenty of them are eligible for use in protein construction. As each amino acid is randomly selected from the barrel, it

*Assembling amino acids into the sequence required to produce a functioning protein is no easy task.*

must bond to the amino acid selected previously. In this way a polypeptide (protein) is formed piece by piece. But there is no guarantee that this bond will occur. In the absence of the proper enzymes (which, in our experiment, do not exist yet since their existence depends on fully functional cells, complete with DNA, RNA, etc.), the chances of these bonds forming are very, very low.

But for the sake of argument, we will take the probability of this bond forming to be 50 percent. To further increase our chances of success, we will calculate the odds of randomly selecting and successfully forming one of the shortest functional proteins that is common to living systems: the cytochrome-C enzyme (a small protein). It is merely 110 amino acids in length, but we will shorten this further to only 100 amino acids. Now for the math. The odds of getting a specific chain of 100 amino acids by chance would be the probability of selecting the right amino acid (1 out of 39 possibilities) 100 times in a row, and with a 50 percent chance of the chemical bond forming between each. In mathematical notation, that is: Probability = $(1/39)^{100}$ × $(1/2)^{99}$.

This comes out to be $(1/10)^{190}$. Written out, that number looks like: 1 divided by 1,000,000,000,000,000,000,000,000,000,000,000,000,000,000,000,000,000,000,000,000,000,000,000,000,000,000,000,000,000,000,000,000,000,000,000,000,000,000,000,000,000,000,000,000,000,000,000,000,000,000,000,000,000,000,000,000,000,000,000,000,000,000,000,000,000,000,000,000,000,000.

*1 in $10^{50}$ would be the same likelihood that every person on the planet would win the Powerball Grand Prize once per second not just for the rest of their lives but for the next 1,000,000,000,000,000,000,000,000 years!*

Numbers with that many zeros are absolutely meaningless to us.[3] For comparison, a probability of 1 in $10^{50}$ would be the same likelihood that every person on the planet would win the Powerball Grand Prize once per second not just for the rest of their lives but for the next 1,000,000,000,000,000,000,000,000 years! Obviously that cannot happen, and yet this wildly improbable scenario is not nearly as improbable as our amino acid illustration above. Or consider the fact that

*If one proton in the entire universe were painted purple, the chances of your randomly selecting it would be $10^{80}$. Even so, this is still far more probable than an amino acid forming by chance.*

scientists have calculated that there are about $10^{80}$ protons and neutrons in the whole universe. If one proton in the entire universe were painted purple, the chances of your randomly selecting it would be $10^{80}$. Even so, this is still far more probable than our amino acid illustration. So what do you think? Did life arise by chance?

## Alternatives to the Design Inference

### Unknown Ordering Mechanism

Recognizing that the chance formation of protein molecules is impossible, scientists are busy searching for a natural "ordering mechanism"—a law of nature—that would cause amino acids to form and link up in the right sequence to produce a protein. As evidence mounts that life appeared quickly (geologically speaking), scientists are assuming that it must be easy for life to form given the conditions that were present on the early Earth. However, all that we've learned up to now argues for exactly the opposite. But for the sake of argument, suppose such a natural law is soon discovered. Would this overturn the need for a Designer? Absolutely not. Such a law, capable of generating such magnificent living complexity, would of itself be a powerful proof of God's involvement.

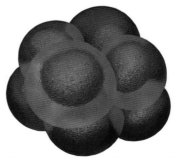

## Summary

Life is complex at the cellular level, where a remarkable biochemical orchestration of replication, transcription, translation,

That we develop from the union of a sperm and egg into a cluster of cells, an embryo, a fetus, and then eventually fully grown humans is one of the greatest of all wonders.

and protein synthesis is daily conducted to sustain the cell's well-being. Surely the psalmist had no idea that his praise of the Creator's handiwork would apply even to a single living cell: "For it was You who created my inward parts; You knit me together in my mother's womb. I will praise You, because I have been remarkably and wonderfully made. Your works are wonderful, and I know this very well" (Ps. 139:13–14).

## Notes

1. This quote is from Kenyon's interview on the DVD entitled, *Where Does the Evidence Lead? Exploring the Theory of Intelligent Design*, produced by Illustra Media, 2003.

2. Harold Urey, interview in *Christian Science Monitor.* (January 4, 1962): 4.

3. The number 1 in $10^{190}$ could possibly be revised downward (toward greater odds) by generously accounting for mitigating factors such as the possibility of different amino acid sequences being capable of a similar enzymatic function, multiple opportunities for a natural environment to perform the chemistry involved, and even the possibility that multiple planets are available for conducting this experiment. However, even if these optimistic factors are included it remains the case that the chances are still less likely than finding the one purple atom in the entire universe! And we are only talking about the chance formation of a single, small enzyme. Accounting for all the other hundreds of molecules and structures required to make a living cell would make the odds all the more impossible.

# Chapter 36
# Impossibilities in Biochemistry: Biological Complexity

## *Beauty and Information*

Humans are awed by great examples of design and beauty. Think of the works of Michelangelo or the night sky and other wonders of nature. It is not so obvious, but underlying all these things are the laws of nature. Even less obvious is the fact that these laws are in and of themselves beautiful and unspeakably complex. This is especially so in the biological sciences where the in-built complexity far exceeds anything dealt with in rocket science. We previously considered the complex design of DNA. Like anything else in the universe, the transmission of genetic information is subject to the second law of thermodynamics. With repeated copying, information degrades beyond recognition. Making photocopies of photocopies is one well-known illustration. What started out as a clear picture becomes

If you make a copy, then copy the copy, and so on down the line, you eventually have a very poor rendition of the orginal.

a blob of ink as the information (quality of image) degrades with each copy event. Information loss is avoided only if a complex repeater system is in place to continuously correct and restore information. Interestingly, the cell provides this service for DNA. Even so, genetic information gets altered or mutated over time.

As information degrades, the products derived from that information also degrade. Hence, complexity decreases as time marches on. Interestingly, that is not the pattern we observe in the historical emergence of biological complexity, where we typically see an *increasing* level of complexity as we move from single-cell organisms to mammals. As the complexity increased, of necessity the information did as well. This is reflected in the different amount of DNA required for lower life and higher life forms. Humans require 23 pairs of chromosomes, whereas the sea slug gets by with only 7 pairs. Humans have about 20,000 genes, whereas 250 to 300 are enough to sustain simple life forms. Where did this increasingly

*Where did this increasingly complex information come from? And how have biological systems advanced against the grain of the second law of thermodynamics?*

complex information come from? And how have biological systems advanced against the grain of the second law of thermodynamics? The usual answer is genetic mutations. But mutations almost exclusively degrade genetic information rather than increase it. Imagine writing a rather poor essay, then giving the file to a monkey to play with on the computer in hopes that the "mutations" it creates will improve the paper. The monkey bangs away at the keyboard inserting all sorts of random changes. By the time he tires of the exercise, the paper will have gone from poor to poorer. Similarly, mutations typically destroy information rather than create it. Following

is a survey of some design complexities that challenge naturalism's claim that the accumulation of small genetic changes leads to increased biological complexity.

## *The Trilobite*

Trilobites lived in seabed environments much like those inhabited by horseshoe crabs today. In fact, trilobites resemble horseshoe crabs in many respects though the ancient trilobite is the more complex of the two. Notice below the trilobed axial symmetry of the trilobite body typified by a specimen of *phacops*. In many ways the trilobite is not all that different from any arthropod one might encounter at the beach today though they have been extinct since the late Devonian era (about 360 million years ago). The Cambrian strata (from the Cambrian era, which began about 600 million years ago) contain an astonishing diversity of life forms and are the deepest, oldest strata to contain significant amounts of multicellular fossils. The Cambrian is the bottom-most layer of the geological column of rocks bearing fossils of multicellular life forms. So in any Darwinian representation of the development of life forms, we would expect to find only simple life forms in those earliest layers of geological history. The abundance of trilobite fossils in the Cambrian strata contradicts

*The Cambrian strata contain an astonishing diversity of life forms and are the deepest, oldest strata to contain significant amounts of multicellular fossils.*

Trilobites are extinct arthopods that included roughly 17,000 species.

this expectation, for it had a very modern arthropod body plan and the most complex visual system known in the entire animal kingdom, living or extinct.

*The existence of the complex trilobite in an ancient strata demonstrates that, contrary to all Darwinist expectations, at least some examples of complex life existed in Earth's earliest eras.*

Each of the many lenses in the trilobite eye has its own separate imaging element. Thus, the trilobite eye forms the optical equivalent of a phased-array radar that can track multiple objects at the same time without moving. This means that while the trilobite eye cannot swivel, it can follow the movement of multiple objects around it through nearly 360 degrees! No other known organism has such a complex visual system.

The Chicago Museum of Natural History displayed a tree of evolution chart some years ago, as sketched here by Hill Roberts. Their chart placed the trilobite at the *top* of the tree rather than near the bottom, based on its astonishing complexity. But it is found in the deepest strata and thus indicates that complex biological information appeared early in Earth history. So in summary we see that biological complexity defeats naturalistic evolution in two ways. First, complexity typically increases over time in the fossil record in ways that are very difficult to account for by strictly Darwinist mechanisms. Second, the existence of the complex trilobite in ancient strata demonstrates that at least some examples of complex life existed in Earth's earliest eras. This is a hard knock against Darwinism since that theory relies on the postulation that life proceeds from simple to complex as small changes build complexity over time.

## Vision

Darwin said the complexity of the eye presents a challenge to his theory of natural selection. "To suppose that the eye, with all its inimitable contrivances for adjusting the focus to different distances, for admitting different amounts of light and for the correction of spherical and chromatic aberrations, could have been formed by natural selection, seems, I freely confess, absurd in the highest degree."[1] Nevertheless, he was hopeful that his theory could account for the eye. More recently, Richard Dawkins elaborated on Darwin's conjecture about the naturalistic origin of the eye in neo-Darwinian terms.[2] First, says Dawkins, by mutation there

Darwin knew the eye presented a serious challenge to the role chance plays in his theory.

came to be an organism with a light sensitive spot that was useful for establishing a day-night biorhythm. Many generations later, one of this organism's offspring produced a dimple overtop this light-sensitive spot. Hence, the basic shape of the modern eye had arisen. This advance imbued the organism with a directional light-detection capability, useful for orientation and food tracking. Natural selection ensured that this advantageous mutation was passed on since it conferred greater ability to survive, thrive, and reproduce. As time passed, a random mutation just happened to

*"To suppose that the eye . . . could have been formed by natural selection, seems, I freely confess, absurd in the highest degree."*

— *Charles Darwin*, **Origin of Species**

cause the dimple to produce gel, and happily the gel actually helped the eye because it increases its light collecting power and provides protection for the light-sensitive cells. Finally, in later generations mutations formed a hardened film over the gelatinous material, thus forming a rudimentary lens to further improve the optic performance.

What are the odds that these things truly happened by mutation? Consider the ostensibly simple light-sensitive spot.

Sensitivity to light requires the following steps: First, a photon enters the light-sensitive cell and interacts with a rhodopsin protein (which just *happens* to be there!). This protein contains organic dyes that adsorb energy from the photon, causing the rhodopsin protein to change shape. The reconfigured rhodopsin is now able to bind to another protein called transducin. This new molecule is unstable, and so a portion of it drops off and is replaced by a GTP molecule which stabilizes the structure.

*What are the odds that these things truly happened by mutation?*

This megamolecule is now able to bind to a molecule of photodiesterase, which is fixed on the wall of the cell's outer membrane. The cell wall has a series of ports which open and close to allow charged ions such as sodium and calcium to cross in and out of the cell. These ports are controlled by a membrane molecule called cGMP. More cGMP keeps the ports closed; less allows the ports to open. When the megamolecule (officially called GTP-transducin-metarhodopsin II) binds to the photodiesterase on the cell wall, some of the cGMP is displaced, thus lowering the cGMP concentration. This allows some of the ion ports to open up, which in turn allows positively charged sodium ions to enter the cell. Since the ions carry an electrical charge, this induces a charge imbalance across the cell wall, which results in a voltage being established across the membrane. The voltage seeks equilibrium

by propagating along the cell membrane until it gets to another cell and jumps the gap to begin the propagation of an electrical signal from one cell to the next.

We have just described the process required to obtain the first step of Darwin/Dawkins's scheme: the light-sensitive spot. Sound like something that can arise by mutation? If any of these steps or components is missing, the process does not work. Hence, everything had to be in place at once, else the system was useless and cannot have been selected by the natural selection process which only selects for functional systems that confer advantage to the organism. Behe calls

*Dawkins's first step on the road map to vision is a step off the cliff of impossibility.*

systems such as the eye "irreducibly complex" because they cannot have arisen by the slow accumulation of successive changes from mutations. It must come into existence as a fully functional whole to have any utility at all. Obviously, this presents a problem for the theory that complexity builds over time as mutations accumulate. Dawkins's first step on the road map to vision is a step off the cliff of impossibility.

## The Flagellum

Imagine you are a naturalist and you are walking along the beach admiring all the things nature has produced through unguided mutation and selection. Before long you find a cylindrical object about the size of a soda can. Its casing encloses a shaft which rotates, thus turning a cordlike appendage which emerges from one end of the shaft. This appendage has connectors at its terminus, allowing it to attach to other equipment. You pry the case open and discover that the shaft has a series of wires that connect through slip rings to a plug on the outside of the shaft. Furthermore, the inside wall of the shaft has magnets attached to it.

Hook (universal joint)

Filament (propeller)

L ring ⎫
⎬ (bushing)
P ring ⎭

Rod (drive shaft)

S ring ⎫
⎬ (rotor)
M ring ⎭

You now recognize that you are holding an electric motor. Though you are a naturalist, would you suppose this were a product of mutation? Not likely, for electric motors require electrical engineers to design and build them. Yet many cells contain such complex motors. One example is the bacterial flagellum, which inspired the above description. The flagellum is the long cord-like appendage at the posterior end of a bacterium. Like the propeller on an outboard boat motor, the flagellum twirls around and drives the bacterium

*Like the propeller on an outboard boat motor, the flagellum twirls around and drives the bacterium forward through the fluid of the cell.*

forward through the fluid of the cell. The flagellum is powered by an electrochemical motor embedded in the bacterium's cell wall. Amazingly, these motors rotate at speeds in excess of 10,000 revolutions per minute!

## Ecosystems

Most of us learned in grade school that the food chain starts with the sun. Plants absorb sunshine and convert it to a form of energy that helps them use the minerals they absorb through their roots to build plant biomass. Plants are in turn the basic food stuff for the animal world. For example, bunnies (herbivores)

Rabbits multiply rapidly. Fortunately, predators keep their population in check.

eat the plants; thus the sun's energy is passed to the plant and then on to the bunny. Far from just serving itself, the bunny is helping keep plants in check by eating them; else the world would be overrun by jungle. But bunnies can overrun the world faster than plants if left uncontrolled, and so carnivores such as foxes are present to prevent this. Foxes eat the bunnies, but they expend an enormous amount of effort chasing them down and therefore lack the energy resources for producing hordes of offspring. Such factors keep the carnivores in check; else they would devour all the lower animals and thereby wreck the ecosystem.

Omnivores such as humans are at the top of the food

chain and are vital in keeping this balance, for they can eat either plants or animals. Furthermore, they expend some of the highest levels of energy of all organisms to maintain their life cycles and thus produce the fewest offspring. The food chain finally loops back around to the starting point when the

*Reason dictates that nature and its products are the work of a Designer.*

remains of plants and animals are chewed up by insects and bacteria, which eventually die and give their materials back to the ground for the plants to reabsorb.

Such "system balance" is difficult to design, for balance must be made between factors such as individual component design and overall system design. The ecosystem and its particulars (plants, bunnies, foxes, humans, etc.) practice give-and-take in order to achieve the most workable design for all parties involved. Otherwise, either the system or its particulars will wield unequaled power. Given the complexity of Earth's ecosystem, it is clearly the product of supreme engineering rather than chance.

## Conclusion

Naturalists insist that each of the above examples can be explained via mutation and natural selection. However, it remains the case that no adequate explanations have been put

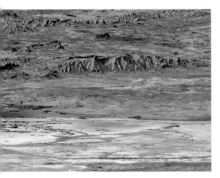

forth. And hypothetically, if scientists are ever able to show that such complex systems can arise as an outcome of merely natural processes, this would only move the question back to an even more fundamental position: how did nature come to be laden with such fantastic capacities? In any case, reason dictates that nature and its products are the work of a Designer.

Earth's ecosystem is comlpex and delicately balanced. In short, it is the work of a Grand Designer. Photo of SRTM Perspective View with Landsat Overlay: Rann of Kachchh, India by NASA/JPL.

## *Notes*

1. Darwin, *Origin of Species*, 1859.

2. See Dawkins's book, *The Blind Watchmaker* (New York: W. W. Norton, 1996).

# Chapter 37
# Impossibilities in Anthropology: The Image of God

We differ from animals in many ways, yet when we stare into the eyes of an orangutan, we see something of ourselves in the strangely familiar face. This can be a deeply moving but also disturbing experience. After all, are we really so different from them? Do we have immortal souls, or are we destined, like orangutans, for the long night of nonexistence? This chapter will explore such questions.

Recognize this guy? The comb-over might resemble your dad's, but are orangutans part of your family tree?

## *Human Significance: What the Naturalists Are Saying*

Popular advocates of naturalism insist that humans are mere animals who have no transcendent purpose to our existence. Here are some examples:

"We are here because one odd group of fishes had a peculiar fin anatomy that could transform into legs for terrestrial creatures; because the earth never froze entirely during an ice age; because a small and tenuous species, arising in Africa a quarter of a million years ago, has managed, so far, to survive by hook and by crook. We may yearn for a 'higher' answer — but none exists."
— *Stephen J. Gould* [1]

---

"The universe that we observe has precisely the properties we should expect if there is, at bottom, no design, no purpose, no evil, no good, nothing but blind, pitiless indifference."
— *Richard Dawkins* [2]

---

"We are the children of chaos, and the deep structure of change is decay. At root, there is only corruption, and the unstemmable tide of chaos. Gone is purpose; all that is left is direction. This is the bleakness we have to accept as we peer deeply and dispassionately into the heart of the universe."
— *Peter Atkins* [3]

---

"The important point about the standard evolutionary story is that the human species and all of its features are the wholly physical outcome of a purely physical process. . . . If this is the correct account of our origins then there is neither need, nor room, to fit any nonphysical substances or properties into our theoretical account of ourselves. We are creatures of matter. And we should learn to live with that fact."
— *Paul Churchland* [4]

## Challenging the Naturalistic Worldview

Obviously, naturalists think humans are essentially indistinct from animals and that the universe is a morally neutral product of chance, time, and matter. But does this really fit with the human experience? The following brief survey addresses this question.

### Quest for Knowledge of Ultimate Things

Humans yearn for knowledge of ultimate things, including God and purpose. But if no such things exist in a naturalistic universe, and if humans are merely the product of such a universe, how is it that we have longings for things that do not exist? The natural world cannot have produced these desires in us. If nature is at bottom wholly indifferent and humankind is nothing but a piece of natural lint, we would be indifferent about God and higher purpose.

Humans yearn for knowledge of ultimate things.

### Evil

In a naturalistic universe good and evil are mere words, not true realities. Does this fit with human experience? The Bible affirms that such things as murder, theft, slander, racism, greed and hatred are offenses against the morality of God Himself. Surely this matches our heart's cry better than naturalism.

*If the universe is the result of random chaos, why do such immaterial things as beauty, math, and logic exist?*

### Order and Beauty

If the universe is the result of random chaos, why do such

immaterial things as beauty, math, and logic exist? Stars and galaxies and morning dew are all explainable from highly precise, logical, and mathematical standpoints, yet they are all beautiful as well. Can materialism explain this? The mathematician James Jeans

Random chance cannot accout for the order and beauty we find in the universe.

once opined that the universe appears to be more of a great thought than a great machine. Naturalism cannot account for this fact.

### Morality

If we are the product of chance, how does Paul Churchland (above) justify saying we "should" come to grips with it?

*There can be no "should" in a material universe, for we are not answerable to any higher power.*

There can be no "should" in a material universe, for we are not answerable to any higher power. By his own worldview, Churchland is nothing more than an articulate blob of carbon-based macromolecules and has no basis for making an appeal to moral obligation.

## The Measure of Man

Humans are like many animals in terms of overall body plan, especially primates. As is widely noted among scientists, we share over 99 percent of our DNA with chimpanzees. In light of these similarities, when anthropologists go to the field in search of human ancestors, they have a list of characteristics to help identify human remains. These include evidences such as:

- A 2–1–2–3 tooth pattern.

- A parabolic arched jaw (instead of V-shaped as in chimps, or U-shaped as in gorillas).

- A large primate brain (on the order of 1250 cc, rather than 300–500 for other primates).

Anthropologists look for a 2-1-2-3 tooth pattern when examining hominid fossils.

- No sagital crest on the top of the skull (versus a rather large one in other primates).

- A rounded occipital bone (instead of a flattened occipital).

- Smallish brow ridges (rather than heavy, thick brows).

- A vertical forehead and chin (rather than sloped ones).

- Bipedal limb structures fit predominantly for walking rather than crawling or climbing.

- Vertical foramen magnum — the skull's hole for the spine (rather than rearward for other primates).

- Opposable thumbs.

- Evidence of massive learning (versus mostly propagation of instinctive behaviors).

- Tool-making as a creative endeavor (versus using the occasional stick to poke at ants).

- Use of language.

- Culture, family, social behaviors.

- Some type of religious belief/practice.

The last few evidences are especially important in helping us define how humans differ from even the most intelligent animals. How many chimps or orangutans talk, philosophize, build cities, read books, decode their genes, or worship God? Those are distinctly human activities. Animals, especially those in the wild, are almost wholly engaged in the processes of getting food and producing offspring. Instinct drives them, not intellect. Blind urges, not moral conviction. In other words, they are not at all Godlike, as humans are. To see more clearly what it means for us to be Godlike, we must look beyond physical appearances into the mind, soul, and spirit.

## Mind and Matter

More than a 2–1–2–3 tooth pattern, bipedal limbs or rounded occipital bones, it is the *mind* that separates humans from animals. MIT's Marvin Minsky once said the human mind is simply "a computer made of meat."[5] This assumes that the mind is exactly the same thing as the brain, but this is mistaken. The physical brain is an organ that allows a nonphysical mind to occupy a physical body.

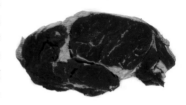

Is the human brain merely a computer made of meat?

Anthropologist Marilyn Schlitz says, "I would take the position of a radical empiricist, in that I am driven by data, not theory. And the data I see tell me that there are ways in which people's experience refutes the physicalist position that the mind is the brain and nothing more. There are solid, concrete data that suggest that our consciousness, our mind, may surpass the boundaries of the brain."[6]

As recounted by J. P. Moreland in Lee Strobel's *The Case for a Creator*, "Neurosurgeon Wilder Penfield electrically stimulated the brains of epilepsy patients and found that he could cause them to move their arms or legs, turn the heads or eyes, talk, or swallow. Invariably, the patient would respond by saying, 'I didn't do that, you did.' According to Penfield, the patient thinks of himself as having an existence separate from his body." Moreland goes on to say, "No matter how much Penfield probed the cerebral cortex, he said 'there is no place . . . where electrical stimulation will cause a patient to believe or decide.' That's because those functions originate in the conscious self, not the brain."[7]

> *The physical brain is an organ that allows a non-physical mind to occupy a physical body.*

With our minds we reason, think, decide, and choose. It is the ultimate point of origin for all our actions, for the mind conceives a plan and provides the impetus for fulfilling that plan. This is why the mind (a.k.a., the will) does more to shape a person than any other part of their being. Getting to know someone is not a matter of becoming familiar with their hair color, height, or body weight. It is getting a grasp of what they think, what they feel, what lights their fires. Science cannot help you there, for grasping a person's mind is not a matter of studying empirical data. There is no test that measures thought. Sure, there are tests that measure brain activity, but the thought itself is not the same thing as the electrical activity that accompanies it. J. B. S. Haldane exposed the fallacy of supposing that the self is merely a complex collection of atoms. "If my mental processes are determined wholly by the motions of the atoms in my brain, I have no reason to suppose that my beliefs are true . . . and hence, I have no reason for supposing my brain to be composed of atoms."[8] Reaching a similar conclusion, Charles Sherrington

*Thoughts, beliefs, and moods are not the mere product of electrical firing in the material brain. The immaterial mind plays an essential role.*

observes that, "A radical distinction has therefore arisen between life and mind. The former is an affair of chemistry and physics; the latter escapes chemistry and physics."[9]

If thought is just the product of firing neurons, we should praise or condemn our neurons for the quality of choices we make.

Fortunately, the mind is not a slave to the motions of atoms in the brain. Mind and brain are interrelated certainly, but in essence the mind is master to the brain. It is from the mind that higher things such as moral consciousness, artistic creativity, problem solving, love, and altruism spring. It makes no sense to say that these things arise simply from the electrical activity of brain cells. For this reason Sir John Eccles, Nobel Laureate in neurophysiology, wrote, "I am constrained to attribute the uniqueness of the Self, or Soul, to a supernatural Spiritual creation."[10]

## The Morality of Man

As mentioned in chapter 7, Dr. Francis Collins heads up the Human Genome Project, which mapped the human genetic library. In an interview with CNN in 2006, Collins shares that he was raised by unbelieving parents and that he had adopted their unbelief for himself.

Dr. Francis Collins, director of the Human Genome Project. Photo: National Human Genome Research Institute (Maggie Bartlett).

But then I went to medical school, and encountered life and death issues at the bedsides of my patients. Challenged by one of those patients, who asked "What do you believe, doctor?" I began searching for answers. I had to admit that the science I loved so much was powerless to answer questions such as "What is the meaning of life? Why am I here? Why does mathematics work, anyway? If the universe had a beginning, who created it? Why are the physical constants in the universe so finely tuned to allow the possibility of complex life forms? Why do humans have a moral sense? What happens after we die?" . . . [I later discovered] that one could build a very strong case for the plausibility of the existence of God on purely rational grounds. . . . But reason alone cannot prove the existence of God. Faith is reason plus revelation, and the revelation part requires one to think with the spirit as well as with the mind. You have to hear the music, not just read the notes on the page. Ultimately, a leap of faith is required.

For me, that leap came in my 27th year, after a search to learn more about God's character led me to the person of Jesus Christ. Here was a person with remarkably strong historical evidence of his life, who made astounding statements about loving your neighbor, and whose claims about being God's son seemed to demand a decision about whether he was deluded or the real thing. After resisting for nearly two years, I found it impossible to go on living in such a state of uncertainty, and I became a follower of Jesus.[11]

C. S. Lewis presents a case for morality in his classic *Mere Christianity*. He argues that everyone has an innate sense of right and wrong. Not everyone agrees on the particulars, but everyone agrees that the categories of right and wrong exist. When we argue over whether a given action is

*The moral law is reflective of God's holiness. In the end, it is God, not the moral law, whom we contradict with our sinful behaviors.*

right or wrong, we make our case by appealing to a universal standard. This standard is moral law, an unwritten code that stands over all of us. Francis Collins was influenced by Lewis's arguments and describes the moral argument this way: "What is being debated is whether one action or another is a closer approximation to the demands of that [moral] law. Those

*Moral law convicts us all of sin, revealing that we fall short of its standard.*

accused of having fallen short, such as the husband who is insufficiently cordial to his wife's friend, usually respond with a variety of excuses why they should be let off the hook."[12]

So the moral law stands over us as judge of our behaviors,

but it also helps us choose the good. If we choose to jump into a river to save a drowning child, risking our own life in the process, it is moral law that helped us make this choice. Moral law confirms that you have done the right thing when you choose the good, or alternatively, it condemns your choices when you choose the bad. Ultimately moral law convicts us all of sin, revealing that we fall short of its standard.

*The only solution to our moral offensiveness is to turn to the very God whom we have offended and ask that He pardon us as we place our faith in the One who paid our penalty, Jesus Christ.*

This is because moral law is reflective of God's holiness. In the end, it is God, not moral law, whom we contradict with our sinful behaviors. This is why the only solution to our moral offensiveness is to turn to the God whom we have offended and ask that He pardon us as we place our faith in the One who paid our penalty, Jesus Christ.

## *Notes*

1. Gould quoted in Ravi Zacharias, *Can Man Live Without God?* (Dallas: Word, 1994), 31.

2. Richard Dawkins, "God's Utility Function," *Scientific American* (November 1995): 85.

3. P. W. Atkins, *The Second Law: Energy, Chaos and Form.* (New York: Scientific American Library, 1984).

4. Paul Churchland, *Matter and Consciousness* (Cambridge: MIT Press, 1984), 21.

5. Marvin Minsky is cited in Lee Stroble, *The Case for a Creator* (Grand Rapids: Zondervan, 2004), 80.

6. Marilyn Schlitz is cited in Lee Stroble, *The Case for a Creator*, 251–252.

7. Cited in *The Case for the Creator*, 258.

8. Haldane's quote originally appears in "When I Am Dead," in *Possible Worlds and Other Essays* (London: Chatto

and Windus, 1927), 209. C. S. Lewis quotes Haldane in his book, *Miracles* (London: Fontana, 1947), 19.

9. Sherrington is quoted in Theodosius Dobzhansky, *Human Culture: A Moment in Evolution* (New York: Columbia University Press, 1983), 67.

10. Sir John Eccles, *Evolution of the Brain, Creation of the Self* (New York: Routledge, 1991), 237.

11. Dr. Collins wrote this as a special article for CNN.com on April 6, 2007. The title is "Collins: Why this scientist believes in God." The article was accessed at http://www.cnn.com/2007/US/04/03/collins.commentary/index.html on 9 January 2008.

12. "Excerpt: 'The Language of God' Author Francis Collins Shares Personal Testimony to Explain Reasoning," from http://abcnews.go.com/GMA/Story?id=2192678&page=3, accessed 18 October 2007.

# Part VIII

# Apes, Bones, and Human Ancestry

# Chapter 38
# Apes and Cavemen: Our Ancestors?

## Who Are Your Ancestors?

If you were given a photo album which included a picture of every one of your ancestors, recent and ancient, you would see some pretty interesting things. Most likely you would discover folks from places and ethnicities you never would have guessed. Big people, small people, brave people, and smart people — people of every variety would compose your album. But if you were to look really far back in the past, would the

1871 cartoon of Charles Darwin.

album include hairy apes and grubby cavemen? Most of us would instinctively say no, but Time-Life published a chart in 1974 that clearly suggests otherwise. You have probably seen it. It depicts a succession of creatures walking one behind another from monkey to modern man.

This chart cemented in popular opinion the idea that we came "up from apes." It also cemented the idea that "cavemen" were not fully human but were instead something between ape and human. On what evidence was the chart based? The text under the chart says it all: "[This chart] is a revealing story not only for the changes it shows, but also because it illustrates how much can be learned from so little." What they don't tell you is that "so little" refers to a mere pile of fossils that could all be placed into a single shoebox. Not surprisingly, this paltry evidence was not enough to justify the chart, and so all the members in the middle portion of the chart (oreopithecus, ramapithecus, austropithecus robustus, and paranthropus) were eventually kicked out of the progression. The evidence, once properly evaluated, fell far short of justifying the famous chart.

## Misfires in the Search for the Missing Link

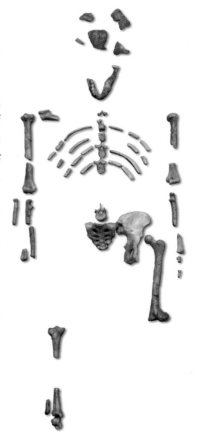

*Ramapithecus* serves as a nice example of the danger of basing far-flung theories on little evidence. When *Ramapithecus* was first discovered, all that was found was a broken upper jaw pallet and a few teeth, yet it was quickly heralded as "The Missing Link." At about the same time cooler heads realized that *Ramapithecus* was really just an ordinary *Sivapithecus,* an orangutan. Hence, *Ramapithecus* was no longer a candidate for human ancestry, but of course this admission was not heralded with fanfare.

After the demise of *Ramapithecus,* other fossil finds were advanced to replace it. The most famous of these is Lucy, known

Replica of Lucy in the National Museum of Natural History in Paris.

scientifically as *Australopithecus afarensis*. "Lucy" is the name given to a nearly complete skeleton found in the southern Afar region of Africa. She has skeletal features consistent with bipedalism (walks on two feet), which you would expect of a missing link, and was dated to 3.5 million years, which fits nicely with prevailing expectations. For these reasons Lucy was immediately a cause for celebration among many scientists. But what of her other features? Though scientists initially downplayed or ignored problematic evidence, the fact that the skeleton is only 3.5 feet tall, has a strictly V-shaped jaw, arms that are longer than her legs, and a brain case the size of a chimp's eventually convinced experts that Lucy is not an ancestor to humans.

## What about Cave Men and Neanderthals?

One picture that emerges from the anthropological evidence is that humans that were modern anatomically and culturally did not show up until fairly recently. Additionally, as is true of every species in the fossil record, humans show up abruptly. There is a gap of several million years

*The biblical narrative and time line indicate that humans were created in the near past.*

between quasi-humanoid candidates (such as *Homo erectus*)

and *Homo sapiens*, who date from only tens of thousands of years ago. In that regard the evidence nicely matches the biblical narrative and time line which indicates that humans were created in the near past, not millions of years ago. One further implication of this evidence is that Cro-Magnon (Cave Man) was not an intermediary between apes and humans but was rather actually human. Cro-Magnon remains are anatomically human in all

Reconstruction of Neandertal at the Neanderthal Museum in Germany.

regards. That they did not leave behind stunning examples of human accomplishment is not evidence against their genuine humanness. What enduring evidence would you leave behind if you had to fend for yourself in the wild? Besides, they did manage to leave behind cave art depicting literal and abstract images of animals.

But what about Neanderthal (a.k.a. Neandertal) fossils? They predate Cro-Magnon fossils by as much as 100,000 years or more. Neanderthals apparently exhibited some behaviors that recall human behavior, such as burying their dead in graves cov-

This is a hypothetical reconstruction of a Neaderthal child based on skeletal remains found at Gibralter. This model is kept at the Anthropological Institute at the University of Zurich. Phtoto: Christoph P. E. Zollikofer.

ered in flowers. Were they human? Prehuman? Scientists are still divided on this issue. However, tests of Neanderthal DNA (extracted from fossilized bones) seem to indicate that the human genome does not include Neanderthal DNA, which means the Neanderthal were not humans. Nevertheless, it seems wisest to say that the jury is still out on Neanderthal. As usual, the evidence is incomplete, and we await the possibility of future discoveries that may help answer outstanding questions. Patience is truly a virtue regarding such issues as this. But

*Patience is truly a virtue regarding such issues as this.*

even if Neanderthal were fully human, then it would still be true that the age of humanity would be measured in tens of thousands of years (a couple hundred thousand at most) rather than millions of years. And it would still be true that there is at least a two-million-year gap between these specimens and the next best candidates now known for human forebears. It is true that an ancient primate dubbed *Homo erectus* appears to have made flaked stone tools and maybe used fire, but that is about the extent of his "human" traits. Chimpanzees use sticks they shape to fish for ants in anthills, and other animals are known to fracture rocks for use in opening shelled foods. Needless to say, these actions do not mean these animals are humans.

## Conclusion

Humans date to less than one hundred thousand years past. It is true that some early men found it convenient to live in caves since they provide good shelter and require minimal maintenance, but these men were no less human for it. Bear in mind that conditions were more difficult then. You ate only what you killed or gathered, and consequently men often had no spare time for building homes. In summary, the fossil evidence has not provided convincing proof of human-ape ancestry, and the so-called cavemen differed from you and me only insomuch as they enjoyed far fewer advantages from technology, medicine, and so forth.

*Science has not been able to provide fossil evidence for human-ape ancestry, and the so-called cavemen differed from you and me only insomuch as they enjoyed far fewer advantages from technology, medicine, and so forth.*

# Chapter 39
# Fossils

## *Fossilized Trees and Noah's Flood*

Fossils are the mineralized remains of dead plants and animals. Except for rare circumstances, most organisms disappear without a trace after death. However, some become fossilized if the carcass is entombed in conditions that prevent decay. This most frequently occurs underwater because lakebeds and seafloors are low in oxygen, a situation that forestalls decay and allows the slow buildup of overlying sediments. We can observe these processes today as large beds of seashells are continually buried along the continental shelf to become limestone. We can also observe the formation of mineralized trees in places such as the hot springs in Yellowstone National Park.

> *Fossils are the mineralized remains of dead plants and animals.*

The trees in the picture on the following page are nearly 100 percent mineralized at the roots and lower trunks. Barring erosion, or some other destructive intervention, they will maintain their treelike form essentially forever. Now imagine that the area where they stand is repeatedly inundated by mudslides or lava flows which subsequently harden into layers of rock. In this case these trees would be found to penetrate

Fully mineralized trees at Yellowstone National Park, Mammoth Hot Springs. Photo by National Park Service/Rosalie LaRue.

multiple strata because they were standing upright in fossilized condition as layer was added to layer all around them until the trees were largely or completely buried. This in fact has happened at Yellowstone, where some forty such layers appear with fossilized trees penetrating strata that were laid down ages apart. Some advocates of flood geology claim that such trees (called polystrate fossils), and all the layers surrounding them were fossilized *at the same time*. But the layers were clearly laid down at different times during different local cataclysms, and the fossilized trees transect multiple layers because the trees were fossilized *before* each of the surrounding layers were laid down and hardened.

## *Fossils and Evolution*

Evolutionists have a love-hate relationship with the fossil record. It is at one and the same time the chief cause of their theories and the chief liability to those theories. Charles Darwin was well aware of the situation when he published *Origin of Species* in 1859. Speaking of the intermediate links which are so vital to his theory, Darwin admitted, "Geology assuredly does not reveal any such finely graduated organic change, and this is perhaps the most obvious and serious objection which can be urged against the theory [of evolution]."[1] Recognizing that this is a serious problem, Darwin offered the following honest assessment: "The geological record is extremely imperfect . . . [and this] will to a large extent explain why . . . we do not find interminable varieties, connecting together all the extinct and

> *"Geology assuredly does not reveal any such finely graduated organic change, and this is perhaps the most obvious and serious objection which can be urged against the theory [of evolution]."*
>
> — *Charles Darwin*

existing forms of life by the finest graduated steps. . . . He who rejects these views on the nature of the geological record, will rightly reject my whole theory."[2]

Darwin himself feared that the "imperfect" fossil record might overturn his theory.

We should appreciate Darwin's honesty. If the fossils don't confirm his theory, the theory should be rejected. So, have fossil discoveries since Darwin's day relieved or confirmed his concerns? David Raup, curator of the Museum of Natural History in Chicago, has an answer. "Well, we are now about 120 years after Darwin, and knowledge of the fossil record has been greatly expanded. . . . Ironically, we have even fewer examples of evolutionary transition than we had in Darwin's time. By this I mean that some of the classic cases of Darwinian change in the fossil record, such as the evolution of the horse in North America, have had to be discarded or modified as a result of more detailed information."[3]

In advocating his own punctuated equilibrium theory of

evolution, renowned paleontologist Stephen J. Gould once revealed what he called "the trade secret of paleontology," which was the "the extreme rarity of transitional forms."[4] He did not mean that there is no traceable variation in fossil-bearing strata or even some apparent intermediate forms. Rather, he was emphasizing the fact that rather than a smooth, linear Darwinian form of evolution (such as required by the laws of genetics), the fossil record is replete with long periods of stasis (stability) punctuated with dramatic shifts and replacements of such magnitude as to obscure any intermediate transitionals as envisioned by strict Darwinism. James Valentine has commented helpfully on this discrepancy:

> One of the issues that is currently being debated among theorists derives from a notable fact observed in the fossil record. That is, when a new species appears in the record it usually does so abruptly and then apparently remains stable for as long as the record of that species  lasts. The fossils do not seem to exhibit the slow and gradual changes that might be expected according to the modern synthesis. For this reason, in part, a number of evolutionists—most notably Stephen Jay Gould of Harvard University and Niles Eldredge of the American Museum of Natural History—have proposed a variant concept of "punctuated equilibria" for species evolution. According to this concept, species do in fact tend to remain stable for long periods of time and then to change relatively abruptly—or rather, to be replaced suddenly by newer and more successful forms. These sudden changes are the "punctuations" in the state of equilibrium that give this concept its name.[5]

If there are no convincing transitional fossils, that means there is no record of any "finely graduated organic change." In this case we should follow Darwin's advice and reject his theory of naturalistic gradualism. Niles Eldredge, paleontologist with the American Museum of Natural History, sums up some of the chief difficulties. "No wonder paleontologists shied away from evolution for so long. It never seems to happen. Assiduous collecting up cliff faces yields zigzags, minor oscillations, and the very occasional slight accumulation of change — over millions of years, at a rate too slow to account for all the prodigious change that has occurred in evolutionary history. When we do see the introduction of evolutionary novelty, it usually shows up with a bang, and often with no firm evidence that the fossils did not evolve elsewhere! Evolution cannot forever be going on somewhere else. Yet that's how the fossil record has struck many a forlorn paleontologist looking to learn something about evolution."[6]

> *If there are no convincing transitional fossils, we should follow Darwin's advice and reject his theory of naturalistic gradualism.*

By this point you may be wondering why these experts are so pessimistic. After all, everyone has seen the comprehensive standard tree of evolution representing all the fossils and living groups that have evolved from the common ancestor. By all appearances scientists have pieced the whole picture together nicely. The diagram above is a typical example. The tips of the branches

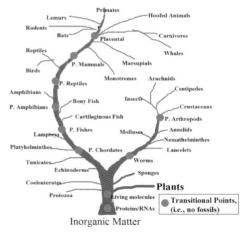

represent living varieties. All the transitional fossils are represented by the various branching points. Grand-scale evolution, where fish are becoming amphibians, for example, occurs at the branch connections. But this is where the problem lies, for these are exactly the points at which the fossil evidence breaks down.

If we were to blank out everywhere on the tree where there

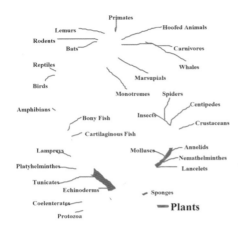

Inorganic Matter

really is no direct supporting data, either in living or fossil form, there is not much tree left. The fossil record appears rather grim if one is committed to the slow process of Darwinian evolution on the grand scale. There are all sorts of microevolutionary "bushes" to be found in the fossil record, but that is a whole different thing from the sort of evolution that includes ape-to-man progression. And one must ask: If evidence for microevolution is so well attested in the fossil record, why would macroevolution not also be well attested?

Alfred Roemer offered a variation of the tree of life, which we include below. It plots the abundance of vertebrates in the fossil record. Geological time proceeds from bottom to top on the chart, and complexity is plotted left to right with the jawless fish on the left and mammals on the far right. The width of the inkblot is a measure of the abundance of the type of vertebrate as represented in the fossil data. The dashed lines show the common ancestral lineage. The inkblots are plots

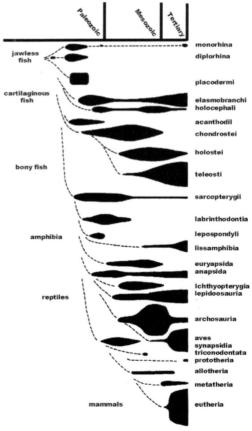

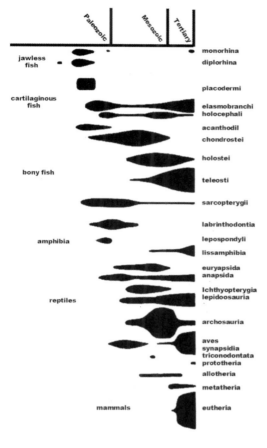

of data. The dashed lines are Roemer's interpolation. This means there is no data for the dashed lines: if there were he would have shown it as inkblot. Why did he include the dashed lines? Well, consider what the chart looks like without them:

Without the dashed lines, the actual fossils show sudden beginnings and then pretty much stay the same until extinction. There are no gradual transitions and thus no links to a single common ancestor. This is why paleontologists such as Gould and Eldredge formed their "punctuated equilibrium" model for grand-scale evolution, as shown here:

Notice how all the various adaptive bushes show up at once with respect to time (vertical direction). This better reflects the actual fossil data than does the older Darwinian trees. The fact that all the bushes start nearly at the same time is a direct reflection of the Cambrian Explosion—a time when new life forms exploded onto the scene all across the globe. Before this era there are very few fossils to speak of. In other words, there are no convincing transitionals leading up to the Cambrian diversification. To put it another way, that horizontal "root" in the punctuated equilibrium model above is an interpolation. No data directly supports it. Again, consider how that would look if we blank out where there is no actual fossil data:

Fossil data gives support to the notion that life appears rapidly in geological terms. The speed with which new life arose is very problematic for all views that do not appeal to supernatural causation. After all, large-scale biological change through genetic mutation cannot occur so rapidly. For that matter, it is difficult to get a series of small adaptive changes to add up to major changes even over millions or billions of years.

## Conclusion

The theory of Punctuated Equilibrium was considered heretical by many scientists when it was first introduced, for while it gives a reasonable account of the fossil record, its postulation of the sudden appearance of life reminds many observers of creationist arguments. On the other hand, the traditional Darwinian view avoids creationism but suffers a lack of evidence in the fossil record. Will the divide between these two parties be resolved anytime soon? British physicist Alan Hayward believes not.

*The theory of Punctuated Equilibrium was considered heretical by many scientists when it was first introduced, for while it gives a reasonable account of the fossil record, its postulation of the sudden appearance of life reminds many observers of creationism.*

The controversy is likely to go on for a long time, since both sides have at least one [strong] suit. Orthodox Darwinism offers a plausible biological explanation for what might have happened, but is in conflict with the evidence of geology. And the alternative theory accepts the geological record but cannot explain how species could arise so suddenly. To the outside observer it seems that both these versions of Darwinism are on shaky ground.[7]

## *Notes*

1. Charles Darwin, *Origin of Species*, Harvard Classics (Collier & Sons, 1909), 334.

2. Ibid., 391.

3. "Conflicts Between Darwin and Paleontology," *Field Museum Bulletin*, 1979.

4. Stephen Jay Gould, "Evolution's Erratic Pace," in *Natural History* 86 (May 1977): 14.

5. James Valentine, "Evolution," Microsoft Encarta97.

6. Niles Eldredge, *Reinventing Darwin: The Great Debate at the High Table of Evolutionary Theory* (New York: Willey, 1995), 95.

7. Alan Hayward, *Creation and Evolution* (Bloomington, MN: Bethany House, 1985), 19.

# Part IX
## Concluding Thoughts

# Chapter 40
# Understanding Creation in the Twenty-first Century

In this book we have seen that the Bible's testimony about creation is one of the most compelling evidences for its inspiration and authority. Though written ages ago, the Bible fits remarkably well with proven scientific theories that have arisen in modern times. In fact, the major scientific breakthroughs of our era have left atheists with little to stand on. Consider what one leading astrophysicist said when summing up the significance of modern discoveries in physics:

*The Bible fits remarkably well with proven scientific theories that have arisen in modern times.*

> This is an exceedingly strange development, unexpected by all but the theologians. They have always accepted the word of the Bible: In the beginning God created heaven and earth. . . . [But] for the scientist who has lived by his faith in the power of reason, the story ends like a bad dream. He has scaled the mountains of ignorance; he is about to conquer the highest peak; as he pulls himself over the final rock, he

is greeted by a band of theologians who have been sitting there for centuries.[1]

Yes, the Bible's teachings beat science to the punch by many centuries. The same cannot be said for the other creation accounts that arose in ancient Mesopotamia. The Babylonians, Egyptians, and Sumerians put forth crude creation myths that are unworthy of God and cannot withstand even a moment's scientific scrutiny. Neither can the modern creation myth — naturalism — withstand scientific, philosophical, theological, or moral scrutiny. It is no exaggeration to say that the biblical doctrine of creation is the *only genuine option* on the table.

Historically, the Bible actually provided the basic worldview convictions that led to the development of science.[2] The beliefs that God is rational, that all the universe is His creation and reflects the orderliness of His mind, and that humans are created in His image with the capacity to think and plan and act according to rational principles, helped the founding thinkers of science come to believe that it was genuinely possible to investigate nature and understand it.

In essentials, unity. In nonessentials, liberty. In all things, love.

## Keys to Understanding Creation

So what is the best path to understanding creation in the twenty-first century? We believe it is by starting with the Bible, which supplies the vital starting points for worldview formation and saving knowledge of Jesus Christ. We also believe it is vitally

*Whether you believe creation is young or ancient, you believe God alone is Creator and Ruler if you call Jesus your Lord.*

important to take a proper accounting of God's other book of revelation: the natural world. In this way we allow the Bible and nature to come together and present a unified message on life's major questions. Granted, it is not always easy to see how God's revelations come together in this way. Nevertheless, we believe it can be done. But it takes more hard work than many people are willing to commit to. And it takes humility. As we have seen, there are many science/Bible issues that Christians struggle with. Our recommendation is that Christians should not focus on what divides us but on what unites us. Whether you believe creation is young or ancient, you believe God alone is Creator and Ruler if you call Jesus your Lord. And whether you understand the flood to be local or global, you know the Bible is telling the truth and that God judged all of humanity except Noah's family in an ancient deluge.

*Whether you understand the flood to be local or global, you know the Bible is telling the truth and that God judged all of humanity except Noah's family in an ancient deluge.*

Unfortunately, it is often easier to focus on what divides us. Despite what some popular teachers say, the issues surrounding the age of Earth and the extent of Noah's flood are not always so black and white. We hope this book has helped you understand the issues and gain respect for the views you do not hold. We also hope you will be encouraged to engage in discussion about these issues with a spirit of humility, Christlike love, and a passion for truth. Greater faith and understanding are the rewards for those who are willing to face the tough questions, lay their presuppositions on the line, and let God's revelation and Spirit lead in our pursuit of the truth. To arrive at that kind of destination, we should be like Job and put our hands over our mouths a little more

*Greater faith and understanding are the rewards for those who are willing to face the tough questions, lay their presuppositions on the line, and let God's revelation lead.*

often. After all, we are not right on all our opinions, but we serve and trust the One who is. And when we do uncover our mouths, let us unite our voices in praise for our Creator and Redeemer. Amen!

## *Notes*

1. Robert Jastrow, *God and the Astronomers* (New York: W. W. Norton and Co., 1978), 116.

2. A good source for tracing the role Christianity played in the development of science is *The Soul of Science* (Wheaton, IL: Crossway, 1994) written by Nancy Pearcey and Charles Thaxton.

# Suggested Reading

## Evolution and Intelligent Design

Behe, Michael. *The Edge of Evolution: The Search for the Limits of Darwinism*. New York: Free Press, 2007.

Dembski, William. *Intelligent Design*. Downers Grove: InterVarsity Press, 2007 (Paperback edition).

Denton, Michael. *Evolution: A Theory in Crisis.* Adler and Adiem, 1986.

Eldredge, Niles. *Reinventing Darwin: The Great Debate at the High Table of Evolutionary Theory*. Indianapolis: Wiley, 1995.

Gonzalez, Guillermo, and Jay Richards. *The Privileged Planet: How Our Place in the Cosmos Is Designed for Discovery*. Washington, DC: Regnery, 2004.

Gribbin, John. *Cosmic Coincidences: Dark Matter, Mankind, and Anthropic Cosmology*. Black Swan, 1991.

Hayward, Alan. *Creation and Evolution: Rethinking the Evidence from Science and the Bible*. Bloomington, MN: Bethany House, 1985.

Johnson, Philip. *Darwin on Trial*. Washington, DC: Regnery Gateway, 1991.

Lester, Lane, and Ray Bohlin. *The Natural Limits to Biological Change*. Grand Rapids: Zondervan, 1984.

Lewin, Roger. *Bones of Contention: Controversies in the Search for Human Origins*. Chicago: University of Chicago, 1997.

Moreland, J. P., and John Mark Reynolds. *Three Views on Creation and Evolution*. Grand Rapids: Zondervan, 1999.

Rana, Fazale, and Hugh Ross. *The Origin of Life: Biblical and Evolutionary Models Face Off.* Colorado Springs: NavPress, 2004.

Thaxton, Charles, W. Bradley, and J. Olsen. *The Mysteries of Life's Origin: Reassessing Current Theories.* New York: Philosophical Library, 1984.

Ward, Peter D., and Donald Brownlee. *Rare Earth: Why Complex Life Is Uncommon in the Universe.* New York: Springer, 2000.

## Age of Earth

Blocher, Henri, and David Preston. *In the Beginning: The Opening Chapters of Genesis.* Downers Grove: InterVarsity Press, 1984.

Dalrymple, G. Brent. *The Age of the Earth.* Palo Alto, CA: Stanford University Press, 1994.

Hagopian, David, ed. *The Genesis Debate: Three Views on the Days of Creation.* Mission Viejo, CA: Crux Press, 2001.

Morris, John. *The Young Earth: The Real History of the Earth—Past, Present, and Future.* Green Forest, AR: Master Books, 1994.

"Report of the Creation Study Committee," Presbyterian Church in America, 2000. Available at http://www.pcahistory. org/creation/report.pdf.

Ross, Hugh. *A Matter of Days: Resolving a Creation Controversy.* Colorado Springs: NavPress, 2004.

————. *Creation and Time: A Biblical and Scientific Perspective on the Creation-Date Controversy.* Colorado Springs: NavPress, 1994.

————. *The Creator and the Cosmos: How the Latest Scientific Discoveries of the Century Reveal God.* 3rd edition. Colorado Springs: NavPress, 2001.

Schaffer, Francis A. *Genesis in Space and Time.* Downers Grove: InterVarsity, 1972.

Weins, Roger. "Radiometric Dating: A Christian Perspective." Accessed 9 January 2008 at http://www.asa3.org/ASA/resources/Wiens.html.

Whorton, Mark. *Peril in Paradise.* Carlisle, UK: Authentic Media/Paternoster Publishing, 2005.

Wonderly, Daniel E. *Neglect of Geologic Data: Sedimentary*

*Strata Compared with Young-Earth Creationists Writings.* Hatfield, PA: Interdisciplinary Biblical Research Institute, 1987.

Young, Davis. *Christianity and the Age of the Earth.* Grand Rapids: Zondervan, 1982.

Zorn, Joshua. "The Testimony of a Formerly Young Earth Missionary." For the Web site of the American Scientific Affiliation, 1997. Available at http://www.asa3.org/ASA/resources/zorn.html.


## Science and Faith

Collins, John C. *Science & Faith: Friends or Foes?* Wheaton, IL: Crossway, 2003.

Henry M. Morris. *Scientific Creationism.* Green Forest, AR: Master Books, March 1985.

Numbers, Ronald. *The Creationists.* Los Angeles: University of California Press, 1992.

Ramm, Bernard. *The Christian View of Science & Scripture.* Grand Rapids: Eerdmans, 1954.

Ross, Hugh. *Creation As Science: A Testable Model Approach to End the Creation/Evolution Wars.* Colorado Springs: Navpress, 2006.


## Ancient Creation Myths

Sproul, Barbara C. *Primal Myths: Creation Myths Around the World.* New York: HarperCollins Publishers, 1979.


## Noah's Flood

Grudem, Wayne. *Systematic Theology.* Grand Rapids: Zondervan, 1994.

Hamilton, Victor P. *The Book of Genesis*: chapter 1–17. New International Commentary on the Old Testament. Grand Rapids: Eerdmans, 1990.

Hodge, Charles, *Systematic Theology*, vol 1. Grand Rapids: Eerdmans, Reprinted, 1993.

Kious, W. Jacquelyne, and Robert I. Tilling. "This Dynamic

Earth: The Story of Plate Tectonics." Available online at http://pubs.usgs.gov/publications/text/dynamic.pdf or in print from USGS Information Services, Box 25286, Building 810, Denver Federal Center, Denver, CO 80225.

Mathews, Kenneth A. *Genesis 1-11:26*. New American Commentary, vol. 1A. Nashville: Broadman & Holman, 1996.

Morris, Henry, and John Whitcomb. *The Genesis Flood*. Phillipsburg, NJ: P&R Publishing, 1961.

Young, Davis. *The Biblical Flood: A Case Study of the Church's Response to Extrabiblical Evidence*. Carlisle, UK: Paternoster Press, 1995.

## *Apologetics*

Craig, William Lane. "The Existence of God and the Beginning of the Universe." *Truth: A Journal of Modern Thought* 3 (1991): 85–96.

France, R. T. *The Evidence for Jesus*. Virginia Beach: Regent College Press, 2006.

Geisler, Norman L. *Baker Encyclopedia of Christian Apologetics*. Grand Rapids: Baker, 1990.

Heeren, Fred. *Show Me God: What the Message from Space Is Telling Us about God*. Wheeling, IL: Day Star Productions, 2004.

Lewis, C. S. *Mere Christianity*. New York: HarperOne, 2001.

Muncaster, Ralph O. *Evidence for Jesus: Discover the Facts that Prove the Truth of the Bible*. Eugene, OR: Harvest House, 2004.

Roberts, Hill. "Evidences That Have Led Many Scientists to Accept an Ancient Date for the Creation of the Earth and Universe," available online: www.LordIBelieve.org.

Strobel, Lee. *The Case for Creation: A Journalist Investigates Scientific Evidence that Points toward God*. Grand Rapids: Zondervan, 2005.

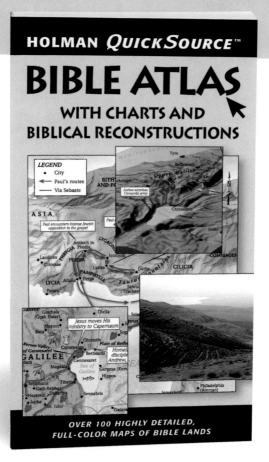

# Have your REFERENCES for Christ prepared.

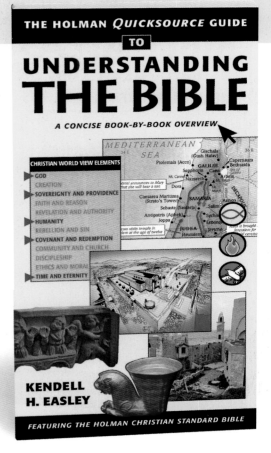

In the *Holman QuickSource™ Guide to Understanding the Bible*, Bible reference resources are provided in quick, easy-to-use formats that are not only beautifully presented, but also filled with reliable and detailed information.

## AVAILABLE NOW

PUBLISHING GROUP

BHPublishingGroup.com

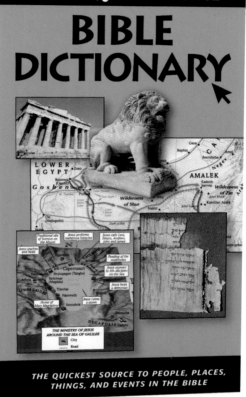

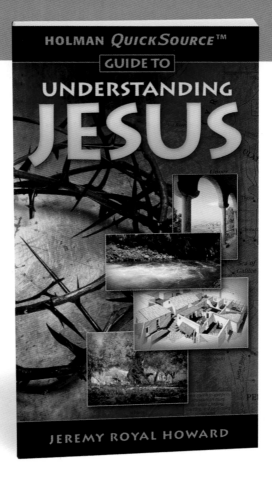